T0357192

COMING
OUT AS
DALIT

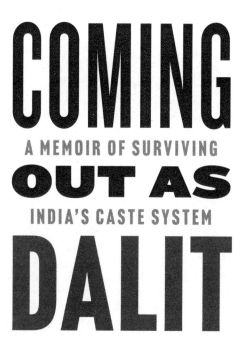

COMING

A MEMOIR OF SURVIVING

OUT AS

INDIA'S CASTE SYSTEM

DALIT

EXPANDED EDITION

YASHICA DUTT

BEACON PRESS · BOSTON

BEACON PRESS
Boston, Massachusetts
www.beacon.org

Beacon Press books
are published under the auspices of
the Unitarian Universalist Association of Congregations.

Copyright © 2019, 2024 by Yashica Dutt
A previous version of this book was published in
India in 2019 by Aleph Book Company.

All rights reserved
Printed in the United States of America

27 26 25 24   8 7 6 5 4 3 2 1

This book is printed on acid-free paper that meets the uncoated paper
ANSI/NISO specifications for permanence as revised in 1992.

Text design and composition by Kim Arney

Some names have been changed to protect people's privacy.

Library of Congress Cataloguing-in-Publication Data is available for this title.
Hardcover ISBN: 978-0-8070-4528-2
E-book ISBN: 978-0-8070-4529-9
Audiobook: 978-0-8070-3509-2

For . . .

My mother, who taught me that I could do anything I wanted and helped me live it, often at a great personal cost.

Rohith Vemula, who lit a flame that made my silence impossible.

CONTENTS

AUTHOR'S NOTE
TO NEW EDITION

The book you're about to read was written under extraordinary circumstances, as most books typically are. Like many authors, I struggled to survive while writing, having immigrated to the US just months before starting this project and working multiple jobs during the day to find time to write in the evening. It was excruciating and laborious and took a lot longer than I expected. But like many books that should have always existed but somehow didn't, this book too carried the urgency of molten lava, that once started could not be contained.

I *needed* to write *Coming Out as Dalit*.

Even before I had any words typed on a laptop, I knew this book would never be mine alone. In the fiercely gatekept space of Indian English-language writing, where dominant caste literary stars were bursting almost daily, Dalits did not exist. Rare books that told our stories also never spoke to us. They addressed a reader who, with the objective distance of their dominant caste, could feign shock or anguish when encountered with the reality of our lived existence.

Writing this book was the one shot to tell our stories in our own words. It was my window to communicate with a people who rarely got a chance to dream and imagine our own narratives without having to factor in the omnipresent dominant-caste reader of the Indian English literary canon. Or even the first-world reader of the Western literary canon. Dalits did not get to write books in English. Faced with the task of writing this rare book that, beyond the debut work of a journalist turned author, was an idea that had finally come alive for millions of us across the world, I wrote *Coming Out as Dalit* for Dalits.

That does not make this book difficult to access for anyone else who is not. In fact, it makes the possibilities of engaging with this work that much more exciting, electric even—to witness the rare power of speaking to a people who have been erased for generations, now considered, understood, and made visible. There are references to institutional policies of affirmative action like reservation, and historical narratives of the caste colonial confluence, that are left unexplained, as they amount to so much of the Dalit everyday life. Bollywood films, Indian pop-cultural characters, and granular details of Indian university systems are presented without description for the same reason. But the stories that run underneath these symbols, of a marginalized community that resisted all attempts at its erasure and refused to be silenced, are universal.

Since its release in the Indian subcontinent in 2019, *Coming Out as Dalit* has been a book that has become more than what's contained in its 250-plus pages. It is now an idea that represents the defiance of a generation of Dalits who have seen their ancestors chip away at a system that refuses to give way. It has evolved into a symbolic aspiration of lower caste, untouchable people who struggle twice as hard as everyone and are yet reminded they will never amount to anything. It is a testament to the power of a Dalit reader that cannot be contained, despite the narrow and unimaginative ideas in Western publishing around whose stories get to be told and who gets to tell them.

That is why I'm choosing to leave this book unchanged, with no amendments or revisions for the global version, with the exception of two additional chapters that focus on the anti-caste progress in the United States. It's a document that records an important turn in the history of global Dalit writing and deserves to be respected as such.

I thank Beacon Press for recognizing why this was a story that *needed* to be told. And my hope is that you get to see that, too.

AUTHOR'S NOTE

I spent close to ten years working as a journalist in Delhi. During that time, writing a book wasn't something I could ever have seen myself doing. I didn't think I had enough to say, that I was willing to share with the world. After I came out as Dalit, I no longer had anything to hide. Everything about my life was connected to a larger narrative. Everything that I had done so far or that had happened to me was somehow related to my caste. But I didn't want to tell just my story. I also wanted to tell the stories of all those Dalits that the media and society at large had ignored. Through their accounts and by making sense of my own life, I have tried to piece together a larger picture of what casteism truly looks like today.

Before I started thinking deeply about it, like most of us, I never saw caste for what it really is—the invisible arm that turns the gears in nearly every system in our country. It's been working silently for so long that we have stopped noticing it, even though it exists all around us. Whether we realize it or not, almost all critical decisions and developments in the country, whether in the justice system, government, or media, are upper-caste decisions. And they almost always exclude lower castes or Dalits. Caste doesn't only come into play with regard to certain issues—manual scavenging, reservation, government jobs, or cow traders. It is part of every aspect of all our lives. What I hope this book will do is let you see how.

In this book, I talk of the lives of a varied group of Dalits: those who live in the cities and in villages, those who read Ambedkar or don't, those who are out as Dalit or not, and those who exist somewhere in between. Clearly, I don't speak for every Dalit in the world. There are thousands of stories I have yet to discover. But as a journalist, a researcher, a writer, and a Dalit woman who spent most of her life in hiding, I hope to speak for those whose voices haven't been heard before.

The only thing I don't do is ask if casteism still exists. And you won't either, once you listen to those who are shouting to be heard.

The descriptors "upper" and "lower" to refer to people who belong to various caste groups are arbitrary, illogical, and offensive. I use these terms since they are widely understood, but I reject the implied inherent "superiority" or "inferiority" that they have come to stand for.

PROLOGUE

Hiding one aspect of your identity is like leading a double life. You don't feel like you belong anywhere. You create masks to wear in each of your lives, and switch artfully between the two. Eventually, the two blur together and you no longer remember who you were.

Pretending to be from a caste that's not Dalit is something like that. And there are so many of us who are living this lie. We avoid talking about caste, hoping to somehow find a place in the world of upper-casteness that has been forbidden to us. We create upper-caste identities—stolen badges—that help us gain entry to a space that will reject us the moment it finds out who we really are. We nervously flash these IDs anytime we are grilled about our origins. Those who fail to exhibit satisfactory signs of upper-casteness and those who refuse to are punished for trespassing, for being where they don't belong. Discrimination, humiliation, oppression are all penalties for not being upper caste, or simply for being Dalit. Our Dalitness is imprinted onto us through the burned bodies of our children, suicides of our PhD scholars and college students, rapes of young girls and women, asphyxiation of our manual scavengers, and "honor killings" of lovers. These penalties are so routine that they aren't even considered worthy of shock and outrage. Newspapers either skip these stories or stick them in the back pages, between the sports and the city sections. Hipster jazz bars don't flinch before announcing a music group called "Bhangijumping" and show little remorse after being informed about its grossly offensive undertones.[1] It's heartbreaking that an upscale jazz club that can painstakingly educate itself about a musical tradition that originated from Black musicians in the United States in the late nineteenth century can't be bothered to understand how "Bhangi" is a term of abuse much closer to home.

"We are post-caste," we are told. "Casteism is over." We are chided for addressing the inequality our Dalitness saddles us with and are sharply reminded of the "unfairness" of reservation.

Caste always colored my worldview, even when I had little understanding of it. When I was a child it puzzled me that my father and grandfather didn't share their last name, unlike other father-son pairs in the neighborhood. My grandfather had dropped Nidaniya—a typically "Bhangi" last name—in his twenties, perhaps around the time he was forced down from the horse he was riding during his wedding procession at swordpoint by caste Hindus in Jaipur. Seventy years later, little seems to have changed as caste Hindus still humiliate Dalit grooms who display any upper-caste symbols of Hindu wedding revelry like decorated turbans or going on horseback to their bride's house.

My grandfather, father, and I experienced our Dalitness in vastly different ways. Dad—the son of a revered civil servant—wasn't forced down from his horse, nor was his wedding party disrupted. Two generations of prestigious government jobs and concealed last names had somewhat diluted the obvious markers of Dalitness. But not enough had changed that I could give a straight answer to the question: "What caste are you from?" My Dalitness still weighed heavy on me; I dragged its carcass behind me through my childhood and into adulthood. As a child, I worked harder to hide it, every tiny nudge throwing me off balance, every new interrogation about caste assaulting my spirit. My civics textbook educated me about "the evils of the caste system" but didn't equip me to deal with its manifestations in my own classroom. It didn't explain the stinging shame that pierced me every time one of my classmates or teachers called someone "Bhangi"—a slob. I didn't even know I was "Bhangi," but I knew it was something I, and not anyone else, should be embarrassed about.

One of my earliest memories of this pretense was watching Mum act the part. She would awkwardly try to explain how she, a Brahmin girl from Uttar Pradesh, married a Dalit boy from Rajasthan, without them ever having met. It was also one of my earliest memories of discovering that this artifice was not easy nor would it always be believed. It was rare for the recipient of that lie—a new neighbor or a classmate's mother—to not see through it. And when they did, they often wanted nothing to do with us. My initial attempts at this pretense often contained the same awkward explanation about my parents' marriage which, as a child, I was terrible at defending. But as I grew older, that narrative cemented into a perfectly crafted, well-rehearsed spiel that I could deliver on command. By that time, the weight of my Dalitness had settled so deep within me that I'd stopped feeling its weight or recognizing its presence.

So it wasn't unusual that when I first saw the Facebook post about a Dalit boy who had committed suicide in Hyderabad University, I didn't open the link. He was not the first Dalit boy who had died and he was not going to be the last. Dalit boys and girls, men and women, children, and old people, have regularly died because of caste violence. It is among the most devastating but far from the only outcome of caste discrimination that endures through Indian societies in the subcontinent and across the world. Even upper-caste men and women who claim that they are not casteist—and perhaps sincerely believe it—often propagate casteism in the name of tradition and culture in various ways, most significantly by insisting on marrying within their own caste. Matrimonial columns in all newspapers are filled with demands for a "Brahmin girl for a Brahmin boy," an "Aggarwal only" girl, or a "well-educated Rajput boy." Even beyond the recent heightened intolerance for beef, vegetarianism has been the gold standard for caste purity. Purity is considered the sole preserve of Brahmins and other "higher" castes whereas those at the lower end—Bhangis, Chamars, Churas, Malodas, Malas, and Madigas, among others—are considered impure and downright polluting. Their touch, belongings, and even their shadows are believed to defile the well-preserved "purity" of others.[2]

Rohith Vemula, raised by his mother, Radhika, was from the untouchable Mala caste. When the news of his death appeared a second time, a third, and eventually became a fixture on my Facebook timeline for twenty-four hours, I thought to myself: Who is this Dalit boy who made all the non-Dalits care? Rohith, a PhD scholar at Hyderabad University, had allegedly committed suicide as a result of relentless caste-based persecution at the university. When news of his suicide broke in the mainstream media in January 2016, my own

Dalit identity was deeply buried beneath layers of convent education, urban upbringing, and a hardened resolve to avoid engaging with anything related to caste.

The day after the news broke, Tuesday, January 19, 2016, I finally read the letter that Rohith had left behind, as I sat at my favorite table at a too cold café in Manhattan's Chelsea: "My birth is my fatal accident." "Never was a man treated as a mind. As a glorious thing made up of stardust."[3] I read it once. Twice. And then once more. I had never read anything written by a Dalit before! I had certainly never read anything written by a Dalit in English—the language I had hoped would help me escape my own Dalit identity. The language I had stubbornly practiced since I was five. Flawless English was supposed to bring me to the same level as my upper-caste classmates in school and college. I leaned on it when the carcass of my Dalitness became too heavy. Later, writing in this language became my career. It is very likely that English was Rohith's crutch too. He was probably still honing it so he could stand tall against those he had decided to take on—those who perhaps equated his Dalitness with an inherent subhumanness.

It's very likely that, like me, he too had recognized that our education was our only strength. With far fewer resources than I had and possibly under more arduous conditions, Rohith sought education as his defense against his caste. Given his hardships, it would have been an easier and perhaps a more obvious choice for Rohith to have taken a job at a private multinational firm, like millions of other Indian graduates. Instead, he chose academia, exploring ideas that could help him interpret his reality as a Dalit. In his excellent report in the *Hindustan Times*, Dalit journalist Sudipto Mondal recounts that for Rohith, his PhD wasn't just a career; he wanted to break new ground in research.[4] Initially enrolled in the life sciences department, he later shifted to the social sciences, pursuing a PhD where he was researching the symbiosis between technology and social sciences. According to reports, he hadn't received the allocated stipend for seven months when he killed himself.

Searching for a photo of Rohith after reading his life story, I looked up his Facebook page, wondering: Who was this boy whose life sounded so similar to mine, but was so much harder? "Remembering

Rohith Vemula" read his profile, instead of just his name, as is customary for posthumous Facebook profiles. The news of his death had circulated a little more than twenty-four hours earlier, but his profile page was brimming with comments from well-wishers. I scrolled for several minutes before his photograph appeared. It was a mirror selfie with Rohith in a red T-shirt. I had seen this somewhere . . . Suddenly, it came to me! Rohith had sent me a friend request two weeks before he wrote his last letter and hanged himself from the ceiling fan in a friend's room in the hostel of Hyderabad University. And I had deleted THAT request, I thought with dismay, a request from someone in whose life I so easily saw my own. My action wasn't unusual. I deleted all unsolicited requests from people I didn't have enough friends in common with.

We had many things in common, but one very vital thing was different. Unlike me, Rohith did nothing to bury his Dalitness. Instead, he used it as a shield to stand up for his fellow Dalit students in Hyderabad University against the caste-based prejudice of members of the administration.

Once I started working as a journalist, the question of my caste lost some of its intensity but none of the fear that came with it: the fear of being caught, the fear of losing friends, respect, and even my bylines. I dodged any and all mentions of reservation—the constitutional affirmative action policy for Dalits—or inter-caste marriages. I ducked whenever someone casually used "Bhangi" as an epithet, struggling to sustain a blank expression and hoping that no one had noticed the actual Bhangi in their midst. The fear that my Dalitness would be "discovered" made me hate it all the more. I wanted to be like my colleagues who were not hiding, not scared, not Bhangi, and therefore better than me. I had to work twice as hard to be half as good and all the trying and hiding had me exhausted before I turned twenty-two. But I couldn't stop hiding.

In Rohith's letter I saw this bizarre possibility that, under a slightly different set of circumstances, his short life could have been mine. The awareness of that possibility forced me to confront my own ways of being in a manner I hadn't in the previous twenty-nine years. In a split second, I evaluated my life and the worth of everything I had done so far. Nothing matched up to those few hundred words in Rohith's letter. Now that he was gone, with his hand virtually extended to me, it was my turn to show up and grasp it. It was at Columbia University that I had recognized a parallel between hiding my caste and the phenomenon of "passing"—the distinctly African American practice of hiding one's (racial) identity and assuming a different (white) one to escape systemic discrimination. It struck me now that I couldn't be the only Dalit passing as upper caste. My journalistic instincts compelled me to look for a deeper narrative. I searched for reports or data about Dalits who had been living as upper-caste individuals, but found none. Dalits only appeared in the media when someone wanted to discuss how "unnecessary" and "unfair" reservation was to upper-caste people. We were largely either pathetic victims or corrupt, immoral opportunists. At that time, I failed to find stories that spoke of the emotional, mental, or physical damage I had experienced daily by trying to hide my caste. There are excellent narratives that address the direct consequences of being Dalit, particularly in the works of Baby Kamble (*The Prisons We Broke*, 2008) and Urmila Pawar (*The Weave of My Life*, 2007). But I found nothing that engaged with the unique anxiety of giving up one's identity to take on another that is seen as superior. So I decided I had to find a place where such stories could live.

I started a Tumblr page where Dalits who, like me, were passing as upper caste could anonymously or openly talk about their experiences. It would be a safe space, without judgment from upper-caste commentators, where our voices would be free to shape our stories the way we wanted. But I couldn't in good conscience be the provider of that space before I dealt with my own identity. Before I could ask anyone to share the truth about their lives with the world, I needed to do it first. I needed to come out as Dalit. Still cautious, I listed the pros and cons of taking such a step. The fact that I was living and working in New York with no immediate plans to return to caste-conscious Delhi/India was a major pro. Within the next few minutes, I was picking out the saffron color to represent the microsite's header. It was a form of resistance to reclaim a Dalit space in the preferred shade of Hindu fundamentalists who often openly affront Dalit rights. I didn't give myself any more time to think as I painstakingly worked on the site for the next two hours, stopping only when I wrote DALIT in a bold size 24 Georgia font. Underneath I defined the word in English and Hindi as "one who has been oppressed." In that moment, I stopped being ashamed. I experienced something I had never felt about my Dalitness: empathy. I knew I was ready. *Documents of Dalit Discrimination* materialized as my first independent journalism project, which I announced on Facebook with a short declaration of my coming out as Dalit. As I was about to hit the publish button, with a mixture of delicious anticipation and radiant pride that had replaced my earlier anxieties, I sensed that it could change my life as I knew it. I was disclosing my lower-caste origins to acquaintances, former colleagues, bosses, neighbors, friends, and even family—practically everyone who was part of my world. I imagined that the bitter caste supremacists among them would be disgusted with the idea of sharing space with a Bhangi as an equal; some would discredit my career as an outcome of my "reservation privilege." I pictured that several among them might also be sympathetic, but I was certain that *no one* would be expecting this. I had pulled the wool over their eyes for years and the effortlessness of my decades-long attempt at passing as upper caste was impressive even to me.

So far, I had escaped the humiliation of being "discovered" as Bhangi and now I was forever taking away their power to do so: by doing it myself. I was putting an end to my constant struggle of hiding behind my education or my career, escaping through my proficient English or my (not-so-dark) skin color. In a way, I was turning my Dalitness into a gold medal of ancestral pride and suffering. I was going to proclaim openly and proudly that I was DALIT. I uploaded Rohith's photograph next to my note and hit publish. Everyone who read it would know I was Dalit. There was no going back. Rohith Vemula, the twenty-six-year-old PhD scholar who concluded defeatedly that his birth was a "fatal accident," made me do it.

Rohith Vemula, the Dalit scholar from Hyderabad Central University, who took his own life on January 18th, wanted to write about the stars. His mind was a "glorious thing made of stardust," whose proof he left in his last letter to the world. In life, his education—a chunk of it financed by his mother's earnings as a tailor—was an act of rebellion. In death, he blazed a trail on Dalit rights, whose brightness refuses to be ignored. By the media, by the bureaucracy, by the Internet and by me.

I was born in a Dalit family in Ajmer, Rajasthan. And I grew up learning to hide it. My convent school education, a non-Dalit sounding last name, and a skin color that was "dusky but still not dirty" eased my passing as a non-Dalit. "Beta, what caste are you from?" "Aunty, Brahmin." A lie I spoke so often and with such conviction, that I not only fooled my friends' mothers but even myself. But I couldn't fool the shame that spread across my face each time someone mentioned "caste," "reservation," "bhangi"—the common slur, which loosely translates to a human scavenger and the name of my exact caste. "This time, they'll find out," I had thought when the undergraduate college I attended tucked my name under the SC/ST quota or when I submitted my birth certificate for my first job at an ad agency. Some did find out, some didn't. Most didn't care. The ones who did (a friend, who along with her parents witnessed my first public admission of being "low-caste" at 15) stopped being in touch. But I always cared. I cared enough to lie about my caste and to create elaborate backstories to protect that lie. I conveniently forgot the last name my grandfather dropped to allow him to pass, almost 60 years ago—Nidaniya.

Until today when I visited Rohith Vemula's posthumous Facebook page. And realized that he had sent me a Facebook request ten days ago, which I had promptly ignored. Maybe he saw some Dalit rights groups I had liked and wanted to reach out.

And reach out he did. He made me "come out" to the people I grew up hiding from, wanting to fit in with. He made me recognize that my history is one of oppression and not shame. He made me acknowledge that my great-grandfather learned to write by scrawling with a stick in the mud because the higher caste schoolteacher forbade him from holding a slate. And he made me proud.

I know I am not alone to feel this. There are many of us whose experiences of growing up Dalit and navigating a society that forces us to feel shame, need to be told and heard. That's why I am starting *Documents of Dalit Discrimination*. A safe space for conversation about caste that needs to go beyond "reservation" and "merit" and voices that echo the hurt so many of us suffer silently. Let us hear stories of pride, of history and ownership against the emotional, personal, physical, and mental toll of the caste system. Let it be known that Rohith's birth was no "fatal accident."

Yashica Dutt (Nidaniya)

http://dalitdiscrimination.tumblr.com/[5]

Everything I had imagined before I published that note turned out to be true. I could sense the shock waves that rippled through my friends, colleagues, and acquaintances from thousands of miles away. The outpouring—of shock, dismay, support, and accolades—was immediate. First, the tweets came in, then Facebook posts, and finally the media requests. The note went viral in less than twenty-four hours. My friends couldn't stop sending me comments and reactions on the WhatsApp group we use to stay in touch. We watched it take on a life of its own. It should have been exciting. But, mostly, I felt nauseous. Away from Twitter, Facebook, and WhatsApp groups, my parents had no clue that I had gone and done exactly what they had protected me from all my life.

As I was waiting for my brief appearance on NDTV to talk about the note, I realized I needed to tell my parents before they found out by watching it on live television. But I chickened out and sent them a text asking them to tune in. I went on air and tried to explain why I felt I needed to "come out." If my choked Twitter and Facebook messages were any indication, I did it well enough. Except, my parents had missed it. They were out and thought my appearance was related to Fashion Week, since I had spent years covering fashion. But they needed to be told and I had to be the one to do it.

When Mum finally picked up the phone, for a moment I lost my voice. Then I blurted, "Maine sab ko bata diya main Dalit hoon" (I told everyone I am Dalit). Mum stayed silent for a few seconds that felt like an eternity. Finally, her voice heavy with tears, she said, "Jee-tay raho, beta" (Live long and prosper, my child). Naturally, she was worried about how this would affect my career prospects and was relieved that I was in New York. My dad reacted with the same mix of joy and caution. Even though I knew publishing that note was the right thing to do, I had felt trepidation. Now, I felt fearless. I could take on anyone because my parents agreed I was right.

As I've said, Rohith Vemula had reached out to me. He showed me that it was possible to be Dalit and proud. I wasn't scared of my Dalitness anymore. And I didn't hate it either. I hoped I could (in perhaps a much smaller way) do for someone else what Rohith Vemula had done for me. Despite the fact that he was dead, Rohith's note made me less afraid. And I hoped that somewhere, someone like me would read my note and possibly feel less afraid too.

CHAPTER 1

THE EARLY YEARS

Until three generations ago, Dalits were denied access to learning. My great-grandfather defied this social order and learned to write by scrawling in the mud with a stick. His son, my grandfather, like many others of his generation, fought every step of the way to enter the civil services.

The Civil Service Exam (CSE)—arguably one of the most popular and among the toughest competitive exams in the country—holds a special appeal for Dalits. Under the reservation policy, 22.5 percent (15 percent for Scheduled Castes, 7.5 percent for Scheduled Tribes) of all government jobs, including those in the civil services, are reserved for Dalits.[1] The Union Public Service Commission (UPSC), the central agency that conducts all CSEs, further allows a relaxation in the cut-off marks, age, and number of attempts to appear for the exam. A Dalit can make unlimited attempts to qualify for the exam until the age of thirty-seven, as opposed to six attempts until the age of thirty-two for general category applicants.

Beyond these constitutional provisions, the civils (as the civil services are called) have, for generations, symbolized—somewhat erroneously—the summit of social acceptability. Many Dalit applicants spend years preparing for the examination, hoping that some of the respect linked with a civil service position might rub off on them and go some way towards negating their Dalitness. The other perks of the civil service—a sizeable pay package and power—are especially attractive to Dalits, most of whom have been denied these perks for generations. But while wealth and official power might become accessible to those who clear the exam, social acceptance largely escapes most Dalits. Instances of subordinates ignoring protocols because of the senior officer's lower caste, the stonewalling of promotions despite possessing the requisite qualifications, and the denial of desired postings are common experiences for Dalits in the civil services. *Governance Now*, a publication covering governance and policies in government institutions, quoted former bureaucrat and Dalit activist P. S. Krishnan, who reported many instances of blatant discrimination in the promotion of Dalit civil servants. "Yes, it [bias against SC/ST officers] is very much there and we all know it," he told the publication.[2]

That explains why none of India's thirty-one cabinet secretaries—the top bureaucratic position for which candidates are selected from among Indian civil servants—have been Dalits. Perhaps 2015 CSE topper and proud Dalit, twenty-two-year-old Tina Dabi, will be able to change that. An article in *Firstpost* contemplated this possibility while reporting that out of "431 officials at the secretary, special secretary, additional secretary and joint secretary levels in various central ministries and departments . . . [o]nly 28 officials belong to the SC category and 12 to the ST category."[3] The news of Dabi's top rank in the examination resulted in celebration among Dalits and allies and, unsurprisingly, bitter criticism from other quarters. The fact that Dabi availed herself of the reservation quota to appear for the preliminary exam was used as the main argument against reservation, with many claiming that she didn't need to do so. (Her outstanding marks in the main exam are higher than those in both general and reserved categories.) The argument was that since her father, Jaswant Dabi, and mother, Himani Dabi, had availed themselves of reservation in their successful careers, Dabi's selection was unfair. Some argued that there was no caste discrimination and oppression in her life. Complaints about her rank circulated across the pages and comment threads of social media platforms for many months.

For the anti-reservation brigade, her top rank was proof that Dalits didn't face discrimination—and therefore the need for reservation did not exist. Every time a Dalit succeeds—most caste supremacists find the concept sacrilegious—this argument is trotted out to induce guilt in them about reservation. Curiously (and reasonably), the same logic doesn't apply to economically backward upper-caste farmers who avail themselves of government aid and subsidies.

Indian society doesn't create spaces for Dalits to flourish. Constitutional reservation allows Dalits to enter and survive in a system that tries to keep them on the periphery. The system is designed to keep Dalits confined to undesirable professions. Dalits who use the reservation policy to advance are accused of being "opportunistic" for using their only option for progress. Thousands of years of religious and social policies that denied education to Dalits are discounted and they are regularly challenged to prove their talent without using the "crutch" of reservation. Reservation allows Dalits entry into the upper-caste system, but only their drive, talent, and ability create genuine, viable opportunities for them to get ahead.

Both my grandfathers used those opportunities in the Indian civil services to secure a bright future for their families at a time when few Dalits could access the education required for it. They both spent years preparing for and eventually passing the CSE with the requisite marks. In the 1980s, as India was slowly overcoming the Emergency, a small number of educated Dalits held high positions in the Indian Civil Service. My paternal grandfather was the first Dalit divisional superintendent in the Rajasthan Police Service and my maternal grandfather was an inspector in the State Excise department in Uttar Pradesh. The civil services were a big part of the reason that my parents' families came into each other's orbit. The other reason was because they were born into the same caste—Bhangi. My parents were engaged within a few hours of my father and his family arriving at my mother's house in Dhanaura Mandi, a tiny hamlet in eastern Uttar Pradesh. Mum had no major misgivings about an arranged marriage, except for one condition: she wouldn't marry anyone who drank alcohol. Mum had witnessed its pernicious effect on her parents' marriage and she was anxious that the pattern didn't follow in her own. My father's family assured her that her potential life partner was a teetotaler.

At the time of their marriage, my mother—the oldest of five children—was pursuing a master's degree in history. A resident student at Gokuldas University in Moradabad, about one and a half hours away from her hometown, my mother lived on campus and came home on weekends and holidays. For that time, and in her small town, it was radical for her to live away from home to study in a different city. She was one of only two Dalit girls in her batch. Despite initial resistance to this idea, her family, particularly her father, reluctantly agreed. And yet, this was a compromise. Mum's heart had been set on Allahabad University, arguably the best university in Uttar Pradesh at the time, whose illustrious alumni included poet Harivansh Rai Bachchan and writer Mahadevi Verma. But Allahabad, which was farther from home, was unacceptable, especially after a distant relative, who was neither a fan of women's autonomy nor quality education, had informed her father that girls at Allahabad University smoked cigarettes and drank alcohol. He suggested that keeping Mum closer to home would make it easier to keep a check on her; unsurprisingly, that idea appealed to her father. This was not the first time Mum had settled for something that wasn't her first choice. Her father had pressured her into studying the humanities rather than science and mathematics, subjects she naturally excelled at. He didn't see the point in her choosing harder subjects when the humanities would be easier to prepare for the CSE—a common myth among civils aspirants. Like many second-generation Dalit children of civil servants, Mum was expected to follow in her father's footsteps. She had seen her father attempt the exam multiple times before he cleared it when she was eleven. Her earliest memories of her father were of him preparing for the exam, first at home and later, when he moved to Delhi to join Rau's Coaching Institute, the oldest of its kind. She had often heard him tell relatives and visitors that he would "make his daughter an IAS officer," a somewhat far-out assertion in a largely patriarchal and conservative household. Mum had different aspirations though: she wanted to join the Indian Police Force instead, like Kiran Bedi, the first woman to become an Indian Police Service (IPS) officer in 1972.

Along with her no-alcohol stipulation, she also revealed her plans about wanting to join the IPS to my father and his family before their engagement. They assured her that she was free to appear for the exam after her marriage and, moreover, that she would have their complete support during the preparation. With her two critical demands accepted, she gave her consent to marrying Dad.

They were married in a lavish ceremony that Mum's neighbors recalled for many years. Both Mum's and Dad's families had acquired material wealth relatively recently, and the wedding was a declaration of that hard-earned prestige.

But less than a year later, these promises lay broken. At some point during the engagement, Mum and her parents had learned about Dad's fondness for alcohol. The news devastated Mum, but she could not think of calling off the wedding, fearful of the fallout, not just for herself but for the rest of the family. She hoped that his family would deliver on their promise to support her as she prepared for the exams. Dad's love for the bottle, combined with his status as the oldest child of a successful, high-powered father and his own newly minted position as an excise inspector (he passed the CSE just before the wedding) grew into full-blown alcoholism soon after their marriage. When I was born less than a year after the wedding, my mother had spent the last few months of her pregnancy in a hospital bed.

Testifying in family court a few years later (they almost separated at this point), Mum said that after months of dealing with Dad's drunken abuse, his family's apathy, and the imminent collapse of her life as she had envisioned it—including her childhood desire to join the IPS—she decided to kill herself.* In the few months it took her to get to that point, she had spent countless chilly evenings waiting for her husband to accompany her to shop for warm clothes—the only thing she had not brought with her from her parents' home. She wrapped herself in blankets even when she wasn't in bed and spent most of her time in isolated corners of the house, as Dad's family ostracized her for being "too proud," "too outspoken," "too confident."

She also testified that while his family couldn't deter her from studying, Dad's drunken violence and abuse did. He would start drinking early in the evening and by the time Mum had cooked and served dinner and finished cleaning up, he would be intoxicated. When she returned to studying after he had passed out, Dad interpreted this as a taunt against his relatively low rank in the exam. She testified that he would drag her from the makeshift kitchen at the back of the house to their room, beating her all the while. One evening when he

---

*The allegations made by Mum about my father on this page and elsewhere in the book were recorded at the Ajmer Family Court on April 13, 2018, and form part of the court record.

slapped her, the impact punctured her eardrum. When she told her father about this abuse, he came to see her. But by the time her father came to visit, she had softened her stance, especially after Dad's father "advised" her to be a good daughter-in-law by not reporting her husband's abuse to her family. So her father left, worried but more or less satisfied with his daughter's decision to stay in the marriage. But things didn't improve as the abuse from my father and apathy from his family continued. Mum knew that if she decided to walk out on her marriage she would have no support—her parents would blame her for ruining the marriage prospects of her siblings. Seeing no way out of the situation, she did what good Indian daughters-in-law in her position do: she decided to kill herself. Seven months pregnant, she jumped from the roof of the house and shattered her left ankle, damaging it permanently. The pregnancy was declared complicated and the doctors doubted the chances of my survival.

Domestic violence against women is not limited to Dalit families. Women across the country face immense physical and emotional brutality from their families. But Dalit women—especially those from rural areas and those who are economically vulnerable, from urban or rural areas—are at the bottom of caste, class, and gender hierarchies. Their lower class, female gender, *and* lower caste make them more vulnerable to violence from their families and from society at large. Caste Hindu men in many regions consider Dalit women as sexual property.[4] "Access to a Dalit man's land comes with access to his Dalit wife" is a familiar sentiment across the country.

Dalit women whose parents use access to education to overcome class barriers also face similar vulnerabilities. Their relative rise in class shields them from direct abuse from caste Hindus. But combined with their lower caste, it often ends up exposing them to a unique and perhaps more vicious strain of patriarchy within their own families.

Until I came out as Dalit, I passed as an upper-caste Hindu. As I mentioned earlier, passing refers to an elaborate posturing by mimicking the customs, traditions, and manners of a majority community and is well documented among African Americans. Black Americans often pass as white by dressing, speaking, and gesticulating like white

Americans to escape systemic racism and violent oppression. Dalits in India have been passing as upper-caste Hindus, especially since the Constitution guaranteed everyone equal rights. They also adopt elaborate lifestyle changes—changing their last names, moving cities, following rigid Brahminical traditions, turning vegetarian, exhibiting excessive religiosity—to appear more like upper-caste Hindus. In the early fifties, sociologist M. N. Srinivas popularized the term "Sanskritization."[5] He was describing the changes in the caste system in modern India whereby lower castes were adopting upper-caste traditions to get ahead. Tellingly, Srinivas did not focus on other important ways by which the lower castes were pulling themselves up—through the acquisition of political power and business clout. In a more liberal, balanced, and incisive analysis, sociologist Dr. Kancha Ilaiah in his canonical text *Why I Am Not a Hindu* (1996) explains how "Shudras"—constitutionally termed as Other Backward Classes (OBCs)—in a bid to acquire greater political power imitate caste structures that closely align with Kshatriyas—the ruling caste. As "Neo-Kshatriyas," they also seem to buy into the notion of caste hierarchy and take to practicing caste supremacy and casteism against Dalits who are directly beneath them in the caste structure. Many educated Dalits adopt a complicated amalgamation of Sanskritized and Neo-Kshatriya values, along with internalized caste supremacy and casteism, often to their own detriment. Lifestyle changes tend to accompany a deeper subscription to Brahminical patriarchy and authoritarianism. Ilaiah explains that this results in placing unlimited power in the hands of the male provider/father, where the women and children in the family recognize him as their "head." Families also place rigid restrictions on women making decisions, and there is a general insecurity regarding women's liberties—in choosing a life partner, career, or level of education. The degrees of subscription to Brahminical patriarchy vary with differences in class and caste. As a contrast, Ilaiah presents the "Dalit-Bahujan" economy. Political leader Kanshi Ram collectively described SCs, STs, and OBCs as "Bahujans." In this economy, men and women are seen as equal providers where, despite the existence of patriarchy, Dalit-Bahujan women have marginally more freedom as compared to non-Dalit-Bahujan women. (Many people erroneously use this argument to conclude that Dalit women are "less oppressed" than non-Dalit women, ignoring workplace exploitation and violence, especially against rural Dalit women by caste Hindu men—which I discuss in chapter 11).

Neo-Kshatriyas and Sanskritized Dalits—like my parents' families—tend to operate within the tentative balance between Brahminical and Dalit-Bahujan ideals. The gender-based oppression of the former and the caste-based persecution of the latter come together to create a difficult environment that dictates life for women like my mother who are born into these families. The Dalit-Bahujan tenet of equal work share inspired her father's ambition for her, but his patriarchal Brahminical ideals valued her matrimony over her desire to join the police force. Much like the patriarchal values of Dad's family that seemed threatened by her ambition but did not seem to mind Mum working poorly paid jobs to support the family because their son wasn't earning.

My earliest memory of Dad is of him drinking. He knew Mum resented it, so he rarely drank openly. He would sit hidden behind a curtain. The breeze from the ceiling fan would periodically release the pungent odor of McDowell's No. 1 whisky—his brand of choice. Those fumes would presage an impending argument between my parents. My grandfather never drank, and while I have heard him rebuke Dad on several occasions, he never actively and resolutely tried to stop him.

My grandfather is the most successful member of his family so far. His father, Dad's grandfather, was the first in the family to defy the strictures of caste hierarchy when he started working as a professional photographer shooting photos of foreign tourists outside Jaipur's Amber Fort. He also challenged the rigid prohibition on Dalit education by attending classes even when the teachers refused to teach him. His protest against the caste system allowed my grandfather to graduate with a degree in English literature. He taught at a high school as he prepared for the CSE. His father and, later, his older brother—Dad's uncle—supported him through the years he studied. He was also supported by his wife. My grandfather's first wife worked as a manual scavenger, cleaning dry excrement from people's homes. By the time he cleared the Rajasthan State CSE to become the first Dalit municipal magistrate in Ajmer, she had passed away without giving birth to any children, and my grandfather remarried. He went on to hold several prestigious positions in the state bureaucracy and gained immense recognition. At eighty, he still works and supports his three children, financially and in other ways, as the bona fide head of the family.

CHAPTER 2

THE CASTE SYSTEM

How It Began

Caste is an established reality in South Asia and South Asian communities across the world. Indian culture, in its broadest sense, while well known for its vibrancy in many aspects including food, dance, music, art, also has the hierarchal order of caste (and its patriarchal view of women) at its center. In the past few decades, ever since Dalits were able to reach out to global communities to discuss their experiences, those belonging to the upper castes have become more vehement in their attempts to distance Indian/Hindu culture from caste. They posit that the caste system was not truly a part of Hinduism until the arrival of the British in the 1600s when they created these artificial categories to divide the local population. As plenty of data and research suggests, that is a cover-up for a much deeper and older malaise.

Chaturvarna, the system that divides Hindus into four unequal castes and pushes Dalits (considered untouchables) outside of that system, was standard practice in the subcontinent long before the seventeenth century. This is not to let the British off the hook. While they (in their avatars as the East India Company and later as the Raj) might not have created the caste system, they did formalize these established categories, even creating new ones, using what sociologist G. Aloysius calls a "statistical sleight of hand."[1] They exploited it to ensure that Indians did not come together against them. They pushed the upper castes into the top of most power structures in the subcontinent. Aloysius calls them "a particularly pragmatic type of imperialists . . . who were careful not to disturb the social order and this policy stood them well."[2]

There are several theories about the origins of the caste system in India. Sociologist and human rights activist Gail Omvedt in her book *Dalits and the Democratic Revolution: Dr. Ambedkar and the Dalit Movement in Colonial India* (1994) looks at the work of anthropologists such as Gregory Possehl, Morton Klass, and Morton Fried to see how caste groups came about.[3] Starting with pre-Hindu civilizations like the Indus Valley, she examines tribes or groups of agriculturists, hunters, and fishers who exchanged surplus goods. Over time, these groups evolved into "jatis." However, these jatis existed mainly among Dravidians (believed to be the original inhabitants of the subcontinent) since there were no caste-like groups among the Aryans (people from Central Asia) when they came to the subcontinent. There is no indication that caste or caste groups existed among the ancient Mundari tribes from Jharkhand, Assam, Odisha, West Bengal, Chhattisgarh, Bihar, and Bangladesh or the Sino-Tibetan tribes of the Northeast. The Dravidians already had caste-type groups and a prevailing notion of purity and pollution. With the converging of the Aryans and Dravidians into one society, the Aryans exaggerated the concepts of purity and pollution and used it to maintain their superiority. The division into the four castes of Brahmin, Kshatriya, Vaishya, and Shudra "was developed to legitimate the way in which divisions among the Aryans were solidifying and indigenous groups were absorbed into a new system."

The British understanding of caste was predicated on the (now debunked) Aryan Invasion theory, also called the Aryan theory of race. European Orientalists, who were convinced of their superiority as white men, argued that Brahmins, Kshatriyas, and Vaishyas were descended from the pure, superior Aryans. Dalits and Shudras, on the other hand, were mulnivasis—the original inhabitants of the Indian subcontinent. The narrative of Aryan superiority was already popular at the time: European Orientalists used it to establish an "ethnic kinship between Europeans and ancient Vedic peoples," and upper-caste Indians declared themselves equal to the "white-skinned conquerors" and some upper-caste nationalist leaders of the time claimed the theory proved "their superiority over the low castes of the subcontinent."[4] Aryan/upper-caste superiority was used as the justification for the existence and continuation of the caste system. Social activist and anti-caste reformer Jyotirao Phule challenged this theory in the 1800s by turning it on its head. He denounced Aryans as invaders who had exploited the rightful inhabitants of the Indian subcontinent—the Dalits and Shudras.

More recently, there has been new evidence that indicates that the "Indo-European language speakers" did not invade but migrated to the subcontinent around 2000 to 1500 BCE.[5] This coincides with the composition of the Rig Veda, the oldest known Hindu scripture. As the religion evolved, Manu—considered the first human by some—is believed to have written Manusmriti, a code of conduct, around 1,800 years ago. This treatise delineates the place of everyone in society. As per Vedic scriptures and the Manusmriti, Dalits were considered pollutants.[6] They lived outside the villages or main residential areas in bastis or wadas, used separate roads and water bodies, and were denied direct association with the rest of society. The caste system's unequal ranking that binds people to certain professions appears to have been created to protect the powerful few. The higher castes could avoid hard manual labor, guaranteeing them and their descendants generations of respected positions and the material wealth that follows from that. But for this to work, it was essential for the lower castes and untouchables to fully accept their existence of servile labor and crushing poverty. The concept of karma—paying for the sins of previous lives in subsequent lifetimes—was one means of accomplishing that. It convinced those who were born as lower caste that their status was a result of their own actions in previous lives. Not only did they have to deal with inequality in this life; they also had to contend with the guilt for what they might have done in the previous one. Karmically defiled, the Dalits had to be the ones to take on the most unpleasant tasks as professions. Their shadows, if cast on an upper-caste person, were believed to defile, and they crouched, bent, and prostrated themselves to ensure that others did not get polluted.

Dr. B. R. Ambedkar also propounded a theory of how untouchability could have come about.[7] According to him, Hindus stopped eating beef and turned vegetarian during the Gupta Period (third to sixth century CE). At this time, Buddhism was finding new followers as a nonviolent religion. In order to compete with the nonviolent teachings of Buddhism, Hinduism adapted, with many spiritual leaders propagating a vegetarian lifestyle. This was a lifestyle that upper-caste people took to easily. But the poorer lower castes had to rely on cheap and nutrient-rich beef. They were termed "impure."

Ambedkar also researched the means and causes that sustained caste in Hinduism for centuries. In his 1916 paper, "Castes in India: Their Mechanism, Genesis and Development," Ambedkar concluded that practices like sati, the dehumanizing isolation of widows, and marriages of prepubescent girls, some as young as five or six, to much older men, in their thirties or forties, were a means to control the problems of the surplus man and surplus woman in a caste and maintain endogamy.[8] Ambedkar argued that all three practices were to prevent upper-caste men and women from marrying outside their caste. He accurately pointed out that these practices were not only harmful to the lower castes but also to upper-caste women. Rejecting all existing definitions, Ambedkar limited caste to a single characteristic—endogamy. In *Nationalism Without a Nation*, Aloysius built on that definition to include ascriptive hierarchy, which unequally ranks different castes to create unstable power structures, and its overall validation by Hinduism, to explain the system of castes.[9]

However the caste system came about, it came to mean that Dalits had no right to education, land, no access to temples or personal vanity. Those who dared to pursue any of these rights, even to wear clean clothes and jewelry, were seen as insulting upper-caste people, and were punished accordingly.

By the eighteenth century, the British had developed their own theories. For all their rhetoric about India's cultural and social backwardness, they did nothing to knock down a system as grossly unequal as caste and, in fact, exploited it to suit their interests. Untouchability was the "rule of the land" and they quickly caught on that if caste divided their colonial subjects, they would never fully unite to revolt. In fact, the British Commissioner of Deccan even admitted in a judgment that "An equalising policy would ultimately reduce British stability." The laws that the British established sided with the upper-caste majority, and they claimed that they did not want to interfere in local beliefs and practices. Whether it was during the Kala Ram Temple Entry Movement in Nasik in 1930, when they banned Dalits from entering because it was "against the established custom," or when they paid damages to upper-caste people after Dalits led by Ambedkar drank water from the public Chawdar tank, British laws let the upper castes get away with noxious discrimination and abuse. Phule and Ambedkar both criticized the British for their spineless policies with regard to caste.

British passivity to caste hierarchies extended to education. Since Dalits were not allowed education under the caste system, the British did not force schools to admit Dalit children. They set up separate schools for Dalits and Bahujans, but the teachers (most of whom were Brahmins) would often refuse to teach them. They argued that if Dalits were trained as teachers, it would have calamitous consequences as the gods would be displeased. Phule in 1872 questioned why no such calamity had hit the country when "ati-shudras" (Dalits) were enlisted in the British army.[10] Even in British-run schools, education was heavily Brahminical and discriminated against Dalits. When Brahmins complained of textbooks that criticized the caste system, the British removed those textbooks.

The British did not simply look the other way, allowing casteism to continue unabated. They built entire systems that they handed over to the upper castes so they could continue to discriminate against and exclude Dalits. The British administration in India comprised a small number of Britons. It was the Brahmins, Kshatriyas, and Vaishyas who became part of the bureaucracy while Dalits were kept to their traditional roles. Brahmins, in particular, became auxiliary rulers of the country (where earlier it had been the Kshatriyas) and were "trained through apprenticeship in the art of modern ruling."[11] It wasn't just administration that the British handed over to the upper castes. They also gave the upper castes power over land and agriculture, the largest source of livelihood in the eighteenth and nineteenth centuries. The British were not interested in administering the colonies, but were interested in the money made from taxes imposed on farmers. The upper castes now began to create policies and subsequently even the entire administrative structure that served their interests. Brahmins were appointed to explain local laws and practices to British judges. This meant that Dalits did not even get a chance to have their cases heard properly. Since the presence of a Dalit was considered polluting, they were not allowed anywhere near the Brahmin assistants of the judges. Instead, they would shout from one end of the room (sometimes from outside the room) and important details were often lost as a result of this practice.

At Independence, the British handed over the bureaucracy, judiciary, agriculture, media, and education to the upper castes. They created the template on which, according to Aloysius, the future of India was to be constructed.[12] At the time of Independence, when most Dalits were still learning to read, upper-caste people had been businessmen, bureaucrats, journalists, lawyers, judges, and politicians for several generations. When the British left, they were trained and ready to take over the reins of the new country. Dalits continued to struggle in the system that was still controlled by the upper castes.

Despite all this, some of the policies that the British introduced unwittingly ended up freeing Dalits from the death grip of caste. Untouchability was not banned, but the British rulers did not see a difference between the various classes of colonial subjects. Even that marginal equality challenged the idea of Dalit "lowerness." Education in British schools that introduced the ideas of equality and liberty allowed Dalits to reject the narrative of upper-caste superiority. The introduction of technology and mass communication—radio, magazines, and newspapers—allowed Dalit printing presses to educate Dalits about their rights. While the British never chose Dalits to lead departments or for administrative work, Dalits could still access public employment. Even at the lowest rungs, it provided some relief from their dehumanizing caste-based professions.[13] My mother's grandfather was able to think of a different future for his family. Instead of our caste profession of manual scavenging, he joined the British Indian army. These professions helped Dalits imagine new futures for themselves and their children.

There were some other ways that the British created some freedoms for the lower castes. Even before the East India Company was established, Christian missionaries from many parts of the world made their way to the subcontinent. Their main mission was, of course, to spread

Christianity in this part of the world. The Anglican missionaries who started coming around the early nineteenth century were abolitionists who wanted the Dalit slaves to not only be free but also recognize themselves as equal to the upper castes. In line with movements the world over, the British abolished slavery with the Indian Slavery Act of 1843. This act has been criticized for being very limited in scope—it made economic activity from slavery illegal, but did not entirely abolish bonded labor. In any case, the British also exploited those "freed slaves" by shipping them to other colonies, like the Caribbean islands, as indentured labor. Former British colonies like Trinidad, Guyana, and Jamaica have sizeable Indian-origin populations from the freed slaves who were sent there between 1843 and 1917.[14]

Once slavery was abolished, some Anglican missionaries began focusing on the newly freed Dalit slaves.[15] The missionaries started "slave schools" where, according to academic Sanal Mohan, Dalit men and women were taught the "word of the Lord" and basic reading and writing. Around the middle of the nineteenth century, probably inspired by their work and teaching, many Dalits converted to Protestant Christianity in what was one of the biggest such mass conversions.

Education was one part of the effort, but the missionaries also focused on improving social acceptance for Dalits. But rather than teach upper-caste Christians to not discriminate against Dalits, they focused instead on improving Dalit habits. They encouraged Dalits to give up eating dead animal meat. All these initiatives were necessary because even though slavery had been abolished, the social prejudices that considered former slaves as "polluting" and "untouchable" did not disappear. The discrimination and abuse that Dalits faced before conversion followed them even after they turned Christian. Dalits had not escaped the social standards where they were considered "low" just by moving out of the ambit of Hinduism. The caste system invaded Christianity, following the same patterns of exclusion and discrimination as it did in Hinduism. When people converted to sects like Syrian Christianity they brought caste with them. They often held on to their upper-caste origins and continued to discriminate against Dalit Christians. Upper-caste Syrian Christians refused to attend the same congregations as Dalits and even decades after Dalit conversion, demanded separation, because of "hygiene issues."[16] By the early twentieth century, Dalit Christians, much like non-Christian Dalits, had little to no access to public facilities like roads, education, the justice system; they were not allowed to own land.[17] When Dalit Christians sought admission for their children in schools, it often caused a violent backlash from upper-caste Christians. Dalits were forced to create separate churches and congregations.

Rejected by traditional religion, Dalit Christians focused on social change through education and reform. They created several radical movements to oppose discrimination from upper-caste Christians and Hindus. In fact, Dalit movements in Kerala started as early as the late 1800s. Among the most significant was the one led by Ayyankali, who was born in a non-slave agricultural Dalit Pulaya family. One of his earliest political acts in 1898 was defying the Dalit ban in public spaces by riding in a decorated bullock cart, which was only reserved for the upper castes. In 1907, he demanded that all students be allowed admission to government schools regardless of their caste. He mobilized several Dalits and organized them into a group that was later called Ayyankali's army to generate support for the cause. Ayyankali's army consistently challenged discrimination against Dalits and engaged in radical acts of claiming public spaces that were banned to them. Upper-caste communities lashed out with violence but, according to Mohan, their acts of rebellion had a "domino effect in mobilizing Dalits" to claim their rights.

At the time of the framing of the Constitution of independent India, according to Rupa Viswanath, academic and author of *The Pariah Problem* (2014), it became crucial to identify who the Dalits were so that reservation policies could be decided. At the time, the benefits of reservation and protection through the Untouchability Offenses Act, 1955, were only given to Dalits under the larger fold of Hinduism. Later it was extended to Sikh Dalits in 1956 and in 1990 to Buddhist Dalits. However, Christian Dalits who face similar exclusion in jobs, landowning, and inter-caste marriages still don't have the same legal status as Dalits. Despite separate Dalit churches, the discrimination and prejudice were acknowledged only in 2016.[18] In 1990, the Dalit Christian Leaders Forum demanded the same legal recognition as Sikh and Buddhist Dalits. But, according to Mohan, since they don't have enough political representation in Parliament, Dalit Christians are still not legally considered Dalits. However, there is an exception for Tribal Dalit Christians. If a member of an ST converts to Christianity, according to a 2005 Supreme Court ruling, they retain the constitutional and legal benefits of being Dalits.[19]

Christian and Muslim Dalits are not a large political force and therefore it seems that their interest matters very little to those in charge. Since their votes aren't enough to make or break an election, political parties often ignore their rights without facing any real consequences. It's hardly a surprise that the issue of their discrimination has gone unresolved this far and they feel the only way out for them is by giving up their religion. Hindu, Sikh, and Buddhist Dalits might be able to avail themselves of constitutional reservation and protection under the SC and ST Act, but the apathy they face from policy-makers and violence from upper castes are just the same. Perhaps this is what Rohith meant in his letter when he wrote: "A vote, a number, a thing. Never was a man treated as a mind. As a glorious thing made up of stardust." For them, we are just Hindu, Muslim, Sikh, Christian, and Buddhist votes "reduced to our immediate identity and nearest possibility."

CHAPTER 3

EDUCATION AND FINANCIAL STRIFE

Ajmer in the nineties was a small town, but it had all the essential conveniences. With a few factories, a robust rail network, and several educational institutions, the city provided the framework needed for those who lived there to eke out a comfortable existence. Unlike the rest of Rajasthan, which was largely part of various princely states before Independence, Ajmer was ruled directly by the British until 1947. Centuries of British rule have left a mark on the city—in the Victorian-style churches, substantial Christian and Anglo-Indian population, and a laid-back, somewhat anglicized vibe. The British also chose to establish several educational institutions in the city, some of which, like the Mayo College, are known for their quality education even today. Apart from Mayo, they also set up many convent schools which, along with a government medical college, an engineering college, and the state Secondary Education Board, have turned Ajmer into an attractive education hub. The hard-to-miss colonial hangover gave the town a distinct sense of quasi-cosmopolitanism that mixed comfortably with the traditional Marwari and Jain culture of the city.

For us—Mum, Dad, and me—the city presented the perfect platform to transcend our caste. After the difficult circumstances of my birth, Mum probably acquiesced in her reality, and attempted to make the best of it. I remember watching her get ready, her eighties-style perm luminous under the fluorescent mirror light, as she applied dark metallic eyeshadow. Sometimes she wore tiny kitten heels when we went out, even though the piercing pain in her injured ankle would make it difficult for her to sleep later that night. A photograph of my parents in the audience of a school function from when I was four shows her wearing a gorgeous pair of cream-colored heels, the crepe bandage still visible on her foot. There are other pictures of her in structured pants, slim-fit shirts, and bold patterned salwar-kurtas—experimental fashion choices that stood out in largely conservative Ajmer.

Movie nights, occasional eating out, socializing with Dad's few friends were among our weekly rituals. They mimicked the upper-middle-class habits of the early nineties, even when our financial situation didn't. They were a curated performance designed mostly by Mum's aspiration to break out from our lower caste. The biggest show of the year would often be my birthday party. Every year till I turned five, Mum baked elaborate cakes from scratch—her 2-kg rabbit cake and a three-tier witch's house from the "Hansel and Gretel" fairy tale were remembered for many years—and prepared a feast for at least thirty guests. It was an occasion to declare our "higher" class status and an attempt to camouflage our lower caste. Classmates who lived nearby, and other kids from the neighborhood I hardly ever played with, would be invited, along with their families. Dad, his younger brother, sister, and my grandfather would invite their friends and associates. Dad's siblings and their friends would spend the day decorating the house with ribbons, fairy lights, and streamers. The party would last all evening, with Boney M and Abba playing in the background. It wasn't your average birthday party for a child; it was an assertion that we were the "equals" of the upper castes.

Fashion and lifestyle choices were a significant but ultimately smaller part of that performance of upper-casteness. The toughest act was speaking perfect English. Dad had studied at one of the English-medium convent schools in the city and spoke decent English, although with the slightly forced accent typical of his generation. Mum was less privileged in her upbringing, as her father only joined the Excise Department when she was thirteen. (He had spent many years after his marriage preparing for the exam while also holding down several part-time jobs while his father supported the entire family.) Mum and her siblings attended the local school in her small town that offered English as a subject but not as a medium of education. There she learned to read and write the language but didn't get much opportunity to speak it. By the time she graduated from college with a bachelor's degree in English literature, Mum could write papers on twentieth-century English authors, but didn't feel confident speaking the language. Being able to talk in perfect English with no trace of a regional accent remains the mark of wealth, pedigree, class, and even intelligence in modern India. A failure to master fluency in the language can often indicate the failure of a person overall. Most Dalits and many non-Dalits, particularly in northern and western India, struggle with speaking that kind of English. Many, like Mum, read and understand it perfectly, but fear being mocked for their accent and grammar. *English Vinglish* (2012), directed by Gauri Shinde, tackled the subject masterfully, with Sridevi playing the part of a homemaker whose children and husband ridicule her incorrect pronunciation or misunderstanding of certain words. Their hurtful remarks routinely upset Shashi (the name of Sridevi's character and also my mother's name) who appears visibly deflated and diffident as a result. She joins an English-speaking course in New York (where she's visiting her sister) where, among non-Indians, she learns to separate her worth from her ability to master a colonial keepsake, and ultimately regains her confidence.

The proliferation of hundreds of English-speaking courses in India underlines the assumed link between English and excellence. These courses would have you believe that knowing English guarantees success, a claim that the current job market seems to back. Undeniably, English is essential to compete in a global economy, but it doesn't supersede education, talent, or intelligence. The citizens of several non-English-speaking countries do just as well in a multicultural world as their English-proficient counterparts. As a developing country, our English-fluent population is among our strongest global resources. Yet, it doesn't justify hurting the self-worth of or denying the ability of a majority that feels less than confident in communicating in English. Ultimately, our unnatural deference to English is a result of our internalized colonial hangover. The British are long gone but we still use someone's facility for the language to gauge their place in society and whether we consider them worthy of respect.

Mum shared that veneration for English with the rest of the country and with good reason. Despite her bachelor's degree in English literature, Dad and members of his family continually attacked her for not "knowing how to speak English." She also knew that anyone—even a Dalit—who spoke "good" English would be treated with instant respect. So she decided that I would speak the language fluently—it would gain me the respect and acceptance that she had not received.

My parents spoke to each other in Hindi, but I grew up mostly bilingual: speaking English and Hindi almost equally well. Even when I was young, I knew the English names and pronunciations for most common fruits and vegetables, even those not yet available in India. At one family wedding, when I demanded a date instead of khajoor (as it's called in Hindi) Mum told me it was the most proud I'd made her. A child growing up in the urban middle-class India of the eighties and nineties might find it surprising that this was an achievement to be proud of. But for a Dalit family living in Ajmer it was aspirational. Even at five, I could sense that people reacted to my ease of expression with a combination of mild annoyance, jealousy, and grudging respect. Maybe that's why I started reading when I was very young. When my parents gifted me a copy of *Oliver Twist* for my sixth birthday (it was too advanced for me and I quickly abandoned it) like most of their peers, they were hoping to inculcate healthy habits in me early, but their impetus was different. Only if I excelled in English—reading, writing, and speaking—could I compensate for our Dalitness. I *needed* to become fluent. So I read magazines like *India Today* and *Femina*, which we subscribed to, paid extra attention in English class, and diligently practiced writing in cursive script. Even staring at the TV when I didn't understand the accent of British shows like *Mind Your Language* or *Yes, Minister* made me feel like I was better than my classmates.

From the time I was very young, I was in training to join Sophia, which was then considered one of the top convent schools in Ajmer. Mum and I would rehearse for the interview every chance we got—when she was pulling on my socks, feeding me dinner, or when we were standing in line at the grocery store. She didn't even want to wait for me to reach the eligible age of four, so we went for an interview when I was three. But perhaps because of all this expectation, or more likely because I was a young child who got nervous, I didn't do well in the interview. So for that year I had to attend a smaller and relatively new public school in the neighborhood. My parents had found it hilarious that when I came out of the interview, I blamed the principal's halitosis for my failure. But I do remember them recounting my flippant response, and I could sense Mum's barely concealed regret. I already knew I hadn't lived up to what they expected of me and decided that I wouldn't allow that to happen again, ever. When I appeared for the interview a year later, it was with a different principal. But nothing would have made a difference since I had decided that, no matter what, I was going to clear the interview this time, and I did. Sophia school's convent education impacted my life in all the ways Mum had imagined it would. I finished most of my schooling there and even got elected as the head of the school council—a minor triumph. But I never forgot that I didn't make it the first time.

My sister and brother were born in quick succession a year apart from each other. Dad's family who had grudgingly accepted a first-born daughter were not so magnanimous when Mum gave birth to a second girl. For all their progressiveness, that was two daughters too many. It was their constant jibes that forced Mum to have another baby, knowing well that raising a third child would be unsustainable in our straitened financial conditions. Her in-laws' response to two girl children wasn't surprising, particularly in Rajasthan, known for its high rates of female feticide and infanticide.[1] During both pregnancies, Mum was often sick; her ill health was exacerbated by the stress from arguing with Dad's family and his constant drinking. But the third pregnancy was particularly dangerous and, after a heated blowup at home, the doctor advised Dad to move her away from this environment. Even though we had already moved out once and then returned once my sister was born, this time it seemed more final. A few months after we moved out of my grandparents' house, Dad came to pick me up from school to tell me that we finally had a baby brother.

Even though our family barely counted as lower middle class, I spent my first five years living the life of a coddled, upper-middle-class kid. In those years when it was just the three of us, Mum tried her best, and more or less succeeded in keeping up appearances. Dad's government salary barely covered the basics. His constant benders cut his small paycheck even smaller. Initially, we survived on a near steady stream of help from Mum's father. When that became less frequent,

Mum began pawning her wedding jewelry, hoping that once we had more money, she would be able to recover it. By the time my sister was born, we relied on the remittance from Mum's jewelry as an alternative source of income. But as the years went by, and Dad received neither a promotion nor a raise, it became clear that it was easier to let the jewelry go instead of paying the high accumulated interest to get it back. Initially, Mum was hesitant about pawning her jewelry. She would use a gold bangle to pay my school fees or a pair of earrings for a sundry medical expense. By the time I was six, she was selling big-ticket items like a heavy gold set for a few months of warm clothes, uniforms, and food. Her family opposed her spending habits. They didn't understand why she couldn't send me to study in a local Hindi-medium school where books and uniforms would be heavily subsidized. Or why we needed to dress in the few good clothes we had, when we couldn't afford them. But for Mum, her jewelry and personal vanity mattered a lot less than the social (upper-caste) acceptance of her children. If she was going to stick with a terrible marriage, she decided that at least we children should come out unscathed.

In 1992, with little jewelry left to sell, Mum decided the only way to keep Dad from drinking was to keep an eye on him at all times. He was now posted in Merta City, a bleak town in western Rajasthan. So that is where she went with a new baby, a toddler, and a seven-year-old in tow. Merta City is a hamlet in Nagaur, which has remained one of the most underdeveloped (officially called industrially backward) districts of Rajasthan. She hoped that staying with his family and seeing his children daily would motivate Dad to drink less and be more focused on his job. Named somewhat ambitiously, Merta City then had a population of less than thirty thousand and almost no decent schools. My parents had decided to enroll me in Sophia's boarding school so as to not upset my education. But they understood that staying away from home at seven was a big ask, especially from their indulged firstborn. Yet, to their surprise, I didn't answer them with a "yes" or "no" when they asked me if I was okay with it. Instead, I remember asking "how"—as in how can you afford to send me to a hostel when paying my school fees is a struggle?

Even at that age, I felt somewhat responsible for the increased stress and the arguments my parents were having while discussing my school fees every quarter. A year earlier, while visiting my Mum's parents' house, one of her brothers had brazenly asked me why I wanted to "inconvenience" my parents with my expensive school fees. I didn't fully understand Mum's reasons, but I knew it was important to have a "good standard" and that we couldn't have that if I went to a bad school. If I needed to stand out, I had to study in Sophia. Despite knowing this, I couldn't help but feel guilty about the way my mum was educating me when she couldn't afford it. For many years after, till I was an adult, that conversation echoed, leaving me feeling like a spoilt, demanding child who thought she was *so* special that she deserved a good education, when as made sufficiently clear by my uncle, I wasn't. I remember wanting to prove to him, and pretty much everyone else, that I was indeed good enough to deserve that education. And even if I wasn't, I would work twice as hard to ensure no one questioned my right to it again. If my mum was indeed doing me a "favor," as my uncle had implied, then I *needed* to return it in full, with excellent grades.

I joined the hostel in the middle of the school year. It didn't affect my classes, except that instead of taking a school bus I could now walk to class from the dormitory. But unlike other girls who had simply left their houses to share a huge hall-like space with seventy-five others, I was also leaving the safety net of my family's upper-caste performance. But that's precisely why Mum chose to send me there. Living with upper-caste girls was meant to train me to be like them. By picking up little details like how they spoke, braided their hair, or tucked in their sheets—some of the markers of upper-caste culture—I would successfully blend in with them for the rest of my life. So far I had not needed much in my armory to convince people that I was like them—middle class and upper caste. A few "going out" clothes, a pair of thin gold hoops and sturdy shoes made me look as middle class and upper caste as anyone I knew. But a boarding school meant that I would need to pretend I was upper caste in nearly every breathing, waking, and sleeping moment—an onerous effort for most adults and nearly impossible for a seven-year-old. But living with upper-caste girls as openly Dalit would shake my self-esteem and perhaps scar me forever, never allowing me to climb out of the caste cage. So the only choice was to maintain the upper-caste aura. Mum feared that without the necessary trappings, my outing as a Dalit would happen in less than a week. So she spent money we clearly didn't have on more expensive things that would make up for my caste. Shoes that lit up with multicolored lights as I walked, the It kid's shoe of 1992, high-quality buckets and mugs made from shiny plastic, and matte gold studs for my ears were meant to convey that we were rich so that no one would wonder if we were the right caste.

We didn't have much money when I was young. But even for Dalit families who are better off, this "performance" of being upper caste is necessary to blend in. "Books were never denied, music was cultivated like a subject. . . . Festivals and food celebrated with aplomb. Clothes and appearances were cared for, shoes were always polished," Neha Bhujang, who is an engineer and openly Dalit, shared her story on *Documents of Dalit Discrimination*. In the same post, she talks about her parents' forced deference to upper-caste villagers through Marathi salutations like "Johar Mai Baap"—you are my mother and father, you are my supremacy and I bow to you. "This was proof that no matter your economic status, caste is like a tattoo on your face that you cannot hide," she wrote. Neha also opened up about growing up like an upper-caste, middle-class girl but never speaking about her Dalitness for fear of being "ostracized."

Even as Mum took me around the city buying unnecessarily expensive daily comforts, she knew there was one thing she had little control over—my skin color. More wheatish/tan than fair, it was close to her own coloring, and she worried that all her effort to stage-manage our affluence and, in effect, our upper-casteness would get upended by my "not-so-fair" skin shade.

We are a society that is obsessed with fairness—the Indian skin-whitening industry was worth around $450 million (3,163 crore Indian rupees approximately) in 2016. We demand that potential brides be "very fair" and are openly bigoted against darker-skinned men and women who don't fit our idea of "fairness equating beauty." These biases are blatantly manifest in educational institutions, workplaces, and, inarguably, the arranged marriage market. The bias against dark skin affects both men and women, but in our patriarchal setup, it is women who suffer its consequences the most. Hurtful and mean comments like "black crow" and facetious concern regarding their inability to land a life partner are a big part of the lives of dark-skinned women. Colorism, or a bias against darker skin, is commonly traced to the British, who used their pale complexions to justify violence, prejudice, and superiority over brown-skinned Indians. The British first ventured into the slave trade in Africa in the fifteenth century where they trafficked African men and women and sold them as human livestock to traders in Europe. They used racism—the idea that dark-skinned Africans were inherently inferior—as a justification for forcing people into subhuman servitude that extended over generations.[2] Scottish philosopher David Hume further rationalized racism in his infamous 1748 essay "Of National Characters." In a footnote, he wrote: "I am apt to suspect the Negroes and in general all other species of men (for there are four or five different kinds) to be naturally inferior to the whites. There never was a civilised nation of any other complexion than white, nor even any individual eminent either in action or speculation."[3] The idea of white supremacy over other races gained strength in later centuries as the British expanded their colonial empire to the Indian subcontinent as well as other countries in Africa and Asia. British writers like Rudyard Kipling and Thomas Carlyle further defended British colonialism and racism: the idea that it was the "more civilized" white man's duty to imperialize (and civilize) nonwhite peoples.[4]

Yet, many are unaware that caste prejudice has been linked to a "darker" skin shade since before the British arrived. Academic Radhika Parameswaran researched transnational media activism targeting colorism, beauty, and sexism in India a few years ago, and talks of a strong cultural perception that links skin color and caste.[5] Classical texts dating to the pre-British era also seem to identify cannibalism with darker-skinned tribals in the subcontinent.[6] The idea that equates fairness with a higher caste had existed long before the eighteenth century. Some Brahmins and Kshatriyas, who were generally paler skinned, used the eugenics argument to justify the caste system and declare themselves as "Aryan" or European. (Humanist thinker and Nobel-prize winner Rabindranath Tagore, who was Brahmin, examined endogamy—the custom of marrying within the same caste—in his work.)

In modern India, caste and color are deeply connected, with both being equated with notions of purity/cleanliness and impurity/pollution. Some scholars still argue that Dalits and tribals are descended from the darker indigenous Dravidians and the upper castes from lighter-skinned Aryans. Unsurprisingly, this theory as well as the heavily debunked eugenics argument continue to be widely popular among caste supremacists. It's alarming to note the regularity with which they appear in the arguments of online trolls hoping to justify casteism, even in recent years. Taunting people, especially women, for their dark skin is so ingrained, particularly in north Indian culture, that a popular comedy show on national television saw nothing wrong in airing an episode mostly centered around ridiculing a dark-skinned actress. Tannishtha Chatterjee took to Facebook in 2016 to condemn her humiliation on the show, where she was invited as a guest:

> Once I was asked: "Your surname is Chatterjee? Oh you are Brahmin. What is your mother's surname? Maitra! Oh . . . She is Brahmin too." And then indirectly he hinted how is my skin tone still dark . . . This is so deep rooted and linked to our perceptions of caste, class and skin tone. Upper caste = fair skin = touchable. Lower caste = dark skin = untouchable.

It quickly went viral and dominated the national conversation for weeks. Promisingly, "transmedia activism" against dark-skin bias, like Chatterjee's post, has become more visible in the past two decades. A-list actors, including Shah Rukh Khan, have been called out by their own colleagues for endorsing fairness creams. Abhay Deol, in particular, has been vocal about how Bollywood is complicit in promoting a bias against dark skin. Nandita Das's "Dark Is Beautiful" campaign has been active for several years and many dark-skinned models have repeatedly criticized the fashion industry's prejudice against casting them. Yet, the contempt for darker skin and a parallel zeal for fairness persist. India's skin-whitening industry, with specific fairness creams for women, men, armpits, and even vaginas, was projected to grow by 18 percent annually in 2015.

But even before Unilever launched Fair & Lovely, arguably India's first and most enduringly popular fairness cream, kitchen remedies worked double shift to make us fair. An entire branch of Ayurveda deals with face packs and masks made with spices, roots, fruits, pulses, and vegetables. While a lot of them are medicinal and focus on treating ailments or skin issues, many promise "glowing" or "fairer" skin. Some of these packs or "ubtans" have mythological and ritualistic roots in Hinduism—Goddess Parvati is known to have created Ganesh from the sandalwood paste she rubbed off her body, the haldi ceremony in Hindu weddings intends to deliver a "bridal glow." Beyond ceremonies, these ubtan recipes have circulated for years, passed down from mother to daughter and, more recently, in the beauty columns of magazines. The letters grown women and teenagers write to these columns seeking advice to "make them fair" are a heartbreaking reminder of how women are mistreated in our society, especially the arranged marriage market, because of their skin color.

While my mother didn't spend most of her childhood and teen years writing in to these columns, she did grow up reading them, almost obsessively. She would try a new ubtan every week and faithfully shielded her arms, face, and other uncovered body parts from the stinging rays of the sun; she still does. Even her mother and grandmother bathed with homemade ubtan instead of soap. But that has made little difference to the color of her honey-toned skin (it has, however, kept it smooth for decades). Dad's family would ridicule her for not being fair enough, even as most of them, except Dad, were of the same skin tone. I was born a light-skinned child who grew up to be progressively darker, until my skin tone was the same as Mum's. This became a constant source of anxiety for her. Before I was old enough to remember or protest, she started bathing me with ubtans—something I had no choice but to follow till middle school.

I hated ubtans, especially the part where I had to sit on a tiny plastic stool waiting for the thick, cold paste to dry. I often tried to outsmart Mum by applying small patches on my arms or legs. Mum quickly caught on, and would come into the bathroom to rub it on me in big, cold goops. Sometimes, when washing it off hastily as I rushed to get ready for school, I would miss some hard-to-reach places like my elbows and behind my ears. By the time the second period started, the paste would have caked into dry flaky pieces that would fall onto my notebooks as well as my classmates'. I hated my classmates' cruel jokes even more than the ubtan. Even if on some confused level I understood that I *needed* to be fair to be accepted, and not "Dalit-looking," there was no way I could explain that to them. So I'd quickly and wordlessly scrub it off when someone noticed that I still had some of my "Dalitness" sticking to me.

While packing my luggage for the boarding school at Sophia, Mum had slipped in a bag of the dry powder I was supposed to mix with milk or water and use during my bath. Before leaving me at the dormitory, she also left unnecessarily detailed instructions on how that was to be done with the seventeen-year-old caretaker who managed the "junior girls" in that wing. I knew the caretaker did not appreciate Mum's directive because she repeatedly reminded me of it for the two years I lived there, often humiliating me in front of my hostel mates. During the common bath time, she would loudly inquire about that powder my mum left for me to become fair. Of all the times my ubtan embarrassed me, those were the worst. My seven years so far had taught me nothing about standing up for myself, or defending what I thought was right. I also lacked the entitlement that a combination of wealth and caste pride allow many, even at that young age, to take on much older, more influential bullies with fortitude. I was poor and pretending to be upper caste in a hostel filled with mostly older girls; I had to fit in. So I joined the raucous laughter in the room or smiled like I was in on the joke she was making at my expense and about Mum, even as a part of me cringed. The caretaker must have sensed that I was hiding something, for she soon added a new element to her weekly routine: asking me if I thought my mother was a bad person. She wasn't content with just mocking me, she also needed me to assure her that she was right.

I didn't tell Mum about this. I knew she would want to intervene or report it to the administration. And I thought that would only make things worse for me. The caretaker might be reprimanded. But after that, living at the hostel could get a lot worse. Pretending to dislike my own mother while blaming myself for not defending her didn't take long to turn into deep self-disgust. That plastic bag of ubtan became its center and source. I would shove it deep into the belly of my locker so no one, not even I, could see it. The bag would sit there unopened during the semester and I would bring it home with me during the break. Even though Mum had half-expected that I wouldn't actually use it, she would still be disappointed. During the weeks I spent at home, she would go through old magazines looking for the least messy ubtan recipes. She'd spend hours searching for the ingredients, and painstakingly blend them either by hand or in an old mixer. I would return to the hostel with a new packet and fresh fodder for the bullying. And as much I wanted to, I could never throw it away either. During those long months away from home, that bag was my connection to my mother.

CHAPTER 4

HUMILIATION IN MUSSOORIE

At the end of my second year in the hostel at Sophia, it closed down. By that time, my family had moved to Gangapur City in the Sawai Madhopur district, where Dad was posted. It was only a slight improvement on Merta City, in the sense that the shops stocked white bread and its well-connected railway station had turned it into a somewhat important small town in the area. Trains that ran between New Delhi, Mumbai, Jammu, and Amritsar—cities that were part of the West Central Railways—often halted there. A handful of railway officials lived in town as a result. One official told my parents about Oak Grove, the Northern Railway-owned and -subsidized boarding school in the hill town of Mussoorie that his daughters attended. He also mentioned the direct train that ran between Gangapur City and Dehradun that made visiting the school in Mussoorie convenient, even though it was 600 kilometers away. He offered to enlist us as his relatives to get us access to the subsidized fees at the school. The idea instantly appealed to Mum, who couldn't think of a better option than a Mussoorie-based boarding school for my education after Sophia. Since we had started living with Dad, our financial situation had somewhat improved, but we still couldn't afford two sets of fees (my sister was ready to start school) at an expensive boarding school, no matter how subsidized. At that time, most middle-class families couldn't either, but that small detail failed to discourage Mum.

My semester at Sophia had overlapped with the winter-based sessions in Mussoorie and we missed the last date to submit the application to Oak Grove by a few weeks. That meant we would not get to take advantage of the subsidized fee structure at that school, but Mum had already spent over two months planning for us to study in Mussoorie. So in May that year, when the five of us boarded the Bandra Express to Dehradun, Mum was *convinced* she would somehow make it work. But it didn't work out that way. Not at Oak Grove at least. The staff at Mussoorie Public School were more helpful—it was among the few residential schools still accepting admissions when we arrived. Mum must have been prepared for the much higher fee since I had heard my parents talking about selling the "Jaipur property" my dad's grandfather had left behind. Dad, his brother, and my grandfather had equal shares in it. My grandfather of course saw no sense in selling property to "educate girls at an expensive school." In fact, he even complained to my maternal grandfather about my mother's "stubborn and wasteful expense." Despite his skepticism, Mum convinced my grandfather to sell the property, but only after months of arguing, fights, and multiple bouts of illness. Mum believed that good schooling was our only ticket into upper-casteness. Even a few years at an expensive boarding school in Mussoorie could be just what was needed.

This steely resolve to do whatever it takes to educate children isn't unusual in India. Most parents who grow up underprivileged, especially Dalits, cherish the life-changing quality of good education. They make do with the bare minimum or sell properties they have painstakingly bought over the years to pay for their kids' tuition. For many Indian parents, their children's education is their greatest achievement. If they happen to be Dalit, it means even more—educating their children after previous generations were cruelly denied any form of learning becomes their life's work. It's also far more challenging since most Dalit children can't really afford quality education. In addition to the financial barriers, Dalits also face hostility from upper-caste society, even more so when girls are being educated. Delta Meghwal's father, Mahendra Meghwal, faced similar opposition because he sent his daughter to a distant town to study. Delta was seventeen when she was allegedly raped by a teacher and murdered at the polytechnic she attended in Bikaner, Rajasthan. Bright and ambitious, Delta was the first girl from her village to complete high school and leave to study outside. Even as his neighbors in the village blame her education for her death, Mahendra Meghwal, a Dalit educator, remains proud of her achievements.

A similar sentiment drove us to stand in front of the principal's office at Mussoorie Public School. My Mum held onto my hand tightly; she must have felt as nervous as other Dalit parents who took an immense leap of faith for their children. She was taking a huge financial risk and had no support from anyone else, except Dad, who kept himself in the background. We didn't have the money to pay the fees, yet we hoped that my sister and I would secure admission. Mum knew she *had* to convince the principal to allow that. I knew I *had* to be good enough for him to do that. Before I went in for the interview, she looked at me and asked: "Ho jayega, na?" (You will get in, right?) I had no option but to say yes, and make it happen somehow.

They gave us three weeks to return with school uniforms, rain boots, bed sheets, evening uniform, and the bulkiest winter clothes I had ever seen. This time, Mum openly told me to hide my caste and answer "Parashar Brahmin" when asked. She wasn't worried about my sister, who was much paler (and could pass for upper caste) and barely three years old at the time. We arrived deep into the spring session, weeks away from the quarterly exams. Even then, we didn't have the fees in full. My grandfather knew he had no choice but to agree to sell the Jaipur property, but dragged his heels. The school administration, that had already done us a huge favor by agreeing to let us pay after the due date had passed, balked when we couldn't pay it in full. We spent the morning and afternoon going in and out of offices and waiting to see the school principal, a silver-haired educator in his late fifties, P. K. Katyal. On his way to lunch, he agreed to meet Mum and Dad, only to tell them he couldn't help. Mum shuffled out of his office wiping her red eyes with the corner of her olive-green chiffon dupatta. She had come so close . . . to be turned away at the gate. Throughout the afternoon, Mum and Dad visited every officer who was in the school administration office, hoping one of them would understand how important this admission was to us.

Each time Mum returned to check on us and sat next to my sister, baby brother, and me, her face bloated from crying for hours, I wanted to scream: "I don't want this!" Except, my screams never made it past my throat. As I sat there, watching the circus of their humiliation with mute horror and shame, I knew I did want the admission as much as Mum did. I knew this education would change my life, and I was willing to let my parents grovel for it. Eventually, Mr. Katyal gave my parents six weeks to pay the rest of the fees and agreed to admit us. By then, the shame had turned into great bitterness. I knew no matter what I achieved, it would be because I had let my mum plead and cry to make it happen. That's why, when weeks later, the same principal, Mr. Katyal, called me on stage to announce to more than four hundred students and teachers that I had scored a high rank in the exams with fewer than ten days to prepare, I felt nothing. To my mind, if someone *like me* could score so well, then this school couldn't be all that great. For years after that, this sentiment persisted—no institution that accepted me could be all that good. I was never good enough for anything, and once I became good enough, it stopped being good enough for me.

For the next two years in Mussoorie, I remained an "outstanding" student, debating, quizzing, and even, at nine, hosting important school functions. Yet, I never saw that as anything more than dumb luck or lack of competition. My understanding of caste was only half-formed at the time, but I knew there was a very real need to hide my caste. What I knew for sure was that no one expected a Dalit to be bright. So it wasn't enough for me to be bright, I had to be the "brightest" to convince them, and essentially myself, that I was their equal. When I wasn't the best at everything I did—which was most of the time—I feared that everyone would easily see through the smoke and mirrors I was working so hard to hide behind.

In *Between the World and Me*, Ta-Nehisi Coates, one of the most acute commentators on race in America, writes about the need for Black kids to be "twice as good." He describes how Black boys and girls have to work twice as hard as white kids to make it as far, and still, many of them are shortchanged—paid less, judged on their appearance, targeted for police violence—because of the systemic racism in the country. Many Dalit kids are conditioned similarly. I had to work harder so "they" could overlook my "inferiority." I couldn't pause to recognize my "triumphs" or take it easy every now and then because then I would fall behind and they would stop respecting me.

Psychologist Alice Miller explains in *The Drama of the Gifted Child* how some children who are "more sensitive" intuitively understand their parents' wishes, often without explicitly being told, and go to extreme lengths to fulfill those unspoken expectations. I first discovered Miller's book while reading a graphic memoir of a former "gifted child" and a truly gifted grown-up: Alison Bechdel. Her long-running comic strip, *Dykes to Watch Out For*, is among the earliest and most influential representations of lesbians in American popular culture. It is best known for introducing the Bechdel Test, which measures gender bias in entertainment. Bechdel went on to write *Fun Home*, an enduringly popular graphic novel that was turned into a Tony-winning Broadway musical, and even was the recipient of a MacArthur "genius" grant in 2014. *Fun Home*, her first graphic memoir, focuses on her relationship with her father, who committed suicide when she was still in college. But it's in her second memoir, *Are You My Mother?*, that she explores her "strangely inverted" relationship with her mother ("This sense that I was her mother") and uses Miller's work to build her argument. With small exceptions, I identified with most of what Bechdel draws on in her second book. Maybe because I was the firstborn or because, like many parents, mine saw in me a conduit for their own aspirations and dreams, I anticipated most of their expectations, especially those about transcending caste. The children Miller describes in her book often assume these expectations as naturally as "the air they breathe." So hiding my caste was something I internalized—it became a part of who I was instead of something I did just because my parents told me to.

By the end of our two years at Mussoorie, the money from the sale of the property had run out. While my sister and I had been away, Dad's drinking had evolved into dysfunctional alcoholism, causing violent fights with Mum. This drove her to take my brother, who was a toddler, and go to Delhi to stay with her brother. There she enrolled in a design course at the Lajpat Nagar polytechnic. Her father had passed away a year ago, and perhaps the financial insecurity that followed forced her to take this drastic step. She and my brother stayed there for several months. There, for the first time, she explored her own ambitions, however short-lived, and perhaps even dared to imagine how different her life could have been. But she knew there was no way she could raise three children in Delhi without support from my father and the rest of her family. In any case, Dad and Grandfather convinced Mum to return before the school year ended. She agreed, but on the condition that we would soon move into a place of our own in Ajmer and live separately from my grandparents.

Back in Ajmer, though, things took a turn for the worse. We were back to living with my grandparents. I was eleven, my sister five, and my brother was now old enough to start school. My sister and I enrolled in Sophia as day scholars and, wanting my brother to get the quality education we had experienced in Mussoorie, Mum secured his admission in Mayoor School, an affiliate of the Mayo College. This was a well-regarded school and one that was a lot more expensive than other convent schools in the city. Dad was now posted in Devgarh, a small town close to Udaipur, and spent most of his time there. In between his visits, money would often run out, and we would spend the week on less than twenty rupees. Even though my grandfather had convinced Mum to return home, he never helped with money or food. Mum started stitching baby clothes and petticoats and blouses again—she had tried it a few times earlier but never sustained it long term. With a new design course degree, she felt more confident in her ability to charge a price commensurate with her qualification, but in the small town we lived in, that didn't take off. The four of us would often eat cornflakes or noodles for dinner. One day when the pantry was empty, Mum rooted around in all the pockets and handbags and came up with exactly four rupees. "Go get some atta (wheat flour) from the shop to make rotis," she told me. "Tell him we were baking a cake and ran out," she added. The only shop open at the time was one where we had an outstanding bill. As I cycled over to the shop I ran through the possible scenarios in my head. I decided that the only way to pull this off would be to stay out of sight until I could whisper my request, not make eye contact, and drop the change and run away as soon as I got the bag. Of course, it didn't go that way, since the shopkeeper, who had previously asked me to remind my mother to pay the outstanding bill, spotted me immediately and demanded to know what I wanted, loud enough for the long line of customers in the back to become interested in the drama. I muttered what Mum had told me under my breath, once, twice. "Bake a cake? For four rupees?" he screamed as the other customers sniggered. I hung my head and said nothing, desperately hoping to somehow become invisible. For years now we had pretended that we were not poor so we could pretend to be upper caste. Now everyone knew how poor we were, and they were laughing about it, just as I imagined they would.

Our return to Ajmer in 1997 marked the beginning of the worst financial crisis of our lives. This, barring a few periods of relief, lasted till I graduated from St. Stephen's and got a job at FCBUlka in 2007. There were months, maybe even a year or two during this period, when Dad actually tried to bring home his salary instead of spending it on alcohol. Each time he did that, I would begin to feel like a normal teenager, thinking that maybe "now everything would be okay," something he said after every fight with Mum. During one such phase of normalcy, when I was twelve, Mum got Laali—a brick-red cow she thought would help bring us the prosperity and good luck we so badly needed. It was another one of her attempts to adopt upper-caste, particularly Brahmin, habits.

Laali lived in the empty garage in my grandparents' house, and Mum, though initially terrified, quickly became skilled at milking her every morning and evening. Over time, a cross-species sisterhood developed between them and Mum even helped Laali deliver two calves. Mum first cared for Laali as a domestic animal and later considered her a sort of friend. She would ask me to fetch her fodder—a burlap sack full of crushed hay—on the back of my bike or got it on her own. My friends couldn't believe that an urban family would keep a cow at home and would come home to check, only to fall in love with her adorable calves. Laali often got restless tied up in the garage, but we had no fields for her to roam around in. So she would walk the streets of the neighborhood, often eating garbage and drinking water from the gutter. On several occasions, the local municipality trucks whisked her away to the giant animal shelters where they kept stray animals, mostly cows. Mum would often have to bribe them to release her. On hearing Mum's voice, Laali would ram her horns into the iron gates forcing them to open. Laali was with us for almost two years and became part of the family. But one day she was taken away to a shelter far from the city and we never saw her again after that—Mum was heartbroken for months.

Neither Mum's nor Dad's family had any experience rearing farm animals, definitely not a cow. Historically, only upper castes or certain OBC communities like Jats have raised cows. Dalit families rarely have cows, and only have anything to do with them once they are dead. Moreover, few Dalits have access to land for farming, so owning cattle isn't a necessity. There was no real reason for Mum to rear a cow; it was just another avenue that could help us become upper caste. So, in many ways, bringing home Laali, just like stubbornly learning Sanskrit, was a defiant middle finger to the casteist rules that told us we couldn't do something just because we were Dalit. But the only reason we were not punished for it was our relative hard-earned privilege.

CHAPTER 5

THE REALITY OF UNTOUCHABILITY

My grandfather's first wife helped support her family and her husband until he cleared the CSE, but didn't live to experience any of the benefits. As I have said earlier, she worked as a manual scavenger, clearing dry excrement from people's toilets. Even today, it is only Dalits who clean dry latrines. Safai Karmachari Andolan, the human rights organization that has been campaigning for the eradication of manual scavenging, reports that people are employed to do manual scavenging by the military engineering works, the army, public sector, and Indian Railways.[1] The Railways has been under scrutiny since 2003 when the Safai Karmachari Andolan filed a public interest litigation in the Supreme Court. However, the Railways has paid no heed to the Employment of Manual Scavengers and Construction of Dry Latrines (Prohibition) Act, 1993, which makes employing manual scavengers illegal and the owners of dry latrines liable for prosecution.[2] The Railways defended the illegal practice with the weak argument that "manual scavenging cannot be totally eradicated" until toilets are updated.[3]

As per the 2011 Socio Economic and Caste Census there are 1.8 lakh Dalit households manually cleaning the 7.9 lakh public and private dry latrines (not the modern flush ones) across India; 98 percent of scavengers are meagerly paid women and girls.[4] An *Indian Express* article described how female manual scavengers in Meerut remove human excreta with bare hands, without gloves, aprons, or safety equipment ever being used.[5] The same practice is followed in many other parts of the country. Among manual scavengers, Dalit women who go door-to-door, cleaning dry latrines by scooping human excreta into cane baskets and carrying them on top of their heads to sewage dumps, are the worst affected. During monsoons, the rainwater seeps through the porous baskets, percolating human filth through to their hair and clothes. They often get paid in leftover food and old clothes instead of money and are forced to rely on odd jobs, like stringing flowers, to earn as little as thirty rupees a day. Some Dalit women make between ten rupees and fifty rupees per house. Dalit men who work clearing sewage pipes, on the other hand, are paid up to 300 rupees per day. Besides economic exploitation, these Dalit women also face sexual harassment from supervisors, sanitary inspectors, and contractors, and are made to work the demanding night shift.[6] Their backbreaking labor is not only nauseating but also remains overlooked and underpaid.

Daily handling of human waste leads to severe illnesses and health issues for the manual scavengers. "Vomiting, constant headaches, skin and respiratory diseases, trachoma, anaemia, carbon monoxide poisoning, and diarrhea," are common among both male and female manual scavengers.[7] Moreover, these scavengers lack access to proper health care and nutrition and, according to the Tata Institute of Social Sciences (TISS), less than 80 percent of manual scavengers live past the age of sixty.[8]

The Safai Karmachari Andolan was initiated in 1995 to eradicate manual scavenging, to defend the rights of Dalit workers, and rehabilitate them in different professions. Its founder, Magsaysay Award winner Bezwada Wilson, collected data from different states between 2013 and 2016, and reported that almost 1,370 manual scavengers had succumbed to their jobs in the three-year period. The Los Angeles Times reported that twenty manual scavengers die in Mumbai alone every month.[9] Various high courts and the Supreme Court have repeatedly stressed the need for protective gear for manual scavengers and the candle flame test to check for the presence of poisonous fumes. This test requires airing out a manhole before letting a worker enter so that the dangerous gases that have built up get dissipated. Often, the manual scavengers die instantly after exposure to poisonous gases such as hydrogen sulfide, ammonia, methane, carbon dioxide, sulfur dioxide, and nitrogen dioxide, like those in the administrative and engineering departments of the Indira Gandhi National Center for Arts in Delhi, where three Dalit workers died inside manholes.

This indifference to Dalit lives and health stems from the long-held idea that as long as they are paid a few rupees, they should be risking their lives to clean society's filth, because ultimately that's what they were born to do.[10] As recently as March 2017, Karnataka's social welfare minister H. Anjaneya called for the re-legalization of manual scavenging, asking for emergency-based employment of manual scavengers to be applied in routine circumstances.[11] The apex court of the country has had to repeatedly remind employers to treat manual scavengers as living, breathing humans who feel the same nausea, disgust, and sickness as any upper-caste person instead of "mechanical robots," who would not be affected by the poisonous gases in the sewage system.[12]

In her groundbreaking documentary *Kakkoos*, filmmaker-activist Divya Bharathi speaks to manual scavengers in over twenty-five cities spread over twenty districts in Tamil Nadu.[13] She follows them through their inconvenient and long shifts and records their daily lives. Through the course of the film, we see many manual scavengers breaking down due to the lack of basic necessities such as food and clothing despite working hard at a dehumanizing job. During the year of filming, Bharathi witnessed twenty-seven manual scavenger deaths in Tamil Nadu alone.

A 2013 law, the Prohibition of Employment as Manual Scavengers and Their Rehabilitation Act, aims to make up for the failings of the previous law. In addition to making the employment of manual scavengers and construction of dry latrines an offense, it also has a provision for the rehabilitation of manual scavengers. Yet, government-led rehabilitation schemes have managed to identify only 12,226 manual scavengers in a 2015 survey conducted under this law. Those identified under this act were to receive 40,000 rupees to help them start over and find other ways to earn money. Rarely does this monetary assistance reach them. Often, the village leaders tasked with identifying manual scavengers nominate their own kin to receive the money or simply fail to identify anyone at all.

Dalits who work as manual scavengers lead rather short lives encumbered with illness, disease, and penury. On average, a Dalit male manual scavenger earns less than 6,700 rupees a month for entering six or seven clogged sewer manholes daily. Often, they don't get paid on time, or at all.[14] As a result, many of them spend their lives hoping to get used to their revolting jobs by using drugs and alcohol but never fully succeed, adding to their laundry list of health issues. The stench of the filth they handle daily never fully leaves their bodies no matter how often they bathe, isolating them further from their communities. Yet, manual scavengers have few options for sustenance outside their dehumanizing and dangerous profession.

If India truly intends to become post-caste in the next few centuries, ensuring no Dalits need to deal with someone's filth just to survive is the place to start.

Not only are Dalits isolated in communities because they are the ones who are forced to undertake the job of manual scavenging, they are further reviled because they eat beef and work with leather. Dalits and Muslims have been singled out for discrimination for decades because they eat beef.[15] But the objection to beef appears to have taken on even more dangerous overtones ever since the Bharatiya Janata Party (BJP)-led government came to power at the center in 2014.

In late September 2015, in Dadri, Uttar Pradesh, a mob of gau rakshaks (cow protectors) lynched fifty-two-year-old Mohammad Akhlaq because they "suspected" he had beef in his fridge.[16] Vichitra Kumar Tomar, one of the accused in the Akhlaq lynching and a gau rakshak leader, told the *New York Times*: "Our intention was to punish [Akhlaq], to slap him or beat him. Just a few slaps. But not to leave him dead." Tomar was then general secretary of the local Akhil Bharatiya Vidyarthi Parishad (ABVP)—the BJP's youth wing, while Inder Nagar, a fellow member of the organization, was its state secretary. Tomar's absurd self-justification aside, almost half a dozen gau rakshak members blamed Akhlaq for his own death since he had incited the mob by slaughtering a cow. The forensic test conducted by the authorities after the lynching concluded that the meat in the fridge was mutton. But none of this mattered. Even the state's BJP chief Laxmikant Bajpai's statements showed no remorse over the death of an elderly man murdered by a senselessly violent mob. He blamed the Akhilesh Yadav government instead for failing to protect cows; if it had, "these men would not have been forced to take the law in their hands." Mahesh Sharma, then culture minister, labelled Akhlaq's death an "accident."

Between September 2015 and March 2016, several northern states—Himachal Pradesh, Jammu and Kashmir, Jharkhand—saw incidents of mob violence against Dalits and Muslims on the charge of "transporting cows for slaughter," "slaughtering cows," or "carrying beef." This devotion for the cow is not a new phenomenon. Hindu Vedic texts consider the cow a powerful animal but don't explicitly prohibit its slaughter.[17] Cow slaughter saw opposition only around the fifth century BCE after Buddhism and Jainism, which preached nonviolence, began gaining prominence. Dr. Ambedkar examines this development in his 1948 text, *The Untouchables: Who Were They and Why They Became Untouchables*.[18] He traces how the cow, from being considered an important farm animal, became a "holy mother" in a few hundred years around this time. As we have seen, Ambedkar explains that upper-caste Hindus, mainly Brahmins, gave up eating meat as a means to compete with the newer religions, which had nonviolence at their core. But Dalits, who dealt with the disposal of dead cows, often depended on the protein-rich meat for nutrition and couldn't afford to give it up. As the cow grew in importance as a symbol, those who ate its meat—Dalits and Muslims—became increasingly reprehensible to a section of Hindus.

Centuries later, the narrative of cow protection gained prominence during the independence struggle—Mahatma Gandhi considered it a central tenet of Hinduism. He ranked "mother cow" even higher than our human mother who "expects us to serve her when we grow up" whereas the cow only wants "grass and grain."[19] After Independence, President Rajendra Prasad, following Gandhi's wishes, wanted a law to implement a nationwide ban on cow slaughter, but Prime Minister Jawaharlal Nehru dismissed the proposal as "unimportant and reactionary."[20] Yet, in 1955, Congress governments in twenty-four states banned cow slaughter.[21] These states restricted the sale, purchase, and slaughter of cows for decades. After the BJP-led government came to power at the center in 2014, they created new laws to ban the sale of beef, which now includes cow, bull, and bullock meat.[22]

Laws to ban cow slaughter had been largely ignored but after 2014 gained new strength.[23] Prime Minister Narendra Modi said on the campaign trail before the 2014 election that he feared that the Congress, if it won the elections, would bring about a "pink revolution," i.e., promote cow slaughter and trade in leather goods. He made no statement on Akhlaq's and other mob-led Muslim deaths until August 2016, when he criticized the mobs as "anti-social elements" donning the garb of gau rakshaks.[24] This statement did not stop more instances of self-proclaimed cow protectors attacking those they suspected of eating beef, slaughtering cows, or transporting cows for slaughter.

In the last week of June 2017, the weekend before Eid, 15-year-old Junaid and his older brother, Hashim, boarded a train from Delhi to Mathura, where they had gone to shop for clothes. An argument over a seat on the train turned into a fight and ended with twelve people stabbing Junaid to death and throwing him off the train because "they ate beef."[25] In a scathing column following Junaid's murder, then Center for Policy Research president Pratap Bhanu Mehta highlighted the alarming consequences of unchecked fundamentalist mob violence. "This violence establishes a new political dispensation, where a group of people claim direct sovereignty: They act above formal law and order institutions, they feel entitled to enforce the morality, and their impunity comes from the fact that they can now stand in for the 'authentic people,'" he wrote.[26]

Junaid's murder was followed by a number of incidents of cow-related violence, which did not go entirely unnoticed.[27] Gurgaon-based filmmaker Saba Khan's Facebook post asking: "Shouldn't there be protests against the lynchings especially after the murder yesterday in Delhi NCR by a mob of a 16-year-old Muslim boy?" resonated deeply with those increasingly frustrated with mob violence. The #NotInMyName protest, which was initially scheduled to take place in Delhi on June 28, 2017, spread to several other cities, including Mumbai, where Bollywood actors like Shabana Azmi and Konkona Sen Sharma joined hundreds of other protesters. In June 2017, the prime minister condemned the attacks on cattle traders, dairy farmers, and beef-eaters saying "killing people in the name of protecting cows is unacceptable."[28]

Of the twenty-eight Indians killed in cow-related violence between 2010 and 2017, 86 percent were Muslim. And 97 percent of those attacks were reported after May 2014, when the Modi government came to power, and almost 52 percent were based on rumors and falsehoods.[29] A recent investigation by Reuters discovered that cow protectors were seizing cows from Muslims, robbing them of their livelihood.[30] According to the report, cow protectors have taken 190,000 cows worth around $36 million (253 crore Indian rupees) from Muslims since 2014. Many of these cows were sold or handed over to Hindu farmers or (in smaller numbers) sent to cow shelters.

While Muslims are currently the prime targets for mob violence, Dalits are fair game too. Gau rakshaks brutally assaulted Dalit cow traders in Una, Gujarat, in July 2016 and paraded them naked for skinning a dead cow. As the video of this assault circulated online, Dalits retaliated with protests—many turned violent. Almost fifteen attempted suicide, and others threw stones and burned down buses.[31] But the violence soon gave way to what was an imaginative and strong protest. The cow protectors were attacking Chamars for moving dead cows, perhaps without understanding that Chamars were the only ones who dealt with the remains of cows. The tanning of the hides of cows is a profession that has been forced on Dalits purely because of their caste—a trade that their families have practiced for generations. After the video went viral, the Chamar community in Una decided to make known their ire. They refused to cart away the cows that died in the area. They loaded the rotting carcasses onto trucks and left them in front of the Gir Somnath District Collector's Office, chanting: "Tumhari maiya tum hi sambhalo" (Your mother, you take care of it) to drive home the significance of their professions.[32] Soon, the agitation spread to other parts of Gujarat, where many other Dalits joined the strike. Nearly twenty thousand mostly Dalit participants gathered to attend the Dalit Mahasammelan in Ahmedabad on July 31, 2016.[33] The simple gesture of Dalits refusing to do the job that the caste system had forced on them for centuries had such a powerful effect that it led to months of protests across the country and ultimately resulted in one of the largest Dalit uprisings in thirty years. Six days after the Mahasammelan, on August 6, thousands of Dalits left Ahmedabad for the Azadi Kooch March. They walked over ten days and thousands of kilometers to reach Una, where they unfurled the tricolor on Independence Day.[34]

When the first Chamars in Una dumped the cow carcasses at the doorstep of the Gir district collector, they were protesting the assault on the Dalit traders. But by the time thousands of Dalits arrived in Una, it was a much larger protest against centuries of discrimination and injustice. Just like the African American protesters who took to the streets during the American civil rights movement weren't only demanding that the seating on buses not be segregated, the protesting Dalits weren't just asking for justice for the traders who had been assaulted. They were marching for equal rights and justice, in particular for the land that had been allotted to thousands of Dalits on paper but was still waiting to be assigned after decades. It was a truly historic event. Mobs of upper-caste men attacked Dalit vehicles, particularly those with Ambedkar signage, "Jai Bhim" or Bhim Blue stickers, and assaulted the passengers. They forced Dalits to chant "Jai Mata Di" and "Gai Mata ki Jai" and hit anyone who said "Jai Bhim."[35] The Dalits neither had warning nor protection from the police, who, according to reports, were present but did not stop the assault. But the historic Azadi Kooch March had done more than rattle upper-caste men into attacking Dalits. It also shook the BJP-led Gujarat government. Then Gujarat Chief Minister Anandiben Patel was removed and even Prime Minister Modi, who had so far remained silent on the cow protectors, was forced to make a statement condemning their actions.

CHAPTER 6

THE LONG ROAD TO ST. STEPHEN'S

By the time I was in middle school we were in a slightly better place financially and with regard to Dad's drinking. After years of haggling, my grandfather had finally released the entirety of Dad's share of the money from the sale of the property. It was enough for us to buy a plot of land in a village far out of the city. This village didn't have public transport, proper roads, or even running water. Even now, almost twenty years later, it only has two of those amenities. As far as Mum was concerned, they were minor inconveniences, and nothing compared to the years of emotional, mental, and physical abuse she had endured living with Dad's family. Decades of little to no control over her circumstances had driven Mum to look for security and reassurance in the divine. She felt that a ritually observed fast, or a money plant placed in a certain corner of the house would change her life for the better. Mum believes in astrology and often relies on it to find answers to questions such as: "When will things get better?" Hinduism has been another way for her to get closer to an upper-caste identity—the deeper her knowledge about Hindu rituals and traditions, the more easily she could pass as Brahmin. So when it was time for her to finally claim her own space after nearly twelve years of marriage, Mum became a rigid follower of Vaastu Shastra. She seemed to believe that by strictly complying with every rule of Vaastu, she could turn the new house into an antidote to our difficulties. But that didn't mean that everything went smoothly—the construction of the house was plagued by delays and dragged on for nearly three years. Funds repeatedly dried up and some portions of the house collapsed even after the construction was completed. But nothing stopped Mum from visiting the construction site nearly every afternoon to oversee the work. Even when the construction halted for nearly three months, Mum visited every week. At that point, the house was a brick and mortar shell with gaping holes where windows and doors would go. Open to the elements, the cement was threatening to crack off the walls, undoing most of the investment and labor of the past few years.

Before the new house was constructed, arguments with Dad's family left Mum feeling powerless. She felt this more keenly after her father died. But now, with an almost complete house, Mum felt like she had options. So after a particularly nasty argument in late December 1998, she decided to put that option to use and moved us out of our grandparents' house into the new one. It took the entire afternoon and five trips in the back of an auto rickshaw, but we managed to transfer most of our clothes, books, essential kitchen items, and bedding to the new house. It wasn't what most people would consider liveable but for Mum and the three of us kids, it was a sanctuary. The house still had debris all over the floor and only one functioning bathroom. We used thick bedsheets as window curtains, and covered the living room floor with plastic sheets and newspapers. The living room did double duty as a kitchen. A single bulb hanging from an exposed wire lit up the area. Dad was then in Jaitaran, a small town in Pali district where he was posted and, from what I remember, seemed okay with our move. The night watchman, who lived in a small temporary house a few feet away, had been sleeping in the house for the past several months; he continued to sleep in one of the rooms. We slept huddled on plastic cots in the room at the back; it was the largest room we had lived in so far. When we climbed up to the roof on the dangerous, half-constructed stairs we could see the Aravallis. There were a few other houses in the neighborhood and some of the kids went to Sophia. So the private bus that came to ferry them to school would now pick us up too. Two months later, I invited some of my new bus-mates home for my thirteenth birthday party. This party was nothing like the grand affairs from a few years ago, except for the cake Mum still lovingly baked and decorated with plain chocolate icing and Gems.

It took one more year before the house looked presentable. By this time, Mum had planted a garden, we had hiked several times through the mountains that were nearly in our backyard, and I had spent countless evenings on the roof dreaming about my future and doodling on the clear blue sheet that was stretched across the top of the house. A Vaastu expert came over a few months later and told Mum that the house had been built contrary to some of the most basic principles of Vaastu. But it didn't matter, because thirteen years after I was born, we were finally home.

For a happy minute between setting up our new house in 2000 until the middle of the next year, all of us bought into the possibility that "this might be it." We thought that this period—when Dad worked consistently for a whole year and brought his salary home—was our reward for the years of struggle and difficulty that had gone before. Of course, we were wrong. Dad was suspended from service in 2001. The newly elected state government was purging all departments and, with a less than stellar track record, Dad was among the early casualties. He immediately contested the decision in court, which blocked the remittance of his severance pay. We had no savings or additional sources of income. Mum hadn't earned money by stitching clothes for a few years, but she did take a candle-making course and tried really hard to push her small business enterprise with Amway. It was a pyramid-style scheme that required her to sell the products by making showy presentations to attract middle-class housewives. We traveled to Jaipur for one such seminar and returned with a bagful of Amway products. They were too highly priced for a small market like Ajmer and sat in our house for years. When Dad lost his job, it was the end of any income for the family.

While Dad contested his case in court (it's still unresolved), Mum decided to apply for a teaching job in a neighborhood school. She was forty-eight at the time, and had no job experience, teaching or otherwise. She got paid less than 1,000 rupees per month but her job at least kept hope alive. My sister and I applied for a subsidy for Sophia's school fees. Because we had no income and Sophia was a convent school that had government funding, we got the subsidy. Mayoor, where my brother studied, was a private institution and did not show the same generosity. Dad's family would throw a stray

500 rupees our way once in a while, and Mum's family gave small amounts when she visited them on Rakhi or Diwali. Beyond that, our day-to-day subsistence depended on credit from neighborhood shops. Mum had taken a small loan to open a boutique, but because of its location—far from the town and close to shops that stocked cement and offered bicycle repairs—it saw very little footfall. Dad initially made a big fuss about looking for work, but eventually gave up and spent his days ferrying Mum between her jobs on the scooter. Eventually, Mum moved the boutique to another location, close to a small neighboring village in a tiny marketplace that had better footfall, but she made hardly any profit because she had to price the clothes that she stitched from scratch almost at cost.

If it sounds like a trite script from an art movie, that's how it felt, too. As deeply painful as it was to live through it, even we recognized the dark humor in our reality—Mum taught in the mornings, went to the boutique in the afternoons, and stitched clothes late into the night. Even though very little changed for the next three years or so until I left home to join St. Stephen's in Delhi, everything about our life somehow continued to feel temporary. It was only Mum's hopeful, uplifting spirit and backbreaking work that made my brother, sister, and me feel that things could change some day—that Dad could find another job and things would instantly turn around. In those grim years, she would create new hope every time an old one died, and each time Mum and Dad started a new venture, we would again start to believe that "this was it." One of their most enduring ventures was the "gas van." They purchased a secondhand Maruti Omni, which ran on the cheaper LPG instead of petrol and diesel, and decided to ply it as a taxi. The plan was to hire a driver, but the more feasible option was for Dad to drive it himself. Despite his anxiety about driving a taxi when just a few months ago he had been commanding a fleet of jeeps at work, Dad started ferrying kids at Mum's school. A few months later, he was driving passengers to towns nearby and even farther away, in Uttar Pradesh, Haryana, and Gujarat.

At my brother's school, most kids arrived in autos or their own vehicles. Dad would often drop my brother to school and pick him up in the Omni. When his classmates discovered that his father was a "driver," they used every occasion to taunt him about it. The status that Mum had worked so hard to create and keep going all these years was shredded, and we were too poor to do anything about it. The marble floors and shiny sofa sets we had paid for over many years in tiny installments weren't fooling anyone—except a friend's mother who was also a teacher at my school who assumed that we were trying to scam the school with the fees subsidy.

The jobs that my parents did weren't typically white collar or "middle class," so they were identified as "menial." Looking back, there was no shame in our parents working hard to feed and educate their children. But at that time, my siblings and I felt ashamed. This internalized shame forced my sister and me to hide what my parents did or lie about it. And when people like my brother's classmates found out and teased him, we didn't defend them. We had been transcending caste most of our lives, but now that we no longer had the armor of being middle-class, we felt vulnerable. Even more than not having enough money to buy food or clothes, losing that seemed like the biggest tragedy of our lives.

This horrific sense of shame that is endemic in the Indian middle class about "menial" work stems from a nexus of casteism, feudalism, and the shockingly low wages paid for labor. Since jobs that require hard physical labor—farm work, cleaning, garbage collection, construction, cooking, serving food—don't pay well, people who do these jobs never live comfortable lives. In 2014, the minimum wage for construction workers living in metros was increased to 215 rupees per day.[1] Yet contractors get away with paying much lower wages by not registering their workers as employees. Arbitrarily decided wages deny many working-class individuals the opportunity to rise to an improved "middle-class" standard of living.[2] "Casual workers" who work for daily wages and form almost 30 percent of the Indian workforce, according to a report published by the International Labour Organization, do not have access to employment benefits or social security. On the contrary, when a "middle-class" person takes up a "menial" job, they are lauded as brave. Case in point, when a Gurgaon-based woman who owned a 3 crore Indian rupees house was forced to sell chole-kulche on the road after her husband suffered an injury, the headlines were shocked and news stories deeply sympathetic.[3] There are thousands of chole-kulche sellers and others who do similar work all over the country, but they are not considered brave and definitely don't receive any attention or empathy for the same job which, given their relatively weaker financial backgrounds, they perform daily under tougher conditions.

Indian society's instinct to look down on manual labor comes from the profession-based inequality that lies at the heart of the caste system. Since this central idea grades people unequally based on their work, it rules out any respect for an industrious work ethic. Non-caste-based societies tend to assign equal respect for all work. Garbage collection, plumbing, carpentry, electrical work, building construction, etc., are well paid and even sought after trades in Western economies. But in South Asian countries almost no middle-class college graduate will aspire to these jobs. Jobs in retail and the service industry that are a rite of passage for teenagers and young adults in developed economies are often too "labor oriented" for most Indian teens. The proliferation of Starbucks, McDonald's, and other MNC coffee and fast food chains don't seem to have changed that perception. In a culture that doesn't value hard work as worthy of respect, it was only expected that political skirmishes would also be fought along those lines. The fact that Congress President Sonia Gandhi had worked as a waitress and an au pair was used to demonstrate that she would be unfit to govern the country in the early 2000s. More recently, Textiles Minister Smriti Irani was attacked for "flipping burgers" before she became an actress. Prime Minister Narendra Modi's background as a "tea seller" being highlighted as a positive during the 2014 election campaign is an exception.

In addition to societal perception about labor, there are too few laws that protect workers in the unorganized sector, including domestic workers, who are among the most exploited labor force in the country. Along with manual scavengers, they also face the most overtly naturalized casteism at the workplace in urban areas. Often, employers in urban areas make it a point to ask potential domestic workers about their caste for "hygienic reasons" and employ upper-caste workers as cooks and Dalits to clean toilets. In a national survey, one in four Indians admitted to not allowing a Scheduled Caste person inside their kitchens. Apart from the casual heartlessness of being served with separate utensils, prohibited from using toilets, and being asked to sit on the floor when family members sit on chairs and couches, they are often not paid their salaries and are even subjected to physical abuse.

In July 2017, Zohra Bibi was reportedly beaten and accused of stealing cash when she claimed her dues from her employers who lived in a high-rise luxury building in Noida.[4] Her story, while common to many domestic workers, hit the national spotlight when almost three hundred workers gathered around the building to protest. Reports suggested that Bibi's employers Mithul and Harshu Sethi were forced to hide in the bathroom with their children when the workers entered their house and damaged their furniture.[5] *The Guardian* called it "a class war breaking out on India's streets" resulting from the apartheid-style system that is in place. The response by the authorities only underlined this class war. While the residents got police protection and were visited by a minister, the "rioters" were physically attacked and called racial slurs. Most of the domestic workers who protested were sacked. Soon after, the neighboring slums where many of the workers, including Bibi's family, lived had their electricity and water disconnected. The slums were eventually razed to the ground on the pretext of "illegal encroachment." If this was a class war, then it had ended predictably—with the rich bulldozing the poor.

These bad years for my family were the most crucial ones for an Indian high schooler. It is during these years that university courses are decided on and students start attending tuition and coaching classes to help them get the edge (and marks) that they need for admission into the college of their choice.

Mum was working two jobs: in the mornings as an NGO worker educating highway truckers and sex workers about the threat of HIV/AIDS and about healthy sex practices, and in the evenings at the boutique. She would travel several kilometers out of the city to visit the truckers and sex workers, and since the NGO paid a pittance, often hitchhiked with truckers to reach there. She would also cook most of our meals since I didn't know how to cook and my siblings were too young. Dad made lunch sometimes but there were many days when she wouldn't have eaten till 5 p.m. since she couldn't afford to buy food outside. Even though I was helpless and couldn't change the situation, it broke my heart and deepened my sense of guilt. Even when I became the secretary of the school council (I became its president the following year, something Mum had hoped for), I hid it for weeks—I didn't feel like I deserved to be congratulated or celebrated. When my sister heard the formal announcement in the school assembly and finally told Mum, we had a small celebration at home. Mum brought crumbled pastry and crushed wafers that she had saved from a work function.

As things got bleaker at home, a determination began growing in me to get out—I almost didn't care where to. As far as I knew, the only way out for me was to study science and attend a medical or engineering college. For the last two years of high school, I was run off my feet, busy with school and after-school coaching for entrance exams to medical and engineering courses. The coaching classes involved a sweltering twenty-minute walk and forty-minute bus ride. I would come back home after classes, race through dinner, and settle down for some late-night cramming. Because I had done well in school so far, I was able to attend a coaching center practically for free. The cofounders of the coaching center, two young twenty-somethings, waived my fees entirely. I continued studying science partly out of an obligation to "repay this debt," which I felt that I paid in part when their annual newspaper ad for "batch toppers" featured my black-and-white passport-sized photograph. Every move I had made after fourteen—choosing to prepare for competitive science exams despite having no real interest in the sciences, scoring exceptionally well in the Central Board of Secondary Education (CBSE) Class X board exams, studying science in high school, and even appearing for medical and engineering admission exams when I'd imagined myself in an English literature class since I was eight—was a small step out the door . . . and into a better life.

I did well enough in the Class XII board exams but performed miserably in almost all the competitive science and maths entrance tests. I had no real interest in becoming a doctor-engineer hybrid. By the time it came to the last few exams, I stopped pretending to care, and didn't even open my books the previous night. Despite all the guilt and self-flagellation I had subjected myself to this far in order to get ahead through education, when it came down to it, I found

I couldn't make myself love the subjects I thought would ultimately shape my career. My back-up plan was similar to those who didn't manage to crack any of these entrance exams. I would take a gap year to prepare until I was eventually accepted into a semi-respectable college, by which time I would hopefully learn to love the subjects. Many students who don't manage to score well in these entrance exams lose hope and tragically cut short their lives by resorting to suicide. In my case, it was thanks to one of the cofounders of my coaching institute that I found my way. My parents had sought advice from him about my "failing career." He took me aside and, for the first time in years, asked what *I* wanted to do. Those few moments became a portal to a different life, one where I too had desires and the permission to act on them. Almost without thinking I answered, "I want to study English somewhere, maybe St. Stephen's in Delhi." Till then I had considered St. Stephen's as a delicious but impossible option, where only rich, cool, urban kids studied. It hadn't even registered that the courses it offered were among the best in the country or that it had a reputation for churning out famous graduates—several politicians, bureaucrats, actors, sportspersons, authors, and academics are its alumni.

When my coach repeated to my parents what I had just told him, Mum's eyes lit up—I hadn't seen that in a long time. She took one look at my face and immediately understood what going to St. Stephen's would mean to me. A future version of me danced in front of my eyes, but I wasn't quite ready to believe it could happen. As always, Mum did believe. After that conversation, my vision for my future became a lot clearer and I knew I couldn't graduate from anywhere but there. In those few brief seconds, I had seen what my future could look like, and was convinced that it would all start at St. Stephen's, Delhi. Mum casually mentioned my plans to attend college in Delhi to her brother who lived there, hoping he would invite me to stay at his house at least for a few months. There was no reason for him not to. I had not been a troublesome child. As I grew up, I even started dressing dowdily so relatives on whose generosity we depended would think of me as a serious, trustworthy person, a young woman who wouldn't think of hanging around with boys. Only a few months ago a random acquaintance had compared my demeanor to that of an innocent cow! My uncle did offer to let me stay at his house. But after I had stayed there for a month, waiting for the college application results, he rescinded his offer. When my parents came to visit, my uncle complained to them that I was sitting in the balcony in the evenings, staring at passersby and trying to attract attention. The only other person in the house was my grandmother who watched endless Ekta Kapoor dramas all day long. Sitting in the balcony people-watching seemed to me to be a perfectly innocent way to pass the time. My uncle and grandmother declared that they simply couldn't take responsibility for me. What if I got pregnant? My Mum yelled at her brother with an anger she usually reserved for the very heated arguments with Dad. Even she knew I was an innocent cow. I was mad, too, at their disgusting misogyny. Mum asked me to pack my bags immediately and in just a little while we were on our way to the bus stand to catch a bus back to Ajmer. In the auto ride from Kalkaji in South Delhi to Old Delhi, I stared at the bright full moon that night, knowing it wasn't the last I had seen of the city.

I had applied to an English Honors course and the now defunct BSc General course at St. Stephen's. I also wanted to take a stab at history and philosophy, subjects I hadn't studied in any depth but knew I would enjoy a lot more than a combined degree in physics, chemistry, and mathematics. But Mum suggested that I could study those subjects *after* I had taken a degree in science. At any rate, I didn't clear the famous Stephen's interview for English, which every candidate needs to go through regardless of their score. With no education in the classics or even a foundation in literature, there was no way I could have. The only way I would now attend St. Stephen's was as a BSc General student, and I had cleared the interview for that. So I took it, even if that meant studying physics, chemistry, and mathematics for the next three years. They were subjects I heartily disliked by then and had sworn never to study again. But I was finally in St. Stephen's, and in all my seventeen years that was the only thing that had mattered, really mattered, to me.

A month after the admission interview, I attended the "first assembly" at St. Stephen's. Mum had hastily sold off the land that had been our backyard garden which she had lovingly tended. The money would cover the rent for a shared PG I was to stay in. As we filled out the admission form, Mum suggested, for the very first time, that I tick the box that said I was an SC/ST candidate. Like so many Dalit students who don't understand how systemic casteism works and buy into the casteist narrative of "proving themselves without a crutch," I didn't think I needed reservation. If I checked that box, I would taint my achievements with the "quota student" tag. My lifetime of lessons to successfully appear upper caste would be rendered useless with that single stroke. But I didn't have a choice. I needed the financial aid and scholarships to pay even the heavily subsidized Delhi University fees. I noticed that other students who had come with their parents to fill in the form were smartly dressed, impeccably accented, and walking around like they belonged there. With my downward gaze and stooped shoulders, I didn't. Mum kept reminding me to look up, walk straight, be confident, even fake the attitude I put on when I really wanted to win a debate or the school president election. In her best but rather outdated sari that hadn't seen daylight in a long while, she didn't look like she belonged there either. But we both really wanted to. And this was the *only* way to do it. So I closed my eyes, ticked the box, and hoped no one would notice.

St. Stephen's is notoriously hard to get into, not only because of the high marks required but also because the screening interview is extremely tough. Given its reputation as a somewhat exclusive club and its lengthy list of illustrious alumni, new students feel like they've "made it" in life by just getting accepted. When I got in, I felt that too, but not for the same reasons. It was because, despite everything, I had finally made it out of Ajmer.

All through the previous year as I had rushed from school to home to the bus stand to the coaching class, it had been impossible to imagine that my life could be different. I had denied myself any joy or pride so far because I was saving it for when I got out. I hadn't taken a summer off since 2001 and had gone to the coaching institute nearly every week until I appeared for the final engineering exam in early May of 2004. Everything I had done so far had been to get to Delhi. And now I was living there. And I had not got here by accepting admission in some third-tier engineering or medical school. I had applied to St. Stephen's College, one of the top colleges of the country, cleared the interview, and got in. In every sense, I truly had made it.

Except my definition of "making it" was about to evolve. The coaching institute cofounder who helped me with my epiphany had also passed on a job—an after-class tuition gig. His cousin, who had just graduated from the course I had enrolled in, used to help a four-year-old girl with her homework for around 400 rupees a month. Two weeks into my first year in college, I was walking from the college campus in the middle of Delhi University in North Delhi to the neighboring Civil Lines area to tutor a kindergartener. As my classmates hung around after class chatting or trying to decide which movie to watch, I would have to leave abruptly because my student would be home from school and waiting for me. It was Ajmer all over again. Despite working hard for it, I still didn't have money or the time to relish my new life. I was still studying subjects that I had not magically grown to love. I would stand in the corridor next to the history, economics, or English classrooms and wonder what it would be like to sit in those classes. Since there were far more subjects in the science courses than the humanities, the latter had fewer classes and students had more free time, while we spent our afternoons in the practical classes in the science block. I had imagined that when I got into Stephen's I would be transformed into a Proust-spouting, self-assured, and stylish Arts student. In reality, apart from my location, nothing had changed.

I lived in the Model Town area with five or six girls from different Delhi University colleges, who not only ate three proper meals a day but also had money for snacks and shopping and other small indulgences. I grudged them their easy lives. I never managed to make friends with them, mainly because of my own insecurities and issues with self-worth. My frustration welled into a deep sadness and ultimately became what I now realize was a dark depression. This darkness persisted until I took a job in a call center after my first year.

When Mum visited me a few months into my first year, I had gained several kilos from eating plain butter when there was nothing else to eat. She instantly knew something was wrong and pulled me out of that makeshift hostel and put me into a bigger, private hostel with almost 150 girls, where all meals were included in the rent. A Sardar couple ran it from their huge house in the affluent BD Estate area and agreed to charge me a lower rent when Mum pleaded with them to let me stay. By this time Mum was used to pleading to get our fees lowered and I was used to feeling small and guilty as a result. I moved into a big room that I shared with two girls from Miranda House. Now I didn't have to travel as much to college and back. Soon after I moved to this hostel, Mum came to check on me again, and she did so frequently through my college years. She would travel all night in the general compartment (which was cheaper than second class) of the train from Ajmer to Delhi and sleep on a thin sheet spread on the floor. When she walked into the room the first time she came to visit, her clothes were soiled from the dirt from the train floor and she was carrying a duffel bag whose strap had broken on the way. It was when I saw the looks on the faces of my roommates that it hit me: Mum was no longer the glamorous, well-dressed woman from my childhood. And with that single look, my roommates came to the conclusion that St. Stephen's or not, I wasn't one of them. And for the rest of the year that I stayed there, I wouldn't be able to overcome this.

After the final exams at the end of the first year, as everyone got ready to go home, I visited employment agencies in Kamala Nagar that could put me in touch with different call centers. As far as call centers were concerned, I was the ideal candidate—I had just graduated from my first year in college, which meant I wouldn't complain too much about onerous working conditions; I looked urban and middle class, so I wouldn't have a hard time understanding the culture of whatever Western country we would call; and I spoke excellent, fluent English, arguably the most important qualification to work at a call center. I soon got a job selling T-Mobile phone connections to elderly Britons living mostly in rural England. Call centers were rather new in 2005 but people already knew of them as rather demanding places to make a quick buck. Most girls in the hostel had a friend who had worked in one. Many knew enough about the profession to advise me against joining a "sales process" where you made outbound calls to customers. This kind of role demanded odd hours and had punishingly short breaks. Employees were frequently fired for failing to meet daily sales targets. But it was the highest paid of all the call center processes, so that is what I opted for.

An air-conditioned cab would arrive at my hostel by 2:30 in the afternoon and travel through South and Central Delhi before heading to Gurgaon where Delhi Call Center (DCC) had its office. The shift that started at 5 p.m. would end at 2 in the morning, with two fifteen-minute breaks and half an hour for dinner. We spent every other minute making calls to England via an automated dial-up connection. With a fake British name and a clumsy English accent (which we were trained to imitate on the first day), I received my fair share of annoyed hang-ups and racial abuse. It turned out, when we told them that we were calling from Gloucester, England, they didn't exactly believe us. It didn't take me long to realize selling phone connections wasn't my calling, and found myself checking the clock every five minutes after I logged in. Despite this, I ended up selling several T-Mobile connections over the two months at DCC, mainly by not sticking to the phony sales script we were supposed to parrot. I didn't love leaving at 2:30 p.m. and returning at 3:30 a.m., among the last few people on the cab route, or staying up till 5 a.m., watching television in the main room of the nearly empty hostel. But when, for the first time in my life, I received a text message alerting me to the 9,200-rupee salary deposit in my bank account, an obscene amount for any nineteen-year-old in 2005, let alone one in my position, I felt numb. I would be able to pay a few months of hostel rent and finally buy some of the things that I longed for. But I also knew that I had earned this money at a job I was driven to in an AC cab, where the hardest part of my day was talking to people. Meanwhile Mum would be hitchhiking to deliver her pamphlets on HIV/AIDS and working for six hours at a stretch to finish a sari petticoat which would fetch her fifty rupees.

Since the opening up of India's markets in 1991, Western economies had identified India as a location for cheap, educated labor and the call center boom of the 2000s was a direct upshot of outsourced back-office work. The Guardian reported in 2003 that several UK-based companies, including Standard Chartered, HSBC, British Airways, and Reuters, were moving their call centers to India.[6] "While British workers will take call center jobs only when they have no choice, Indian workers see them as glamorous," the newspaper had reported. Even though the companies were paying Indians much lower wages than their British counterparts, salaries were rather high compared to starting salaries in other industries. The outsourcing not only created more wealth for young English-speaking Indians; it also birthed a new urban culture of recreational spending. Young adults often earned as much or, in my case, much more than their parents, and many experienced "wealth" for the first time with jobs that rewarded an English-medium education. In DCC, where I worked that summer, there were at least ten other undergraduate students from Delhi University who were working a summer job before classes began. Almost all of us spoke fluent English and consistently sold mobile connections even though we had no background in sales. Several older call center workers who had more sales and overall work experience would struggle to get the same results. *The Guardian* noted that a new "middle class is developing in cities previously dominated by caste." This was not entirely correct. A new middle class was emerging but not by displacing caste. The "new middle class" had in fact emerged out of the older existing structures of caste. While some Dalits (like me) speak good English as they attend English-medium schools, most still communicate in Indian languages. English-medium education, which is often privatized and costly, is not available to most Dalits. In the "new" India, speaking good English was the mark of the new upper caste. But this did not mean that those of the lower caste would necessarily have a chance to improve their lives because those who were already upper caste were the ones speaking good English and could access these jobs. At the call center, caste found its way into pre-shift conversations. When I refused to disclose mine, saying that my parents were progressive and didn't discuss these things at home, most of my colleagues assumed I was upper caste because of my English. I quit the job after two months and swore never to go back to a call center again. But along with the money I so badly needed, it also brought me the validation I had been looking for all along. I didn't need to prove that I was upper caste anymore. I was passing so well that people easily believed I was one of them. "The most marketable skill in India today is the ability to abandon your identity and slip into someone else's," *The Guardian* story had observed (albeit in a different context). If that were true, as it was for me, then passing was the best thing that could have happened for my résumé.

Mum didn't want me to send her any money, though it would have gone a long way to easing my guilt. Since Dad had been suspended in 2001, we had bought hardly any new clothes except for the few necessities Mum had purchased when I moved to Delhi. I spent the money I earned from DCC first on rent for the next year and indulged in small luxuries—eating a pizza for the first time, buying moisturizer and cheap high street fashion that all college students sported. I was particularly excited about the new jeans and trendy tops I had bought with my first paycheck. I walked into my room carrying several large and small bags filled with my new possessions to find one of my roommates there. Her father, an IAS officer in Jharkhand, stayed in good hotels when he came to visit her. She had strong opinions and, unlike me, had no trouble standing up for herself when she felt she had been wronged. I could feel her eyes on my back as I walked the short distance from the entrance of the room to the wardrobe at the far end. "How could you buy all this when your mother does so much for you?" she shot at me before I could turn around. I froze and shut my eyes tight and rested my forehead on the thick paper bags. In hindsight, I realize she had no business lecturing me about what to do with money for which I had worked six days a week for two months doing a job I hated. But in that moment the guilt that had been gnawing at me took hold. "It's actually not like that," I muttered and left the room, feeling that I deserved to be called out for spending the money on myself instead of sending it home. I accepted that this person, who I wasn't friends with and who knew nothing about my family except for briefly meeting my mother, was right to chastise me for my selfishness. I used the moisturizer but pushed the clothes to the back of my cupboard and never wore them.

After working at the call center, I didn't want to go back to teaching kindergarten students for very little money. So I started teaching a high school student instead. I would travel almost ninety minutes to East Delhi to teach her Class IX maths, chemistry, and physics. Despite my sincerity and desperate need for money, this job lasted less than a month. I could barely muster enough interest to clear my own exams, let alone teach someone four years younger than me to do the same. Mum had tried to justify pressuring me to study science by holding up that high school tuition gig as a benefit. When it ended unexpectedly, she never brought it up again, even when my grades dropped to the lowest they ever had. Luckily for me, a form of private sector "reservation" kicked in soon after.

Reservation for upper castes functions with connections, networks, and contacts that go back decades. As a nineteen-year-old second-year college student trying to stay afloat without much financial help from home, I learned that quickly. Some girls I knew often took up ad hoc jobs like ushering at events and exhibitions. For a full day of work that involved standing for several hours and smiling brainlessly, the pay was never more than 300 rupees. Certain gigs paid higher if the "models" were prettier. While I never conformed to Eurocentric standards of beauty that help with entry into the world of modelling, fashion, and, especially, films, I turned out to be useful for events that required more "Indian"-looking girls. We would meet at the modelling agency that an influential event promoter ran out of her sprawling home in Greater Kailash. We were taken by cabs to our assigned events and sometimes dropped back in the city after the event ended. For several months, I welcomed people at weddings, woke up at 4 a.m. to cheer runners at half-marathons, and even represented West Bengal at a corporate event with twenty-five other girls from different Indian states. It was through the connections I made at these jobs and events that I got my first job in journalism.

Amir Rajpal, a celebrity photographer who had worked with several Bollywood and fashion celebrities from the seventies to the nineties, was looking for someone to ghostwrite articles for the *Delhi Times* supplements. He worked from his second-floor home, smack in the middle of Connaught Place (real estate gold), shooting portfolios of aspiring models. I would arrive at his house after classes and ring up local fashion designers, socialites, models, theater stars, and businesspeople from his landline. The articles were mainly about their plans for Christmas, New Year, Diwali, or whatever festival was on the calendar. The strange accent I had inherited by pretending to be "Ruth from Gloucester" at DCC, which made me sound like a rather pretentious, rich, South Delhi teenager, worked in my favor. Aspiring models would silently wait for Mr. Rajpal as I politely nudged the celebrities to give me something better than "I plan to have fun."

After Mum managed to borrow some money for the college fees, I attended a media course that a highly respected private journalism institute ran from the Stephen's campus. It was an eight-month course and focused on print, radio, documentary, online and photo journalism, and advertising. I knew Mum had struggled to arrange the fees and that I needed to start earning full-time right after graduation. I couldn't afford a specialized master's degree in journalism that everyone told me I needed. So I held on to the ghostwriting gig even though it paid less than a hundred rupees per article and I couldn't add it to my résumé, since I wasn't getting a byline. I would spend several hours collecting the quotes I needed and then write the articles by hand, which someone would type up in a cyber café. I would then edit and proofread them, and send back the changes, a process that I had to repeat several times when the typist couldn't understand my handwriting. It was a tough job that didn't really pay the bills. And with theory and practical classes that stretched long into the afternoons, I often struggled to submit the articles by the deadline. Yet, it was the most useful training in journalism I received outside of grad school. I was my own researcher, writer, fact-checker, proofreader, and editor—the articles would be lightly edited before they were published. Even as a nineteen-year-old who was yet to graduate from college, I knew this experience was priceless. And it set me on the path to real journalism.

CHAPTER 7

THE ARGUMENT FOR RESERVATION

Through the three years I spent at St. Stephen's, I was worried about people finding out about my caste only when the result lists went up on the notice boards and my name was tucked under the SC/ST category, or towards the end of the course when my classmates began discussing how easy it would be for a reserved category student to get into a good MBA college. I stayed silent through most of these discussions because I didn't know how to tell them why that wasn't true. I wasn't entirely sure myself how reservations worked. But I felt deeply ashamed about "grabbing the resources" that belonged to those that rightfully deserved them. I had internalized the argument that anti-reservationists make when they claim that reservations ruin the chances of (deserving) upper-caste people in the college and job market. Of course, I thought, they were right to be upset about that. But beyond these few moments of anxiety, my caste didn't bother me too much. That would not have been the case had I attended other Delhi University (DU) colleges.

In most colleges in DU, the annual student elections, often criticized for being "flashy" and "dramatic," are heavily backed by the student wings of prominent political parties—BJP, Congress, CPI (M), JDU, ASU, etc.[1] These elections are often fought along caste lines, with candidates from certain castes being fielded for certain posts. The elections have been criticized for allowing "caste, money factors [to] rob campus politics of [a] level playing field."[2] These elections are banned at St. Stephen's, and therefore its students are shielded from the caste-based bullying that's common in several DU colleges during elections and the rest of the school year.

Other colleges of Delhi University, like several universities across the country, are steeped in caste discrimination, where Dalit students and faculty alike have to jump through hoops. Their identification as lower caste because of reservation makes them particularly vulnerable to discrimination and abuse from college authorities. Application forms get lost in the mail, theses are not approved in time, and scholarships remain stuck in the back offices for months and even years.[3] Not just in Delhi University, Dalit students face institutional bullying in most other state and central universities that are required to follow the reservation policy.

At Hyderabad University, Rohith Vemula faced such discrimination: his grant was severely delayed until he ran out of money and was forced to live off the generosity of his friends and well-wishers. Most Dalit students understand the power the university system wields over their education and choose to duck their heads, blend in, and comply. Unlike them, Rohith was an outspoken advocate for social justice and a student activist leader. He not only refused to overlook the systemic discrimination against Dalit students but also vocally asserted his rights. In fearlessly announcing his Dalit identity and demanding justice for himself, Rohith possibly challenged a fundamental idea that many upper-caste professors hold—that Dalit students study in Indian colleges and universities on their largesse, so they should be grateful for whatever crumbs they are thrown instead of taunting them by demanding more. In fact, Giri Shankar, an upper-caste assistant professor at Kerala's Ernakulum Law College, screamed something along these lines at twenty-four-year-old Dalit student Vaishakh D. S. in December 2016. Vaishakh had questioned the professor's criticism against male and female students dancing together at an art fest organized on campus. "You belong to SC/ST category and you are studying here and staying in the hostel out of the mercy of the government and people like me," he had reportedly retorted.[4] Vaishakh was immediately suspended for "verbally abusing his professor" as he, along with most other students present, had chanted a derogatory slogan that has circulated among the college students for decades. He only found out that charges had been made against him (none of the other students were charged) when he went to complain about the professor's casteist insult.

The notion that constitutional reservation is an unfair government "handout" to Scheduled Castes and Tribes, who "obviously don't need it," is absurd. It is a corrective measure that reflects the socialist policies of the nation state and is a thousand years overdue. This idea of "undeserving students" didn't spring up in a vacuum. It originated and was widely disseminated during two critical events in modern India's history: the Mandal Commission protests of the nineties and the anti-reservation protests of 2006. The All India Institute of Medical Sciences (AIIMS) in New Delhi was the main hub for the 2006 protests, and they were widely covered by media channels. I remember watching those broadcasts on television as I saw the action unfold around me in real time in Delhi University.

The protests took place in the summer following the release of Rakeysh Omprakash Mehra's *Rang De Basanti* in late January the same year. In the movie, five easygoing Delhi University students turn into activists who lead an agitation against government corruption. This storyline is cleverly juxtaposed against the narrative of freedom fighters (played by the same actors) from the 1900s. Flashbacks of the five famous freedom fighters smoothly cuts to present-day scenes of the same five actors—Aamir Khan, Soha Ali Khan, Sharman Joshi, Siddharth Narayan, and Kunal Kapoor—conspiring to take down a corrupt minister and attempts to justify their actions as patriotic and in the larger national interest. Several scenes were shot in and around Delhi University, including at St. Stephen's, and many students appeared as extras in the film. The five actors had spent part of the year touring various DU colleges and the prerelease publicity was intense many months before its release. Unsurprisingly, the movie opened to packed cinema halls, and became a must-watch for all Delhi University students who felt represented on screen. Moreover, the India Gate sequence, which had charged shots of the lead actors protesting against a corrupt system and the police brutality against them, resonated widely. In particular, police violence against sixty-year-old Waheeda Rehman, who plays the mother of R. Madhavan's character, the slain pilot of a crashed MiG-21, had a lasting impact on the audience. The movie was celebrated for reviving the patriotic spirit in nonchalant early millennials. In this charged atmosphere, when the United Progressive Alliance (UPA) government announced its plan to introduce additional reservation for OBCs in April, Youth For Equality (YFE), a student group based in AIIMS, found it easier to mobilize the usually apathetic students. Cell phones were flooded with text messages urging students to gather at India Gate to stand up for what's right, i.e., oppose reservation. Their message was so effective that even I, someone who steered clear of politics, particularly reservation, wondered if I was neglecting my "patriotic duty" by not attending these protests. Many students who were away for the summer didn't make it to the actual protests. But the message that "quota students have it easy" was reinforced.

Despite limited participation, the protests, which began when YFE called for a nationwide strike on May 13, 2006, had some impact. AIIMS was the epicenter, and the college administration openly supported the protesting doctors and students, providing them with tents, pillows, mattresses, and water coolers.[5] The protests also spread to the students of the Indian Institutes of Technology (IITs), Indian Institutes of Management (IIMs), and some other medical and engineering colleges. AIIMS had no more than a handful of protesters, yet they grabbed national media attention by turning away patients, and even denying emergency health care at one of the most important hospitals in the country. Meanwhile, the pro-reservation protests, which also took place at the AIIMS campus, were brutally shut down by the police, since the administration allegedly did not permit any agitations within 500 meters of its campus.[6] They had relaxed that rule for the mostly upper-caste doctors and students who were protesting reservation. Anti-reservationists shouted casteist slogans. They swept the roads and shined shoes to demonstrate that they were in fact the "new Dalits."

Television news channels ran the footage almost nonstop. Television coverage did not call out the protesters on their casteism and allowed the viewers, most of whom opposed reservation, to frame a new narrative against it. The pro-reservation protests taking place a few meters away barely received any coverage. After almost a month of coverage in print and television news, the Supreme Court ordered the doctors to call off their strike on June 3, 2006.

After the protests died down, the Ministry of Health and Family Welfare asked then University Grants Commission (UGC) chairman Professor Sukhadeo Thorat to look into complaints of caste-based discrimination and abuse against the AIIMS faculty and administration. Thorat's report was released in 2007 and found that 85 percent of SC/ST students disclosed that they did not have proper access to faculty, who were indifferent to them and paid more attention to their upper-caste classmates in practical and viva exams.[7] Almost 76 percent reported that examiners wanted to know their caste, and several students said that their grades dropped once it was known that they were from an SC or ST background. Around 88 percent of SC/ST students reported receiving lower marks than they expected in theory papers. Postgraduate students complained that they were not assigned thesis guides, which made it difficult for them to access external academic opportunities like scholarships and conferences. SC/ST students reported suffering abuse not only from their teachers but also their peers, who would bully them because of their lower caste. Students talked about revolting ragging practices where new students were forced to reveal their caste in front of all students and when discovered to be from a lower caste, senior students would yell invective and casteist slurs, asking why they didn't choose to study elsewhere. SC/ST students would be forced to sit on the floor, while others sat on hostel room beds because they had "earned their seat by merit." SC/ST students would also have to recite "Ten Reasons Why I Don't Belong in AIIMS" and were abused both physically and verbally if they didn't.

These targeted hazing rituals ensured that even students from caste-neutral backgrounds would become hyperaware of the differences, creating casteist hierarchies where they didn't exist before. These hazing rituals are designed so that SC/ST students would start their years at AIIMS, and their careers, feeling inferior, while upper-caste students held on to their sense of superiority. This kind of ragging, which is common in medical and engineering schools across India, is horrifically isolating and aims to dehumanize its victims so the "oppressors" will share no sympathy with them. They are created to duplicate the original rules of the caste system of denying education to Dalits in modern India. Specific to AIIMS, these patterns of abuse and humiliation often follow SC/ST doctors into their careers. Many of them, like Mumbai resident Dr. Rohan Kamble, who wrote in to *Documents of Dalit Discrimination*, are terrorized into giving up higher education.[8] This also leaves a lasting impact on the students' mental health and, as many of them come from poorer backgrounds, they find it impossible to thrive in a toxic academic environment. Of the sixteen Dalit student suicides in North India between 2007 and 2013, two were at AIIMS.[9] Balmukund Bharti had topped his school in Bundelkhand and scored a high rank in the IIT entrance examination, which he gave up to join AIIMS. Bharti belonged to the Chamar community and came from Kundeshwar, a remote village in Madhya Pradesh. He committed suicide in 2010 after repeated incidents of caste-based harassment. The college principal allegedly told him "You can never become a doctor [because] you don't have the brains." Dalit activist and documentary filmmaker Anoop Kumar in his documentary series *Death of Merit* interviewed Bharti's parents who recalled their son's terrified reaction to the principal's diatribe. Despite the obvious harassment, the college administration refused to take any responsibility for his death, instead blaming his lack of English language skills and his inability to cope with coursework. Less than two years later, in 2012, another ST student, Anil Meena, who was the second topper in the Scheduled Tribes Category of the All India Medical Entrance Exams, also killed himself. Kumar's documentary both examines their deaths and holds the college directly or indirectly accountable for them.

But AIIMS doesn't seem to reserve its casteism for its students alone—the SC/ST faculty also complained of illegalities in their hiring and promotion according to the Thorat Committee report.[10] While Dalit professors were denied rightful promotions, the empty seats were filled from the general category applicants in a willful neglect of the mandatory reservation policy. The AIIMS administration dismissed the findings of Thorat's report, questioned its methodology, and called it "biased and unsubstantiated."[11]

Allegations of discrimination and intimidation are not unheard of in other higher educational institutions as well. Rohith Vemula's death at Hyderabad University was not a one-off. Eight Dalit students had committed suicide there between 2006 and 2016 alone.

Rohith's death was categorized as institutional murder for many reasons.[12] Chief among them was that many students believed that then university vice chancellor Appa Rao Podile had a history of casteist neglect and antagonism towards Dalit students and many hold him directly responsible for Rohith's death.[13] Hyderabad University, like AIIMS, encourages the isolation of Dalit students with "lack of merit" scare tactics like outing the SC/ST students with a star under their name, even if they have not availed themselves of reservation.[14] Deepthi Krishna, a PhD student at Hyderabad University, narrated her mother's ordeal in *Documents of Dalit Discrimination*. When her mother was a student there decades ago her roommates set fire to her room. Terrified of similar harassment, Krishna refused to avail herself of reservation even though she was entitled to it as a Dalit student. Like at AIIMS, in Hyderabad University, Dalit postgraduate students are frequently denied thesis guides and find their scholarships blocked. These scholarships, for many Dalit students like Rohith, not only support them but also help sustain their families. Senthil Kumar, who had pursued a PhD despite his difficult financial background, committed suicide in 2008 when the university repeatedly denied him a guide and withdrew his fellowship.[15] Kumar was from Salem, a small town in Tamil Nadu, and the entire family had worked hard to send him to college. He was the first in the family to pursue higher education. Like Rohith's mother, they depended on the money he sent home. It's not hard to imagine Kumar's helplessness and frustration that drove him to take his own life. Similarly, Madari Venkatesh, another Dalit PhD student, killed himself by consuming poison in 2013 when the Hyderabad University administration hadn't allotted him a permanent guide or a laboratory.[16] Former Supreme Court justice K. Ramaswamy reported in 2016 that these delays in allotting guides were based on "ambiguous procedures" and mostly affected SC/ST students in the university.[17] Earlier, in 2013, a group of twenty-nine academicians had identified "administrative indifference and hostile regulations" as a cause of marginalized student suicides in Hyderabad University.[18] But the university's administration asked for "scientific proof" for sociologist Sasheej Hegde's analysis that students from marginalized backgrounds were alienated in the university.[19]

All these universities seem to be following the same playbook on how to exclude Dalits. The academic performance of the students seems to be less important than their lower caste status. Ragging, institutional bullying, and lack of support for Dalit students causes many of them to commit suicide and discourages other Dalits from applying to these important centers of learning, leading them to be excluded from these fields. This sends a clear signal to young Dalit aspirants that these prestigious colleges have no place for them, regardless of what the reservation policy dictates. The toxic belief that "quota students" are innately less able or talented than "mainstream students" is at the heart of this exclusion.

The IIT-JEE exam, which aims to test a student's aptitude for engineering, is not only tough but also vastly different from the central or state board exams that high school students clear in school. The problems challenge logic and theory in a way that makes it almost impossible for anyone who is unfamiliar with its "code" to solve them. The coaching institutes, including the one that I attended, teach the patterns, codes, and techniques to finish the examination paper in three hours. About 82 percent of Indian students either take additional coaching for IIT-JEE and other science-based competitive exams at the numerous coaching institutes that dot every small and big town or directly go to Kota, Rajasthan, to study at one of the 150 "cram schools," which pretty much guarantee you a spot on the list if you are admitted and follow their instructions.[20] Even local coaching is expensive, costing about 2,000–3,000 rupees per month nearly sixteen years ago in 2001–03 when I took these classes. The fees for the Kota schools can go up to one lakh rupees a month, which doesn't include the cost of living—making it prohibitively expensive for students from marginalized backgrounds. It's not that students can't clear these exams without coaching; many SC/ST students in fact do, but since they come from marginalized backgrounds, they lack other support structures. That, along with their government school education, often leads many SC/ST/OBC students to drop out or be expelled for low grades. In 2015, 90 percent of the students that IIT–Roorkee dismissed on account of low grades were SC/ST/OBC.[21] Added to this is the distress, discrimination, and systemic failure that "quota students" face at these prestigious institutions.[22] Nearly 80 percent of student suicides in IITs till 2011 were of Dalit students.

IIT students have a long history of opposing constitutional reservation and several members of YFE in 2006 were from its various colleges. Many used the IIT–Roorkee dropouts incident to argue that "quota students" are inherently talentless and don't belong in the colleges, instead of examining the conditions that led to their dropping out. IITs across the country admit a disproportionately high number of upper-caste students in the general category, which Harvard-based anthropologist Ajantha Subramanian argues isn't as casteless or "meritorious" as it seems. Using IIT–Madras as a case study, she examines how when the number of European engineers in India decreased at the beginning of the twentieth century, Tamil Brahmins were the single largest group in Madras Presidency to replace them. They also filled over 70 percent of the seats in regional engineering institutes despite forming only 3 percent of the population and were disproportionately represented in most modern professions along with other upper castes. At IIT–Madras, not only the students but also the faculty are overwhelmingly upper caste, with 464 professors drawn from the "general category," 59 OBCs, 11 SCs, and 2 STs. She argues that association of "general category" with merit is biased because the students from that category are assumed to be upper caste. During her interviews with several former IIT students, she discovered that many believed that while general category students got bad grades because they were "having fun," reserved category students simply didn't have the intellectual capability to do well. Unsurprisingly, the administration supports that idea, especially former director P. V. Indiresan who believed that "the talented" upper castes deserved "rights of their own" compared to the "socially deprived" who demanded special privileges.[23]

The idea that upper castes are inherently "talented" while the reserved category SC/ST/OBC students are meritless is as hollow as it is casteist. In an anonymous study on the state of female Dalit students in a prestigious Indian university, PhD candidates and research fellows complained that they were discouraged from applying to the generous Rajiv Gandhi National Fellowship for SC/ST students. They were told that they didn't "deserve free fellowships."[24] And the faculty impose their casteist ideas in the universities in many ways.

The University of Hyderabad's "Brahmin well," which was dug in the 1980s for Professor V. Kannan is a ridiculous example of that.[25] Kannan only allowed other upper-caste students and professors to access it and lower-caste students and faculty couldn't come anywhere near it till he retired in 2014. Upper-caste professors not only discriminate against their lower-caste colleagues but also question their "merit" and their right to their careers. Professor Vasant Tarade, a former principal of Mumbai's Sydenham College, recalled that a Brahmin professor refused to use his chair after he retired.[26]

Years of being accused of caste-based discrimination have had some impact and institutes have created some systems to support the reserved category students. The AIIMS website informs us that the campus has a SC/ST grievance cell, while Jawaharlal Nehru University (JNU) has a personalized academic support system and the IITs have English language classes to help students from vernacular language backgrounds. Yet, as Professor Thorat notes, these institutes "lack the will to implement them in full."[27] Universities and colleges should be centers for learning new ideas and questioning the status quo. Instead, they become places of discrimination, exclusion, and institutional harassment. Young minds are bred with hate, ready to assert their caste hierarchy over the next generation. Students are not taught why reservation is essential for those from the lower castes, who have been excluded from education, art, culture, and even owning property, to reach a somewhat level playing field. Without reservation, Dalits will remain on the fringes, unable to access even the most basic opportunities.

The toxic and dangerous narrative about merit that exists around reservation can be traced back to a 1980 report. Setting up our new nation state in 1947, our leaders looked to the humanitarian ideals of secularism, liberty, and freedom. We led ourselves to believe that casteism was also gone with the British. Especially after Dr. Ambedkar's heroic parallel struggle for Dalit rights and Gandhi's "Harijan" upliftment campaign, a new narrative of post-caste India was crafted, even as the reality looked entirely different. While some Dalits, like my grandfather, were using reservation to get into colleges and government jobs, many others were still forced to live in segregation, with no access to public water, education, and, most importantly, dignity. The discrimination had changed shape to fit into the modern post-Independence narrative. Now it was more subtle and, in the case of universities and other private establishments, institutional. Dalit students were not forced to sit on the floor in class but were relegated to the back benches where they could be ignored. Their caste-based professions no longer enslaved them, but they were turned away from most employment except public service jobs, where they could be denied promotions or, if they were officers, disobeyed openly. Now Dalits could move into colonies where upper-caste families lived, only if the owner would rent to them. Untouchability has been illegal since 1950 and discrimination against Dalits could lead to an arrest under the 1989 SC/ST Act but casteism found ways to continue unchecked in insidious ways.

In 1980, Bindeshwari Prasad Mandal, ex-chief minister of Bihar and head of the Second Backward Classes Commission, produced a report which highlighted this reality. This report proposed adding a 27 percent reservation for OBCs at all levels of government service—SC and ST reservation was 22.5 percent. The report took into account the huge OBC population that was unable to access public sector jobs. The report, considered problematic even when it was created, remained buried till 1990, when the pro-reservation prime minister, V. P. Singh, decided to introduce it as a bill. When Singh announced his decision to enforce the "Mandal Commission" recommendation, middle-class, upper-caste, educated Indians took to the streets to protest against the government for taking away their "rights" (privilege). Students from most colleges in the country joined in hartals, bandhs, and dharnas that took place over months. Various upper-caste groups forced shopkeepers to shut down, and intimidated people into staying home. Intense violence, looting, and curfews across many cities created an emergency-like situation in the country. Through the turmoil, Singh stuck to his position, even as his party members deserted him and his cabinet found itself incapable of handling the violent riots and protests.[28] After several weeks, when it appeared that the anti-Mandal protests would die down naturally, a Deshbandhu College student, Rajeev Goswami, set himself on fire, reigniting the protests.[29] Even though he survived, Goswami's immolation triggered a series of similar protests in cities across the country, ultimately forcing Singh to withdraw the bill.

Indian students, who had been rather apathetic to Indian politics since Independence, shattered windowpanes and burned buses because they felt "punished for the sins of their forefathers." The additional reservation that the Mandal Commission proposed did not apply to educational institutions, promotions in government jobs, defense, or paramilitary forces. It only aimed to allow OBCs to enter government jobs. The private sector was not required to comply with this reservation requirement. But upper-caste students made the illogical leap that this would affect their chances in all jobs and industries, hence the widespread protests. But the report was suggesting a 27 percent reservation for backward classes that made up almost 52 percent of the population of the country.[30] Along with SC/ST reservation, only 49.5 percent of entry-level seats would be reserved for those who represented almost 75 percent of the total population of the country. The report took into account not just social backwardness, but also education and economic deficiency to calculate which castes deserved a boost. Genuinely poor and uneducated caste groups that were not able to access these jobs on their own would largely benefit from the commission. But that made little difference, since the anti-Mandal protests were never about actual issues—one high school student who set himself on fire admitted later that he didn't even know what reservation was.[31] In a survey conducted between 1990 and 2000, the National Sample Survey Organization discovered that while Hindu upper castes formed only 37 percent of the population, they formed more than 60 percent of the graduates surveyed in medical, engineering, and agricultural sciences.[32]

Without a doubt, these protests were only about protecting the caste system that ensured the "rights" and privileges of the upper caste. Anti-Mandal protests were regressive in more than their casteist ideology: instead of protesting the lack of jobs like most of their male counterparts, "feminist" groups and female students protested the "lack of good husbands." They argued that upper-caste men would not be able to get jobs, thereby making them ineligible for marriage. Universities that had been seen as apolitical and casteless became openly casteist during the anti-Mandal protests, creating the narrative of meritless "quota students." Students naively complained that the Mandal Commission was forcing them to "think along caste lines," unlike earlier when they had conveniently ignored systemic casteism.

But it wasn't only the students or politically motivated groups who poured out onto the streets that were responsible for the anti-Mandal agitation. The largest and perhaps the most powerful anti-reservationists of the time sat in courthouses as lawyers, ran companies as executives, and, most disappointingly, published newspapers. They either took to the streets to protest or published stinging editorials against the recommendations. The national mainstream media, in particular, which is supposed to stand up for the marginalized and dispossessed, or at the very least present factual, unbiased, and ethical reporting, opportunistically abandoned its principles to twist logic and present half-truths to oppose the Mandal Commission. In the nineties, when there were no online news outlets and both All India Radio (AIR) and Doordarshan were state-owned mouthpieces, newspapers were powerful tools to shape public opinion. During the anti-Mandal protests, many newspapers used that power to create a narrative that was not only anti-reservation but also openly casteist. High-profile editors and opinion makers of the time wrote articles explaining the "gross injustice" of Mandal's report. Former minister and World Bank economist Arun Shourie, who was then the editor of the *Indian Express*, led the charge by writing "casteist articles and editorials," according to activist K. Balagopal.[33] Almost the entire English-language media banded together in support. Even "forward-thinking" academics like Columbia University South Asian studies professor Sudipta Kaviraj (then a professor at JNU) argued that caste-based reservation would be like punishing people for the "follies of the past generations."[34] None of these experts mentioned that Brahmins, who are barely 5 percent of the total population, are overrepresented in the cabinet or that upper castes almost exclusively run Indian embassies across the world. Their (upper) caste was invisible and considered irrelevant, when it was their caste that had allowed them to control the entire country's bureaucracy. But the lower castes of the OBCs and Dalits came into focus when it was used to get them parity in the most basic sense—with entry to a government job. Other recommendations of the report, which called for a ban on private ownership in industry and agriculture to unburden the poor farmers—some of them even upper caste—who were almost enslaved to the rich landowners, were ignored.[35] The articles chose to focus only on the reservation argument, which they dismissed as unsophisticated and poorly constructed. The report was criticized for relying on census data and blurring the lines between castes and classes. The deaths, violence, discrimination and structural backwardness, illiteracy, and poverty that almost exclusively burden the lower castes were clearly not enough proof that casteism hadn't, in fact, magically disappeared with the British.

The print media's all-out attack on the Mandal Commission and its casteist rhetoric was hardly surprising since most newspapers at the time were upper-caste-owned. Journalism, like several other modern professions in India, has been disproportionately upper caste since the nineteenth century. Phule had protested the Dalit-apathetic, propaganda-based journalism back in 1873.[36] As Ambedkar pointed out, the Associated Press India office in the 1900s was filled with "Madras Brahmins."[37] The pattern continued and a few decades before Independence, upper-caste businessmen established media houses like Times Group and HT Media, among the most powerful media houses even today.

Both the anti-Mandal and 2006 anti-reservation protests contested the need for an increased OBC reservation. They argued that instead of a guaranteed entry for "historically backward castes" into some public sector jobs, reservation should instead apply to those from financially weaker backgrounds. Those who were "economically disabled" should have reserved seats, since many OBCs were "rich" and didn't need the reservation. The arguments were only partly right. Many OBCs, who have long been considered part of the lower castes in the hierarchy, but not untouchable like Dalits, have indeed succeeded in availing themselves of opportunities and blending in with the upper castes. In fact, some castes like the Jats are not only deemed upper caste but also practice the same level of loathsome discrimination against Dalits as other upper castes. Banias, Rajputs, and some OBC castes have been known to discriminate against Dalits. Dalit academic Kancha Ilaiah identifies this sociological change as part of the process of "Neo-Kshatriyization," where lower castes tend to adopt the habits, culture, and sensibilities of castes that are directly above them in the hierarchy so as to assimilate better.[38] (They end up adopting their odious casteism as well.) This has allowed several OBC individuals to break through the caste barrier and enter what the Supreme Court has termed the "creamy layer." OBC individuals like Prime Minister Modi who are heads of state, presidents, bureaucrats, doctors, etc., are part of that creamy layer. This creamy layer does not get the benefits of the OBC reservation under the reservation bill that was passed in 2006. Only those OBC castes that have been identified as heavily marginalized based on their social and economic status have been granted that access. Even within this group, children of "successful" individuals are not eligible for reservation.

Both OBCs and Dalits have been marginalized by the caste system. But there is one major distinction between them: untouchability. Discrimination and abuse of individuals increases as we go down the caste hierarchy, and Dalits lie deep at the bottom. While a handful of Dalits managed to enter some vocations before Independence, like my mother's grandfather who was a soldier in the British army, most entered free India illiterate, poor, and with no sizeable land or property. Through access to education and government jobs, many Dalits, for the first time, gained the kind of financial stability that was normal for most upper castes.

Even with reservation, Dalits are discriminated against, regardless of their economic background. Reservation forces the upper-caste system to accept Dalits and it's clearly not happy about it, since it constantly hits back—institutional discrimination in universities is only one example. That's why so many of us hide our caste identity. Without the hand of the law, even those Dalits who have made some progress would easily slip back to the fringes of society. And that is where the majority of Dalits still find themselves. Both financially stable and economically deficient Dalits need antidiscriminatory laws and equal access to the system, which can only happen through reservation.

The fundamental idea that many anti-reservationists fail to understand is that no matter their economic status, Dalits still face social discrimination. Those opposed to reservation tend to attack any Dalit who appears middle class and avails himself or herself of reservation. The "creamy layer" of the OBCs does not exist for Dalits as social discrimination undoes any economic progress. Anti-reservationists used this faulty logic to criticize 2016 IAS topper Tina Dabi for using reservation. They claimed that she was part of the "creamy layer" (since both her parents were engineers) and used her case to slam reservation for all Dalits. But caste bias pervades almost every stage of the UPSC examination: SC/ST candidates consistently score lower than general category students in the interviews, even if they score much higher in the written examination.[39] Even Dabi scored poorly in the personality test interview but topped her written exam.[40] Any Dalit candidate who chooses to avail themselves of reservation is essentially using it to offset this inevitable discrimination.

It's extraordinary that constitutional reservation gets the amount of attention that it does even though it only applies to universities and government jobs, which fall under the rapidly shrinking public sector. Even before the Indian economy opened up to foreign investment in 1991, the private sector was already shooting ahead of the public sector in terms of job creation. Since then, the private sector has gained hugely on the public sector and, according to World Bank Data, contributed almost 52.2 percent to India's gross domestic product (GDP) in 2015.[41] In just six years between 2006 and 2012, the private sector added 3.13 million jobs and grew by 35.7 percent, while the public sector shrank by 3.3 percent.[42] Even in the public sector it takes the arm-twisting provided by the Constitution to accept Dalits, and glaring inconsistencies continue to show up in their grading, hiring, and promotions despite it. The private sector, which is largely controlled by the upper castes, is a lot more unwilling to open its doors to Dalits. In fact, data suggests that the private sector actively works to keep Dalits out as much as possible. In 2007, former UGC chairman Sukhadeo Thorat and Paul Attewell conducted a study of the hiring patterns of Dalit and Muslim candidates in private sector companies in Delhi, Mumbai, Hyderabad, and Chennai. Fake résumés of similarly qualified candidates with Dalit, upper-caste Hindu, and Muslim last names were sent to seek entry-level positions in these companies. Despite there being no difference in their education or experience, they discovered that Dalit applicants were called 33 percent less and Muslims 66 percent less than upper-caste candidates.[43] That study sent shock waves across industries and companies fell over each other to reiterate that they hired people only because of their "merit."

Academics Surinder Singh Jodhka and Katherine Newman interviewed twenty-five HR managers who represented companies that employed a total of 1.9 million full-time workers and 63,000 subcontracted workers.[44] These HR managers also reiterated that they hired based on merit. Yet, the study discovered that apart from their qualifications, candidates were also judged on their "family backgrounds" and "cosmopolitan attitudes," which is code for an urban, middle-class, upper-caste upbringing. The only category of jobs where Dalit "merit" seems to shine is the clerical class III jobs or class IV jobs like drivers, attendants, or sanitation workers, where Dalits form a majority.

The private sector in India does not have a reservation policy, nor does it adhere to self-imposed policies of diversity, inclusion, or affirmative action like in the United States, Northern Ireland, or even South Africa. In 2004, the UPA government suggested including more candidates from SCs and STs in the private sector. CEOs and chairmen of companies large and small immediately condemned the move, making the old argument that SC and ST employees would "dilute" private sector merit. The media seemed to support these casteist arguments. The CEOs, many of whom had degrees from global business schools, seemed to believe that these multimillion-dollar industries would become inefficient by including a few "meritless" individuals in lower- and middle-level jobs. Vishnu Dusad, then MD of Nucleus Software, told *Outlook* magazine that multinational companies wouldn't understand why they were being asked to increase the diversity in the workplace.[45] Many multinational companies in India are funded by US companies that are required to report their workplace composition under the Civil Rights Act of 1964. It showed how little most Indian companies understood international diversity practices, since not a single businessman *Outlook* interviewed in 2004 saw that more talent and diversity could be good for business. They used terms like "mass scale massacre," "racing with hands tied behind," and "artificial division" to describe how employing more Dalits would ruin their companies. Eventually the UPA government scaled down its suggestions when 218 companies signed a letter promising to have greater caste diversity.[46]

In 2007, when the Confederation of Indian Industry asked companies to share data on the castes of their employees, 95 percent did not even respond. Later, in 2011, when a private sector caste survey was finally conducted, it showed that barring Kerala and Tamil Nadu, Dalits did not adequately represent their populations in the private sector workforce in any states.[47] In 2014, politician and Infosys cofounder Nandan Nilekani was viciously attacked for suggesting that the private sector have more inclusive policies. While some sections of the media misinterpreted his comment as demanding full-scale reservation in the private sector, his ex-colleague Mohandas Pai attacked him for "selling his soul for power."[48] An informal study conducted by Jodhka in 2016 showed that Brahmins or Banias filled almost 94 percent of top jobs in fifty thousand Indian companies.[49]

However, since the UPA government's initial suggestion in 2004, the demand for private sector reservation or at least some level of inclusion has only grown louder. Several bills have since been presented to enact an Equal Opportunity Commission in the private sector, the most recent of which was in 2013 by the UPA II government.[50] In 2016, the National Commission for Backward Classes proposed to implement a 27 percent OBC reservation in the private sector, which was backed by several opposition parties and even welcomed by the BJP government.[51] Even many private sector companies have stepped up their inclusion policies. The Tata Group not only has a diversity program but also an affirmative action program that hires employees and contract workers from marginalized sections. Meanwhile, ICICI has set up a Probationary Officer Program for underprivileged students, which grooms entry-level students and imparts soft skills.[52] Infosys also runs a program to enhance the technical and communication skills of engineering graduates to make them employable in companies besides its own. After a more recent 2019 study by the Azim Premji university concluding that SC/ST communities were "over-represented" in low-paying jobs and "under-represented" in high-paying positions, India Inc. announced its plans to adopt the Voluntary Code of Conduct (VCC) to implement social-justice-oriented measures within its organizations.[53]

While the organized private sector is decidedly upper-caste driven, the unorganized sector is equally challenging for Dalit small business owners and entrepreneurs. Yet another study by Jodhka of Dalit business owners in Panipat, Haryana, and Saharanpur, Uttar Pradesh, revealed that in 2010 business was still considered an upper-caste career.[54] While non-Dalit businessmen were identified by their products and sector, Dalit businesses were identified by their castes. Names like "Chamaron ki dukaan" or "Chudon ki factory" discouraged customers from doing business with them. The study also found that upper-caste businessmen supported each other and resented Dalits entering their space. While there are some massively successful Dalit entrepreneurs like Kalpana Saroj, who turned around Kamani Tubes after taking it over, or Santosh Kamble, who made a fortune supplying nylon and leather, for most Dalit businesses it is a tough climb. In 2006, Thorat found that only 27 percent of businesses in urban areas and 12 percent in rural areas were SC-owned, while 22 percent and 5 percent were ST-owned respectively. To counter that, he suggested that government and private contracts give preference to Dalits, especially in food-related products and businesses where they were most discriminated against.[55] Interestingly, Dalit businessmen were allowed to thrive under the British. Columnist Chandra Bhan Prasad recounts how Agra Dalits who had historically worked in the leather industry, trading with the British, were edged out by upper-caste businessmen soon after Independence.[56] Even Dalit daily wage workers are often considered unfit for jobs that involve physical contact with other workers or customers. Dalits currently form almost 25 percent of India's population. Keeping 201 million of us out of business or away from work based on the illogical notions of caste isn't just unjust, it's also bad for business.

In 2015, Dr. Shashi Tharoor, MP from Thiruvananthapuram, argued at an Oxford University debate that Britain owes India and other former colonies "colonial reparations." The entire upper-caste establishment cheered this heartily. Even Prime Minister Modi shared a video of Tharoor's speech from the PMO's Twitter account. Following this, Tharoor wrote the best-selling *An Era of Darkness* on the same topic. But most Indians failed to see the irony in demanding compensation for nearly two hundred years of colonial rule while refusing any reparation for thousands of years of discrimination against their own citizens. "If paying collective reparations for collective guilt is appropriate, then how about India 'atoning' for thousands of years of its caste system?" senior policy analyst Shikha Dalmia asked in her column for *Time* magazine.[57] The difference between the British and the Indian upper-caste establishment, Dalmia noted, was that the British were at least willing to reflect on their history. The upper castes, be it during the Mandal Commission protests, the 2006 anti-reservation protests, or the private sector's protest against reservation, can't even stand the idea of compensation for the discrimination and violence that still affect millions of Dalits today.

As we have seen throughout this book, reservation is called unfair only when it attempts to get Dalits and OBCs the same opportunities, education, and degrees that the upper castes have had easy access to for decades. The culture and wealth collected over the years has created generations of lawyers, doctors, and businesspeople, while Dalits couldn't touch pens, pencils, and books or enter courts, temples, and many other public places. Before international companies set up shop in India (and often even after) it was customary to pass down the father's job to the offspring, in both private and public sectors. But while most Dalits would pass their lower-level office jobs to their children, upper-caste employees were handing over high-level managerial jobs, some of which would stay in the same family for generations. *Golmaal*, the popular 1979 Amol Palekar-starrer, even had a subplot around this. This upper-caste reservation, where most high-paying managerial jobs would pass on to the employees' children or relatives, was the way most companies hired candidates. Even today, 60–70 percent of jobs in the private sector are secured because of family connections and networks.[58]

Most private sector companies, like Jodhka's survey discovered, have often valued family background and "culture" over education and ability. Culture, which is code for upper-caste taste—in dance, music, theater, literature, art, poetry, and even cuisine—has been off limits for Dalits. They were excluded from these upper-caste pursuits and were forced to build an alternate "Dalit culture" with locally developed forms of art, music, dance, and theater. While these upper-caste values have come to define Indian culture, Dalit culture was rejected as lowbrow and inelegant. The private sector has, by and large, adopted a global work ethic—this has forced it to open up to anyone who discovered the new ethic through Western television, Internet, college friends, and batchmates. Urban, English-speaking, mostly upper-caste candidates have a better chance at landing private sector jobs than Dalit and OBC applicants who live in rural areas and speak Indian languages. Ironically, this shift, however small, made it easier for people like me to pass as upper caste. It was different from earlier when Dalits (like Mum's father, who took on the name "Victor" when he worked at the Oberoi, Delhi) found it much harder to pass as upper caste.

By building systems that (without constitutional reservation) favor upper castes, becoming part of the dominant culture remains impossible for most Dalits and OBCs. Upper-caste privilege—which is not always about how much money someone has or how much property they own—is, as feminist and anti-race activist Peggy McIntosh describes, an "invisible package of unearned assets."[59] This "invisible package," which is attached to their not so invisible upper caste, opens doors for jobs, bank loans, business opportunities, and education that are often closed for Dalits. Even when a Brahmin has no money, he or she almost always has education, a poor Bania nearly always knows how to run a business and has the financial acumen to multiply wealth, an economically challenged Kshatriya will likely have management skills and political know-how. Far from being caste-based stereotypes, these are highly profitable skills that are passed down between generations in each caste. These skills allow poor individuals from upper castes to reasonably elevate their financial condition in a way that's not available to Dalits. French philosopher Pierre Bourdieu defined cultural capital as dispositions, attitudes, values, and behaviors that parents can pass on to their children. Upper castes have had access to cultural capital for centuries, from which they continue to benefit and from which Dalits are excluded.[60] An upper-caste family in the same financial situation as mine would have had a better chance of success had they made as many attempts as Mum did to start a small business. In fact, many upper-caste families who lived in our neighborhood did use the same tactics to generate a decent amount of wealth. Mum's multiple attempts failed because she went into them entirely blind, with no support or understanding of how to run a business. The caste-based skill that her mother could have passed down would be manual scavenging, had she not been adamant that none of her children would follow in her line of work. Dalits like my Mum who turn to upper-caste skills without a formal education, support structure, or access to networks have additional challenges to overcome when compared to upper castes. These skills, as well as access to most institutions that are run by people of their caste or other upper castes together create upper-caste privilege. It is so deeply embedded into our society that it's almost invisible. And it is this invisibility that makes upper-caste privilege even stronger and harder to tear down.

CHAPTER 8

CULTURE CACHE
AND ONWARD TO COLUMBIA

Because of my experience as a ghostwriter for newspaper supplements (before graduating, I had published close to fifteen articles), I felt I had a fair chance of landing a job as a reporter. But unlike many upper-caste, middle-class college graduates, my parents couldn't reach out to their friends to get me an internship or a job, and I had no relatives who could ask their coworkers to give me a "tour" of a newspaper or an agency. I didn't get any tips from my parents to help me find a job; their collective career expertise was limited to the "civils." But what I did have was the Stephen's stamp, which afforded me a different type of reservation. As a fresh graduate with a science degree and a certificate course in media studies, I had two leading ad agencies offering me jobs. Unlike constitutional reservation, which offered a one-time, entry-level advantage in universities, colleges, and government jobs, this would last my whole life. Hordes of Stephanians who are multinational CEOs, chairpersons, and management executives in the private sector would recognize me as one of their own and pick me over non-Stephanian candidates applying for the same job. I could ask a Stephanian working in the company I wished to join to help make an introduction. Non-Stephanian hiring managers would also grudgingly place my résumé at the top of the pile and the St. Stephen's brand would go far in getting me hired. I would get into exclusive alumni networks and groups and discover jobs that are often only advertised in these closed groups. Hiring tactics like these are common to the IITs and IIMs, but very few undergraduate colleges in India besides St. Stephen's can claim the recognition and reach of its alumni network. It was the only undergraduate college where both FCBUlka and Ogilvy & Mather, leading advertising agencies, had come looking for candidates. Top international firms like McKinsey and KPMG regularly pick fresh Stephen's graduates, offering them almost the same salaries as top IIT and IIM graduates. Some of my batchmates who joined such firms after college stuck with their first jobs for almost a decade, and now have outstanding careers with company-facilitated degrees from universities like Harvard and Yale.

I had job offers from both FCBUlka and Ogilvy & Mather and chose to join FCBUlka. When I joined, I was offered a higher salary than the average college graduate. The high salary along with the company's preference for Stephanians led some of my coworkers to label it the "Stephanian quota." They called us the "company damaads"—sons-in-law—and declared that we didn't need to work as hard as everyone else since we weren't hired "on merit." It was ironic that their argument was exactly the same as the one upper-caste students made about Dalit and OBC students in government colleges and universities. Except here they were hitting out at Stephanian privilege, which clearly exists, while "Dalit entitlement," much like reverse racism or reverse casteism, is a myth, as I have tried to show. Colleges like the Shri Ram College of Commerce, St. Stephen's, and Lady Shri Ram only admit students whose marks clear their prohibitively high cut-off lists. In many colleges, however, some seats are earmarked for legacy students who have a parent or sibling as alumni, or for those with deep pockets for the "management quota" seats. Both these reservations are often unavailable to Dalits who, for the most part, can't afford the management quota fees and don't have generations who have graduated from these prestigious colleges. My great-grandfather was able to attend school and get an education, yet it took four generations for a member of the family to enter St. Stephen's College. Admission forms clearly ask students to mention if they had a family member or close relative attend the same college. The alumni and management quotas are essentially upper-caste reservations but neither of them get even a fraction of the malice or hate that is directed at constitutional reservation.

At FCBUlka I learned about marketing, branding, and how Indians buy things—with their emotions. I had picked copywriting because, as a twenty-one-year-old, I thought it would be more exciting to write radio jingles and catchy ads than cover courts traffic or the municipality, like my batchmates, who had started working with newspapers were doing. But after only a few months of writing clever slogans that the client would ultimately reject to choose the most clichéd option on the list, I began to miss reporting and writing articles. Since I couldn't afford to join a master's program in journalism, I came to the conclusion that I needed to learn on the job. I also knew that racking up experience at a big ad firm would come in handy while convincing editors to hire me without a journalism degree. So as I learned copywriting at Ulka I continued ghostwriting articles on the side. But I wanted to learn to write better, and without access to a proper editor or teacher, I realized the only way to learn was by reading well-written articles. I didn't have a computer at home, so when I wasn't working, I started reading US- and UK-based magazines and newspapers, most of which were available for free online. My degree in science had left me rather uneducated in history, politics, or social issues. But culture I could understand. And if my time at St. Stephen's taught me anything, it was that being in the know about music, films, theater, literature, and fashion that came from the West would convince people that you were "with it." After attending an elite college, where no one would ask directly about your caste or class but could ascertain it from your clothes, accent, and what you knew of "cool" music bands, movies, and literary magazines, I wanted to be so with it that no one would think of questioning my caste or class again. I decided that I was not only going to know and understand culture; I was going to become an expert in it.

I had noticed that most forms of writing about culture, whether it was music, literature, art, or theater, were written by experts in those fields. But I felt that I could write about fashion without being an expert. Indian fashion was on the rise, but its coverage in newspapers—there were hardly any blogs or websites—was limited to the most controversial outfits, wardrobe malfunctions on the runway, or salacious accounts of after-parties. The kind of fashion criticism I had found in the pages of the *New York Times*'s *T Magazine* or *New York* magazine's "Style" section—where writers reviewed each show in a global, political, and cultural context, building on what the designer had showcased in the previous seasons—was not seen in India. More recently, fashion coverage has become the mainstay on almost all news channels, websites, and outlets. At that time, it made the news only during fashion weeks. While Bollywood celebrities and socialites cared about looking stylish, regular people didn't wear designer outfits, or have their hair professionally styled and make-up expertly applied each time they stepped out of their homes. Even local celebrities in Delhi and Mumbai, who would often get photographed for the party pages of newspapers, didn't seem to care about the "perfect" look (and even repeated outfits).

That changed almost overnight. In 2007 two US-based Indian bloggers, Payal Pasija and Priyanka Prasad, started the blog *High Heel Confidential*, where they analyzed and criticized the fashion choices of celebrities. Payal and Priyanka would often question what a certain actress or a female socialite was thinking when she decided to choose a "boxy/rectangular/tapered silhouette"—wrong for her particular body type. Or they explained, often politely, but sometimes not, how that princess bun hairdo was totally wrong for that flower-print sundress at an afternoon event, especially with those kitten heels. Working directly with fashion photographers, they turned their critical gaze on the famous and semi-famous. At a time when most media outlets walked on eggshells around Bollywood celebrities, Payal and Priyanka criticized anyone who they thought "could do so much better" with their look. Top Bollywood female actors at the time like Kajol, Vidya Balan, Preity Zinta, and Rani Mukherjee were routinely rounded up on their blog for looking "rather frumpy." Even stars like Kangana Ranaut and Sonam Kapoor, who are among some of the best-dressed famous people today, were often pulled up on their blog for not wearing the "right" outfits.

Despite their somewhat unkind criticism of celebrity fashion, Payal and Priyanka's writing was sharp and funny, their wit masking the heavy design and fashion terms that are often used to describe the clothes. But, naturally, their comments upset those they were writing about. So far, Indian celebrities had dealt with compliant journalists but having these two overseas bloggers dissing their clothes "just for fun" was new for most of the Bollywood set. Payal and Priyanka toned down their acerbic wit as their popularity increased. But, by then, their notoriety had made them extremely popular with readers in India and abroad.

Following the success of *High Heel Confidential*, more fashion and entertainment websites like *Pinkvilla* and *MissMalini* cropped up, and soon the supplement sections of newspapers were following their format of identifying female celebrities by their clothes, often carrying them as front-page stories. It was the start of a new kind of celebrity journalism in India. Even as celebrity sightings moved to the inside pages of the supplements, *High Heel Confidential* graduated to more serious fashion coverage and *MissMalini* and *Pinkvilla* grew into general celebrity gossip and news sites—opening the gateway for a hyperaware celebrity culture that was so far absent in India.

In 2007, when Payal and Priyanka started *High Heel Confidential* to discuss "bags and shoes," they were taking a leaf out of the many celebrity websites and blogs that were covering Hollywood in a similar way. Whether in India or the United States, blogging was a relatively new pursuit. But even in those few years since the early 2000s, several bloggers, whether they covered politics, food, tech, or fashion, had quickly amassed huge readerships, often overshadowing even traditional media outlets. Traditional newspaper journalism rightly felt threatened and, perhaps for the first time in the history of journalism, younger professionals who had a better handle on this type of writing had a chance to compete with more experienced reporters. It was in this space that I thought I should try my chance.

So with no formal experience in a newsroom and only a handful of music album reviews and celebrity interviews in my portfolio, I began to apply for jobs at every entertainment supplement and lifestyle magazine. Finally, I heard back from a relatively new magazine that discussed art, lifestyle, celebrities, and fashion. After several rounds of interviews, I finally joined their editorial department as a features writer in early 2009. The recession had just hit the previous year, and after hundreds of layoffs most people in media were holding on to their jobs for dear life. Finding a new job in those times that not only paid relatively well but gave me the chance to work with some of the most exciting writers around who would go on to become well-known lifestyle and entertainment journalists was a rare gift. It was my first time actually covering fashion, something I had wanted to do for so long. I dived into my first piece—about the latest collections of designers at the just concluded Fashion Week. I wanted to do a good job and prove to my editor that she had done the right thing by assigning that piece to me. But as I started working on it, it became clear that I neither had the experience nor the vocabulary to tackle it. So I went back to what I knew—interviewing celebrities. I attended parties, spoke to designers, and wrote about what people wore. I expanded my repertoire and wrote about travel, food, and nightlife in Delhi as well as décor and design tips for people's homes. Soon I moved on to beauty and make-up, which I felt needed less technical understanding than fashion writing. I did maybe one more fashion piece in the year I worked there. It was only when I moved to the daily tabloid *Asian Age* and was forced to attend five fashion shows a day, then return to the office to submit the copy before the edition went to press, that I finally got better at writing about fashion. With almost five fashion weeks that we covered in a year and two stories per day, I was a proper fashion reporter by the time I joined *Brunch*, the Sunday magazine of *Hindustan Times*, in 2011. At *Hindustan Times*, where journalists were breaking important stories almost every day, the perception was that fashion reporting wasn't "real journalism." So rather stubbornly I decided I was going to change that. I focused on researching big talking-point pieces, which my editor then generously ran as cover stories of the widely read Sunday magazine. I investigated where popular trends came from, how Indian fashion was moving forward, and even how we could develop an authentic sense of style that wasn't just a rip-off of Western trends. But as a lone journalist who wished to be taken seriously for writing on a popular subject, I didn't make much headway. But I finally understood that fashion had always been an elite, largely upper-class interest in India.

Fashion is rarely merely a reflection of individual taste. The clothes we choose or can afford to wear are often telling signs of our class, and sometimes even caste. Trends are often created in a small bubble of fashion magazines, fashion blogs, and ramp trends. This trickles down to high street stores. Most of us who want to be fashionable pick up trends from one or more of these sources and look for them in street-wear or designer stores. But those who are neither keeping tabs on fashion nor can afford to spend 3,000 to 5,000 rupees per outfit on daily wear at a high street store don't have the option to be fashionable.

When we judge someone's sense of style, what we are mocking is their lack of access to networks where trends are created and understood and their ability to afford them. Moreover, "style" is something that children pick up from their parents. Fashion magazines often have wistful accounts of stylish women recalling moments when they watched their mothers get ready for parties in sumptuous saris and pearls. In a culture where Dalits are still attacked for flaunting a moustache or wearing jewelry, having style is also a subtle code for being upper caste. It was only during the years of covering fashion that I understood that Mum's stubborn emphasis on looking stylish was so that we would look upper caste. With the Internet, how we access and understand style has changed, but it's still a largely elitist interest. I was able to write about fashion because my mother made it a point to stand out with her style for as long as she could afford it. But for many Dalits, especially those who live in rural areas, the freedom to express their personality through their clothes is not an option. I never picked up on these nuances when I was still writing about fashion, but even then I started questioning how I could criticize someone for not having "style," when with the class and caste divisions we have, most people have no way to understand what it really means to be stylish.

After graduating from St. Stephen's, I was convinced that I didn't need a master's degree to become a good journalist although Mum was keen that I do a postgraduate course. My argument stemmed from my desperate need to keep working and sending money home. And I wasn't ready to go back to being as punishingly poor as I had been during my student years. I wasn't off the mark about the degree, though. Some of the best journalists in India and across the world don't necessarily have degrees in journalism. But having one certainly helps. Especially for someone like me who had decidedly rejected my science education and barely knew anything about the social sciences, practically a mandate for good journalism, it could change everything.

During the years that I worked as a journalist, I sent money home, and would feel the pinch by the time the end of the month hit. I wasn't broke but I wasn't doing well either. While I could afford to live in a cramped barsati in Lajpat Nagar and go out occasionally, I could not manage the same lifestyle as my peers, even those that were journalists themselves. I knew I couldn't afford to stop working either. For a few years after I left Ajmer for Delhi, Dad had moved into his parents' house. Mum's salary from her work as an insurance agent and a part-time NGO worker ran the household. When my sister graduated from high school, she got admission to the Indian Hotel Management Institute in Mumbai, which was then the top hotel management college in the country. Even though it was government funded, the fees were substantially higher than at Delhi University colleges. Like with me, Mum didn't let that get in the way. She took an education loan for my sister. A few years later, my brother graduated and got into St. Xavier's College in Mumbai. Some portion of the money that I sent home went towards helping them stay in Mumbai. In the ten years I spent in Delhi, money was always short and I kept ignoring Mum's tips to invest. I went to the more affordable markets in Sarojini Nagar for clothes and bought a somewhat expensive jacket or a dress maybe four or five times in all those years. But I had managed to build a life in my little Lajpat Nagar apartment, filling it with a fridge, television set, and an air conditioner that I paid for in installments over a few years.

But my mum kept prodding me every now and then about doing a master's. Before I joined *Brunch*, I had not thought of going abroad to study, especially to get a degree in journalism. Apart from a few non-journalist friends who had spent years at Oxford, I didn't know many people who went abroad to study. I assumed that only those who had deep pockets or huge savings could apply to international colleges. But when I saw a colleague at *Brunch* successfully go through the process of applying to New York University and gather funding, I realized that it could be done. It was then that I started looking into possible postgraduate courses in journalism, idly wondering if I should give it a shot. But after almost seven years in journalism, I didn't want to apply to courses where I would be in class with those who had just graduated from undergraduate college. I wanted to go to a school that would elevate my skills and allow me to stand among the best journalists in the world. If it hadn't been for that colleague at *Brunch* (who returned to a successful career as a tech journalist) and others I knew in different departments who had done the same thing, it might have never occurred to me to apply to one of the top journalism schools. Finally, I decided to see if I could make this happen and sent in my application to Columbia University for a master's program in journalism.

When I applied to Columbia, I had no way to pay for it. The fee for the course was around $80,000 (about 56 lakh Indian rupees) for a nine-month course. And I would need money for living expenses as well. I barely had enough money to pay for the GRE test. But with blind optimism, I had to try. And maybe the money would somehow show up. Crazy as that plan was, it's pretty close to what happened.

I got accepted to the course! Once that happened, it all seemed more possible. But I had to get together the funding. Those were stressful weeks that made me wonder—was I going to lose it after coming so far? Most middle-class students in my position would turn to their parents for help. Parents would either have money saved up for this exact purpose in bonds and fixed deposits, or would have assets that they could sell or put up as collateral. Indian banks offer education loans to students who get accepted to US universities. But even after getting a substantial scholarship from Columbia, the banks wouldn't loan me enough to cover the rest of the fees and the cost of living in New York unless we offered our house as collateral. My mother had built that house over two decades, and the final touches had only been completed sometime in 2012. I had never earned the kind of money where I could pay off a huge monthly installment towards a loan this big. And even with a Columbia degree, I didn't know that I could. I couldn't risk the house.

But Mum, as usual, believed that we could make it happen. While she was working to get the loan processed in Ajmer, I wrote to the scholarship department, asking if there was any way I could get more funding. They had replied saying that they would get back to me. But when I didn't hear back for weeks, I wrote to nearly every professor in my department at Columbia, begging for help to get more funding. In the emails I told them about the life I had lived so far and how unthinkable it was for me to be writing to ask for money. I explained that this course had the potential to change my life in ways that I couldn't even enumerate. Some professors replied to say that only the scholarship department could help me. Others ignored my emails.

I tried many scholarships and programs, including the Rajiv Gandhi fellowship for SC/ST students but came up empty. Many journalists my age would tap into international fellowships and research programs abroad. After covering fashion for years instead of "serious" beats like politics, education, health, or science, I didn't think these were even an option. I wasn't part of the networks that circulated information about international scholarships so I either missed deadlines or wasn't fully prepared to send in my application. It was already July and I was supposed to leave for the program at the end of August. While some of my Columbia batchmates were spending time with family and preparing for a gruelling year at grad school, I was still in flux, unsure of whether I was going to get there.

On a dark, rainy day in July I opened my laptop late one morning to check my emails, but I had given up . . . Until I saw a new email in the inbox. I don't think I fully read it before I threw myself back on the bed. I couldn't believe it. I had just received a full scholarship to attend Columbia. I still needed a loan to cover living expenses in New York for over nine months with no job, but that was less than half the original amount I had needed. I was finally going to Columbia!

Now it all started to feel real. But I still didn't have all the money I needed. I didn't know how I was going to come up with the money for the flight tickets to New York in under a month. Nor did I have enough savings to buy the things I would need to settle in a new city. I was still waiting for the loan to be approved so I could apply for the student visa I needed to enter the United States, when I got a call from a high-ranking editor I had worked with earlier at *Hindustan Times*, asking to meet me. I had approached him a few months earlier for information on scholarships and he had kindly promised to find out what he could. By this time, I had received news about a fair number of scholarships I had not won. I assumed he wanted to deliver the bad news in person—that yet another scholarship had not come through. But he told me that he was going to buy my flight tickets to New York and that I could not refuse. He also promised to give me a small loan to cover other expenses. Soon after, the editor I had worked with right after I left Ulka called me to give me another loan to buy winter clothes. Both indulgently asked me to pay them back later when I started making enough money. Both times, I couldn't say enough to thank them or let them know what their support meant to me. That chain of generosity didn't stop with them. A few weeks later, I was at my friend Aditi's house. When I was paying the fees for an important document, my credit card was rejected. My friend's older sister generously offered to pay the 15,000 rupees, saying I could pay her back later.

The years I spent in Delhi were financially hard and sometimes didn't feel worth it. But these gestures of generosity and kindness from my friends and senior colleagues at a time when I needed it the most revealed the strong network of support I had built in those years. I worked hard in all my jobs and tried to learn as much as I could without a formal education in journalism. My friends and bosses perhaps saw that and the hardships I had to cope with in trying to make it on my own in journalism while supporting Mum.

I am so thankful to all of them. And I know how important a role my college networks played to help me get hold of opportunities that are not as easily available outside these spaces. For people who are not in similar networks, career-building breaks like these are hard to reach. Often the first in their family to attend college, most lower-caste people don't know how the system works and have no mentors to guide them. Without access to such well-connected networks, many lower-caste people never get the same chances as upper castes, especially in private sector jobs, even when they might have similar backgrounds and abilities. That's why even when someone is not actively discriminated against for their lower caste, generations of being denied these networks holds Dalits back from truly succeeding in their careers.

CHAPTER 9

DALIT MOVEMENTS AND AMBEDKAR'S LEGACY

As we have seen, Dalits make up one-fourth of our population of over a billion Indians. Yet they are hugely disadvantaged and looked down upon by the upper castes. Any progress they have made is because of the efforts of extraordinary Dalit leaders who fought to change the reality of Indian society.

Dr. B. R. Ambedkar had to fight tooth and nail not only against the upper-caste system but also the giants of the freedom movement to get them to recognize Dalits as equals. After decades of struggle and leadership, he was able to give Dalits a seat at the freedom table and later secure reservation, changing our destiny. He was the one who made the most far-reaching contributions to the Dalit cause, but before he arrived on the scene there were other leaders, too, who were responsible for Dalit upliftment.

Leaders like Periyar Ramasami and Jyotirao Phule and movements such as the Namasudra in Bengal, Paraya in Tamil Nadu, and Adi in Uttar Pradesh and Punjab had been actively addressing the inequalities in Indian society since the nineteenth century. As early as 1873, Phule had formed the Satyashodhak Samaj to challenge upper-caste superiority and create an egalitarian society. Phule was born in a lower caste (but not untouchable) Mali family of gardeners and experienced discrimination. However, due to a British-run high school education, he was deeply influenced by political theorist and activist Thomas

Paine's ideas on governance and administration. He used Paine's theories to call out the British on their grossly neglectful policies with regard to social inclusion and challenged them for not doing enough to dismantle the caste system. His deep understanding of European and American philosophies of equality and freedom made Phule way ahead of his time. He protested the Brahmin monopoly in education, bureaucracy, and governance.[1] Much before Ambedkar, he suggested affirmative action for Shudras (it is argued that he was referring to both Dalits and Bahujans) in jobs like education, since Shudra teachers would be better suited to give quality education to Shudra students. Moreover, he demanded a freeze on recruiting Brahmins into government services until enough Shudras had joined the system. Phule's ideas were equally progressive on women's rights and the grave gender inequality in nineteenth-century India. Married to Savitribai at thirteen, when he was in high school, Phule helped her learn to read and write and supported her in getting a formal education. Savitribai went on to write books and poems and became one of the first Indian teachers to be recognized by the British in 1845. She worked extensively for women's rights and is considered one of the earliest feminists in Indian history. Savitribai also protested the abuse of widows, particularly young girls who had barely attained puberty—at the time it was common for young widows to be sexually exploited.[2] She marched against barbers who ritually shaved the heads of widows. Savitribai opened a care center for women and girls who were forced to abandon their babies born out of assault. Both Jyotirao and Savitribai were strong advocates of education and, according to sociologist and academic Omvedt, understood that it was the "way to change 'eastern morals' and bring about a cultural revolution, as well as a technological one." In 1848, the Phules became the first Indians to start a school for women in Pune. They revolutionized Indian education with inventive ideas like using short stories and poems for lessons and stipends to prevent students from dropping out. The couple even introduced a regular "parent-teacher meeting" and a midday meal scheme (which is part of the 2009 Right to Education Act) so as to focus on the holistic development of their students, many of whom were from poor backgrounds and couldn't afford proper meals. By 1851, they had three schools where Jyotirao and Savitribai nurtured many Dalit and

Bahujan girls, who were often discriminated against in upper-caste and even British schools. While they were pioneers in education who introduced ideas that continue to shape modern Indian education even today, they threatened the abusive patriarchal and casteist structures of Indian society. They were labelled as "outlandish" and consistently ran into problems in running their schools. Upper-caste men would often hurl abuse, stones, and even rotten eggs at them, and Savitribai was known to carry a change of clothes with her at all times because she was attacked so often. Even beyond education, Phule's ideas on farmers and new technology in agriculture were exceptional and truly ahead of their time. He advocated the mechanization of agriculture and spoke of new irrigation methods for better farming. Moreover, he consistently demanded that the British government subsidize farmers or at least give them direct benefits since they were paying the heaviest taxes at the time. Omvedt notes that Phule's vision became reality about a hundred years later with the green revolution.

Earlier, in the late 1800s, movements like the ones started by the Brahmo Samaj and the Arya Samaj also addressed similar issues but stopped short of trying to dismantle the caste system. Neither addressed the Chaturvarna system, which divides Hindus along a sliding scale of four unequal castes. The Brahmo Samaj movement, which is considered radical for its attack on caste and support for the rights of women, essentially created "a modernizing lifestyle for English-educated 'upper' caste Indians," according to Omvedt. She notes that while its followers might have rejected caste and didn't outwardly associate with Hinduism, they definitely identified with the idea of the Aryan "Golden Age" and implicitly considered the period of Muslim rule as "a period of medieval darkness" which was to blame "for the degeneration of India." This framework that the Brahmo Samaj created—outwardly rejecting caste while not necessarily acknowledging its origins in Hinduism or engaging with it beyond terming it a "social evil"—is still the model followed by English-speaking urban upper-caste India. The Arya Samaj, the other contemporary social reform movement, was even more problematic with regard to its views on the caste system. It found immense popularity among Punjabi upper castes and later even Dalits for correcting untouchability. Yet, their solution to caste was deeply offensive and, in fact, reinforced the caste system. Arya Samajis promoted Hindu rites and rituals and believed in a "purifying" ritual whereby Dalits could become upper caste. To them, being Dalit was a curse that needed to be "fixed" or "cured." Moreover, the Arya Samaj was deeply rooted in Hinduism and the Chaturvarna ideology was considered a foundational concept.

The assertion of Dalit rights and Dalit movements became possible because Dalit issues were pushed to the forefront of nation-building at the time of Independence. With freedom from foreign rule we were also winning equality for all Indian citizens, regardless of their caste. The mood of the times demanded that Dalits finally get their due as equal participants in a new India. Textbooks, nationalist narratives, and even certain historical narratives will have us believe that this change happened overnight and almost spontaneously. And what we know of resistance to caste is limited to Gandhi's Harijan upliftment movement and the Congress's policies of social inclusion. It's almost as if when India stepped from darkness into light at the midnight hour, it also shed its old casteist skin to emerge as a land of equals, with no bias and prejudice. Except that this yielding to the idea of Dalit equality was neither spontaneous nor willing. It was a result of laws that forced people to deal with Dalits as one of them, at least in theory. These laws, notably the law banning untouchability in 1950 and reservation, which came with the Constitution, were possible only because decades of struggle for Dalit rights had preceded them. The person who more or less single-handedly led that struggle by accepting nothing less than absolute equality for Dalits and insistently pushed Dalit rights and their marginalization into the national and international spotlight was none other than Dr. Bhimrao Ramji "Babasaheb" Ambedkar.

It was his relentless organizing, diplomacy, and statesmanship since the late 1920s—much before Gandhi's participation in the freedom movement—that made Dalit rights into an issue that the larger national movement could no longer ignore. He emerged as an undisputed leader of Dalits and fought for our rights with the British at a time when Congress leaders such as Bal Gangadhar Tilak were engaged in establishing "kinship" between the British and the Brahmins.[3]

Yet, his life's work is often glossed over when compared to national leaders like Nehru and Gandhi, who contributed to nation-building in similar ways. Reductively labelled as the "leader of the Depressed Classes," we are barely taught about his achievements beyond his role as the "architect of the Indian Constitution."

Bhimrao was born the fourteenth son of a British army subedar and his wife, into a Dalit Mahar family in 1891. Like other Dalit students, he studied by sitting outside the classroom, away from upper-caste students, and could get a drink of water only when an upper-caste employee poured it out for him. He went on to become the first Dalit student to enter Mumbai's Elphinstone High School in 1907 and moved to New York in 1913 to work on his master's thesis at Columbia University (my alma mater). For the next decade or so, he moved between India, England, and the United States, acquiring many degrees. He got a doctor of science degree from the London School of Economics in 1923 and returned to India before becoming the first Indian student to get a PhD from Columbia University in 1927.

Through his years in academia, Ambedkar worked in the area of caste, exploring its origins and development in the Indian subcontinent. So it was not surprising that soon after his return to India in March 1927 he organized the first conference for the Depressed Classes in Mahad to alert Dalits to their civil rights.[4] In those early years, Ambedkar made an effort to appeal to the conscience of upper-caste Hindus and asked them to join the cause for Dalit rights at the Mahad conference. By all accounts, it was a fairly typical gathering of Dalit men and women, and some caste Hindus, none of whom could have had an inkling that they were about to witness an event that would change the course of Dalit rights in India.

At the time, Dalits were discriminated against in nearly every sphere. In most places, Dalits were not allowed to use the roads or drink water from the same water tanks as upper-caste people. However, four years before the conference, in 1923, the Bole Resolution (named after S. K. Bole, the MP who proposed it in the Bombay legislature) had hoped to change that by declaring all public tanks and reservoirs open to "untouchables." The Mahad municipality, where the conference was underway, had also passed the same resolution, opening its Chawdar tank to Dalits. Despite the legal order, Dalits were hesitant to use the tank for fear of harassment. At the end of the two-day conference, on March 20, 1927, Ambedkar decided to lead the Dalit men and women who had attended the conference to exercise their legal rights and drink water from the Chawdar tank. The event, which saw participation from only a few hundred people, was low-key. But what followed turned the simple act of Dalits drinking water from a public tank into the "Mahad Satyagraha." As it turned out, the participants had correctly anticipated an upper-caste backlash for using public water tanks, because as soon as upper-caste Hindus in Mahad heard of the event, they spread rumors that Dalits were also planning to enter Hindu temples and "defile" them. Angry caste Hindus lashed out by attacking Dalit men, women, and children who had attended the conference. Messages also reached caste Hindus in neighboring villages to "appropriately punish" Dalits who had visited Mahad for the conference. A religious ceremony was organized to purify the tank. The "Chawdar Tank March" and the subsequent violence against Dalits made news across the country, turning both the Depressed Classes Conference and the seemingly simple act of Dalits drinking water from a public tank into an assertion of Dalit rights everywhere.

The act of Dalits drinking water from the same source as upper castes was neither simple nor ordinary. It was downright revolutionary since it directly attacked notions of purity and pollution, one of the most fundamental ideas of the caste system. Certain upper-caste Hindus at the time didn't even tolerate a Dalit's shadow on their person, much less make physical contact with them. Food and water have a sacred context in Hinduism. Regardless of what the British laws at the time allowed, Ambedkar perhaps understood the radicalness of leading Dalits to drink the same water that upper-caste people also consumed. With this seemingly small gesture, Ambedkar defied a sacredly held caste belief and asserted the absolute equality of Dalits. It's noteworthy that Ambedkar's Chawdar Tank March occurred almost three years before another important political protest that was heavy with symbolism and was a turning point in the Indian nationalist struggle against the British. In 1930, Gandhi led a crowd of supporters to Dandi in Gujarat to produce salt at a time when the British imposed a heavy salt tax on Indians. With the Dandi March,

Gandhi asserted a collective Indian defiance to the British. Through the Chawdar Tank March Ambedkar introduced the radical idea of Dalits inherently having the same rights as everyone else. Both were similar in their significance and impact if not the scale. Yet the Dandi March is considered a singular event in Indian history and the Mahad Satyagraha is barely discussed outside the Dalit community—another example of the unequal regard for Ambedkar and Gandhi.

After the Chawdar Tank March, and the upper-caste purification ritual, caste Hindus filed an injunction to close the tank once again to Dalits. This led Ambedkar to lose faith in the upper-caste Hindus who he had hoped would join the Dalits in their struggle for their rights. So at the end of the year, on December 25, 1927, he announced the second "Mahad Satyagraha" conference for Dalit rights. Far more aggressive and provocative than its first version, the second Mahad conference called for "absolute equality" for Dalits and had over three thousand Dalit "satyagrahis" in attendance. At the conference, Ambedkar compared the event to the National Assembly in France in 1789 that spurred the French Revolution that overthrew the monarchy to establish a first of its kind republic. By comparing the ongoing Dalit movement to the French Revolution, Ambedkar sent a clear message to the caste Hindus that Dalits under his leadership were ready to revolt against the tyrannical oppression of the caste system. At the time, the idea of Dalit rights was limited to removing the practice of untouchability. Ambedkar dismissed this soft-pedaling approach, calling it a "low aim" and asked for Dalits to be recognized as equal in every sense to any Brahmin, Kshatriya, or Bania.

Having been let down at the first conference, Ambedkar now asked Dalits to stop expecting "Brahmins to rise in revolt against the caste system" and encouraged Dalits to tear down the "man-made" barriers on their own. To underscore his ideas and further inspire Dalits to reject the artificial inequalities of the caste system, he invited G. N. Sahasrabuddhe, a Brahmin, to read out the most offensive sections of the Manusmriti. Then, in his boldest and most direct attack on the caste system and its roots in Hinduism, Ambedkar and the Dalit satyagrahis collected dozens of copies of the Manusmriti and set them on fire.[5] Burning a Hindu religious scripture that many upper-caste Hindus consider an important treatise on various aspects of life, in particular the caste system, signalled the beginning of Ambedkar's fight for Dalit rights. In 1938, he told author T. V. Parvate that even though he knew he jeopardized his life with the Manusmriti bonfire, he did it because "it was a symbol of injustice under which we have been crushed for centuries."[6] While the Manusmriti bonfire became the highlight of the second Mahad conference, Ambedkar had initially planned to lead the three thousand Dalit satyagrahis back to the Chawdar tank and reclaim it for Dalits by drinking from it. But since the tank had been closed by a British injunction, this satyagraha would mean civil disobedience against the British instead of a revolution against upper-caste Hindus, which could lead to the imprisonment of thousands of Dalits. Instead, on January 5, 1928, he directed Dalits to the Gangasagar tank that had also been declared open to Dalits.

Ambedkar often chose symbolic gestures over violence. Academics such as Anand Teltumbde argue that these soft actions set the tone for the Dalit movement, which could never fully face up to challenging caste Hindus.[7] Yet, the burning of the Manusmriti, which Dalits have turned into an annual tradition that takes place on December 25 every year, was a powerful move that squarely blamed the oppression of Dalits on the reductive ideas of Hinduism. Ambedkar's symbolic gesture established a new narrative in the fight for Dalit rights where anything less than complete equality was now unacceptable.

With these two conferences at Mahad, Ambedkar quickly became visible as a leader of the "Depressed Classes." But the Congress party that was leading the nationalist movement against the British had paid little attention to him or Dalit rights beyond Gandhi's efforts against untouchability and for the "upliftment of Harijans." In 1928, when the Simon Commission arrived to introduce constitutional reform and included no Indian members, the All Parties Conference Committee proposed an alternative constitution called the Swaraj Constitution. Also known as the Nehru Report, after Motilal Nehru who chaired the committee, the committee neither asked any Depressed Classes political parties for suggestions nor did it include separate representation for them. Dalit rights might have never been taken seriously if Ambedkar and Rettamalai Srinivasan hadn't represented them at the First Round Table Conference (RTC) in London in 1930. The Congress did not participate in the first RTC since most of its prominent leaders including Gandhi were in jail following arrests during the Civil Disobedience Movement (that began with the Dandi Salt March). Other parties, including the Muslim League and representatives of other states and provinces, stayed in London for several months to discuss the new constitution of India. Grabbing his chance not just with the British but also Indian representatives and Indian and international media in the house, Ambedkar introduced Dalit rights with an intensity that forced everyone to sit up and pay attention. He not only represented Dalits as significant minorities whose discrimination by upper castes deserved attention, but also as powerful stakeholders in the building of independent India's future. "Their voice was to echo for the first time in the history of two thousand years, and more so in the governance of their motherland," he wrote about the conference.[8] Ambedkar presented an in-depth argument detailing the ways in which upper-caste Indians discriminated and practiced violence against Depressed Classes, which not only stunned people in India but also had the British press talking about him for days. It was also the first time the global community learned about India's heinous abuse of human rights through casteism and untouchability. Ambedkar outlined the future of all Dalits in India when, in 1930, he asked for their right to directly elect their own representatives in a separate electorate and for "adequate representation" through reservation in government services. The conference was declared a failure and the Second RTC was announced a few months later in 1931, but Ambedkar's demands for the "untouchables" became a talking point that dominated conversations for months after and got Dalit rights a permanent seat at every discussion on the new India.

Ambedkar's intense spotlight on Dalit rights at the first RTC had threatened the Congress party's claim of representing all Indian Hindus. Even though it was mainly an upper-caste party, as was evident from the Swaraj Constitution, the members of the Congress party were against "dividing Hindus." This led Ambedkar and Gandhi to clash several times over the next few years, most notably right before they were to leave for the second RTC in August 1931. It was remarkable that despite working in the same circles and on similar issues, the two had never met before. In fact, Gandhi did not know Ambedkar was Dalit and assumed he was a Brahmin with a deep interest in "Harijans." By the time they met, Gandhi, who was aware of Ambedkar's Dalitness and his fiery presentation in London, refused to acknowledge Ambedkar with even "normal politeness."[9] Several historians and biographers, including Omvedt, have written about this historic meeting, where Gandhi asked Ambedkar why he wouldn't support the Congress and accused him of going against the "homeland." He reminded Ambedkar that he wasn't the only one concerned about the Depressed Classes and that the Congress had spent lakhs of rupees in dealing with the "untouchability problem." Ambedkar refused to be intimidated and retorted that while the Congress party recognized untouchability, it was not sincere in its efforts to do away with the practice. He then said the now-famous line, "Mahatmaji, I have no homeland. No self-respecting Untouchable worth his name will be proud of this land," and walked out.

When Indian political representatives gathered in London in September 1931 for a second time to discuss the new constitution, the demands on the table were vastly different from earlier. Along with universal adult suffrage, the Muslim League asked for separate electorates for Muslims, the Sikh leaders did so for the Sikhs, and Ambedkar did so for the Dalits. Even the princely states demanded autonomy if they were to become part of the new federal Indian Constitution. The Congress and other nationalist leaders agreed to most of these demands, including autonomy for princely states and separate Sikh and Muslim electorates. But they refused separate electorates for the Depressed Classes. Ambedkar refused to support the form of federal government that the Congress leaders were proposing. He declared that he would only support a government that was "of the people and for the people," where the Depressed Classes had all the fundamental rights as well as a separate electorate.[10] While Gandhi wanted to safeguard a majority for Hindus, Ambedkar wanted equal political representation for the Depressed Classes so as to protect their rights. Omvedt describes what followed as "a confrontation between Gandhi and Ambedkar" that would decide who truly represented the Dalits. Gandhi refused not only a separate electorate but also special representation for Dalits in the legislature. He convinced the Muslim League to oppose Ambedkar in exchange for his support for a separate electorate for the Muslims.[11] Further, Gandhi dismissed Ambedkar as a British nominee who had no claim to represent the Dalits and their "vital interests."

Omvedt argues that "Gandhi was *not* speaking from their [the Dalits'] perspective; he was not even speaking as a *national* leader; he was speaking as a *Hindu* at the second Round Table Conference."[12] Gandhi believed that giving separate rights to Dalits or Depressed Classes "will create a division in Hinduism which I cannot possibly look forward to with any satisfaction." Gandhi didn't want a political division among Hindus and Dalits, but he "ignored the division that already existed; in his warning against the spread of violence, he ignored the violence already existing in the lives of Dalits," Omvedt wrote. She also argues that while Ambedkar demanded political power for Dalits, Gandhi wanted their "protection and reform from above." Even today, several upper-caste arguments follow the same reasoning, asking that we "not create divisions" whenever Dalits highlight structural caste-based violence in universities, cities, or villages.

In 1932, Gandhi wrote to British prime minister Ramsay MacDonald saying that separate electorates were "an injection of poison that is calculated to destroy Hinduism."[13] Gandhi's objections made little sense, even to journalists in India who couldn't justify his actions. "To say the least, it is unreasonable and extremely irritating. If there is any community that needs the fullest protection, it is that of the Untouchable classes," wrote T. A. Raman, a prominent journalist of the time.[14] Despite Gandhi's intense opposition, the second RTC ended with the Communal Award (made by MacDonald), which was declared in 1932 and granted separate electorates to not just the "Untouchables" but also the Forward Castes, Lower Castes, Muslims, Buddhists, Sikhs, Indian Christians, Anglo-Indians, and Europeans. Ambedkar had argued that a separate electorate would allow the Depressed Classes to select their own candidate, one who wasn't merely a Dalit representative of some upper-caste political party. Without reservation, a Dalit candidate would get no upper-caste votes. By allowing the Depressed Classes to vote twice, once for a general candidate and the second time as a minority for a Depressed Classes candidate, the Communal Award allowed the political power Ambedkar was hoping for, even if it severely reduced the number of seats that Dalits could win.

Gandhi agreed to separate electorates for the Forward Castes, Europeans, Indian Christians, and Anglo-Indians, as well as the Sikhs and Muslims but dug in his heels when it came to the Depressed Classes. He was so against giving a separate electorate to Depressed Classes that would "[punish] Hindus" that he declared he would fast unto death if the award did not remove that clause. Gandhi had, by this time, undertaken many fasts against the British and everyone understood its impact on the Indian public. The rattled Congress leaders organized several public meetings to mobilize opinion against the separate Dalit electorate and pressure the British into withdrawing it. The British, on the other hand, left the decision to the leaders who had attended the RTC, namely Gandhi and Ambedkar. Congress leaders turned to Ambedkar to withdraw or at least scale down his demands, but his reaction was vastly different from the usual responses of fear, sympathy, or anxiety that Gandhi's fasts had elicited so far. Ambedkar called Gandhi's fast an intimidating "political move" that would have no sway over his decisions that were intended to protect the interests of the Depressed Classes. Perhaps realizing the high stakes of the situation, he declared, "If Mr Gandhi wants to fight with his life for the interests of the Hindu Community the Depressed Classes will also be forced to fight with their life to safeguard their interests."[15] He questioned why a well-wisher of the Depressed Classes would stake his life "to deprive them of what little they have got." As the declared date for the fast approached, caste Hindus across the country grew anxious for Gandhi's health and began turning on Dalits. The national leaders had failed to convince Ambedkar to withdraw his demands. He stood his ground and even criticized Gandhi for "releasing reactionary and uncontrollable forces" against Dalits who would face a savage backlash if Gandhi perished from the fast. The leaders also failed to convince Gandhi, given his delicate health, not to risk his life to prevent the "separation of untouchables from the Hindus." On the day before the fast was to commence, Ambedkar declared: "I shall not sacrifice the rightful demands of my people just to save the life of Mahatma Gandhi."

Gandhi started his fast unto death on September 20, 1932. At this time, he hadn't even agreed to Dalits having reserved seats in the joint electorate but judiciously left that decision to the All India Hindu Conference. By then caste Hindu opinion had fully turned against Dalits, and Ambedkar, worried that it could result in violent massacres, agreed to scale down his demands. He gave up the demand for a separate Dalit electorate and the double vote and asked for more reserved Dalit seats. Instead of political parties choosing their Dalit representatives who would serve mainly upper-caste interests, Ambedkar demanded an electoral college where Dalit voters would decide who would represent them in those seats. The electoral college nomination of Dalit candidates was to continue for ten years, after which parties could nominate them on their own. Ambedkar demanded that the reserved seats continue unchallenged for at least fifteen years, after which Dalit voters would review it through a special referendum. Gandhi and the Congress leaders agreed to all these demands. But Gandhi refused to yield to the fifteen-year period after which the reserved seats were to be reviewed. "Five years or my life," he famously responded.

While these demands were laid out after the first day of Gandhi's fast, it took three more days until Ambedkar finally gave in to Gandhi's demand to reduce the time period to review the reserved seats from fifteen to five years. On September 24 in Pune's Yerawada Jail where Gandhi was imprisoned, he and Ambedkar came to an agreement on what is now known as the Poona Pact. After the news of the agreement broke, most people were relieved as Gandhi's health had worsened quickly since he started the fast. But the pact itself made no one happy. Omvedt writes that some upper-caste Hindu leaders even thought that the severely watered-down version was "selling out . . . Hindu interests." Even the left-leaning leaders of the time, she notes, were not pleased with the outcome. They felt that the Poona Pact was taking away from the necessary cause of nation-building by focusing on the "mundane cause of the upliftment of Harijans"—this was how Communist Party of India leader E. M. S. Namboodiripad described it in his book *History of Freedom Struggle*. Omvedt quotes Namboodiripad in *Dalits and the Democratic Revolution* and adds that while the communist- and socialist-minded leaders of the time had enough influence to participate in such a "crucial political process," they didn't because "they were uninterested in it. Marxists did not take part, not because they were unable to, but because they did not see the issue of caste and untouchability as important."

The Depressed Classes were deeply disappointed with the outcome. Ambedkar wrote in *What Congress and Gandhi Have Done to the Untouchables* (1945) that the final agreement of reserved seats was no match for the separate Dalit electorate that the Ramsay MacDonald award had originally proposed. With the double vote, parties would have been forced to field candidates who truly stood for Dalit interests, since only Dalit votes would get them elected. Now with both Hindu upper-castes and Dalits voting for the same candidates, Dalit interests could easily be overlooked. Even if the separate Dalit electorate had a limited life span, it would be crucial in setting a political precedent for Dalits in the new country. Ambedkar knew he had been forced into a huge compromise to maintain the peace. Dalits continue to mourn the signing of the Poona Pact and observe September 24 as a dark day when their political rights were coerced away to protect the privileges of upper-caste Hindus.

Despite bringing only a fraction of the political power Ambedkar argued for, the Poona Pact ultimately forced national leaders to take Dalit rights more seriously. Many of them, having realized that Dalits were indignant about losing crucial political rights, immediately started working to regain their support. On September 25, 1932, a resolution was passed that declared that Dalits were no longer "untouchable" and had the right to use public wells, schools, roads, and other public property. It was also announced that it would be among the earliest acts of the new constitution. Five days later, Gandhi launched the All India Anti-Untouchability League, which later became the unfortunately titled Harijan Sevak Sangh—Servants of the Untouchables. While the league set out to remove untouchability, it did not take any effective action that would ensure that untouchability would be eliminated. As per its own records, the Anti-Untouchability League focused on tasks like digging public wells, starting scholarships, and other education-related activities. Ambedkar initially joined the league but quickly left when he realized it was just a front to win over Dalits without doing any of the hard work that would remove untouchability or even inconvenience caste Hindus. For instance, if a Dalit student wanted to benefit from the scholarships, he/she would have to prove that they weren't anti-Congress (as the Dalit community was suspected of being).[16] Ambedkar called it a program "to kill untouchables with kindness" since the league had no real interest in removing untouchability, but only wanted to do "constructive work" that would make Gandhi look like a benefactor of the Depressed Classes while not hurting his popularity with caste Hindus. In *What Congress and Gandhi Have Done to the Untouchables*, Ambedkar criticized Gandhi for saying that Dalits had little political consciousness and that he wanted to "save them against themselves." Academic Rupa Viswanath argues that for Gandhi, Dalits were Harijans, a "vulnerable childlike sub population . . . require[ing] parental succour."[17] That explains why neither the Congress programs for Dalits nor Gandhi's Harijan Sevak Sangh had any Dalits in leadership positions. Ambedkar notes that most Dalit welfare campaigns that came out of the Harijan Sevak Sangh did not lead to any actual progress for Dalits: "The work of the Sangh is of the most inconsequential kind . . . It neglects most urgent purposes for which the Untouchables need help and assistance. The Sangh rigorously excludes the Untouchables from its management. The Untouchables are no more than beggars, mere recipients of charity."[18] Ambedkar wanted a broad civil rights organization that would be under the control of Dalits themselves. "Instead, Gandhi envisaged a paternalistic organisation, controlled by caste Hindus working for the 'uplift' of Untouchables," Omvedt noted.[19] Ambedkar also concluded that the Dalits saw the Sangh "as a foreign body set up by the Hindus with some ulterior motive . . . the whole object is to create a slave mentality among the Untouchables towards their Hindu masters." Omvedt explains that there was a "fundamental difference" between the goals of Gandhi and Ambedkar. Ambedkar wanted the annihilation of caste and saw untouchability as "a fundamental result of it," whereas Gandhi thought that the "benign aspects of caste . . . could be maintained while removing hierarchy and the evil of untouchability." While eradicating manual scavenging was one of the goals of the Sangh, Rupa Viswanath writes that Gandhi insisted on caste Hindus treating manual scavenging as "ennobling," even while very few could earn a living from this. Gandhi and Ambedkar's disagreements on Dalits weren't based on mere ideology, but stemmed from a far deeper difference. Omvedt explains: "Gandhi did not see untouchables as individuals born into a particular community but rather as somewhat unthinking members of an existing Hindu community . . . Ambedkar, in contrast, put the individual and his/her development at the center of his vision."

While the Harijan Sevak Sangh didn't do very much for the cause of the Dalits, its description of Dalits as Harijans (children of God) caught on. While it seems harmless enough to call a group that is discriminated against God's children, it has deeply problematic undertones. By connecting Dalit suffering to divine fate, it lets upper-caste Hindus, who are the ones perpetrating the suffering, off the hook. It also indicates, quite damagingly, that the Harijans' lower caste is somehow related to their karma. Unfortunately, many Dalits at the time bought into that severely harmful explanation of their caste and the resulting discrimination and even passed it down to their children. Like Silicon Valley techie Benjamin Kalia, who grew up Gandhian believing that he was of lower caste because of the sins he had committed in his past birth. Ambedkar found the term "Harijan" extremely offensive and chalked it up to Gandhi's strategy to bring Dalits closer to Hinduism after the fallout from the Poona Pact. In 1938, he called it "practically equivalent to the term 'asprishya' (untouchable)" and walked out of the Bombay legislature to protest its continued use.[20] Since then Dalits have repeatedly rejected the term "Harijan" to describe them and consider it deeply offensive. The Indian government eventually banned it from official communication in 1982, yet it continues to crop up not only in the odd government circular but also in upper-caste descriptions of Dalits.

National leaders continued their efforts to win over Dalits well into the next year. In 1933, Ranga Iyer introduced the Temple Entry Bill. The bill stipulated that trustees of various temples would have to allow the entry of Dalits if a majority of municipal and local board voters in the area around a temple voted for it. Three years earlier, in 1930, Ambedkar had started the Temple Entry Movement when he led Dalits to launch the Kala Ram Temple Satyagraha in Nasik. Temple entry had been a major issue during the Chawdar Tank March. As we have seen, there had been rumors that Dalits were planning to enter temples, which led to violent assaults on them. Ambedkar wanted to use this satyagraha to test "whether the Hindu mind is willing to accept us as human beings." Clearly it wasn't, since Hindus reacted somewhat predictably by punishing Dalits with violence and banning Dalit children from public schools. As the Temple Entry Movement progressed against the backdrop of the RTCs and the Poona Pact, the British government ultimately declared it illegal for Dalits to use holy water sources and enter temples since it was "against the established custom." Gandhi wanted the Temple Entry Bill to become a resolution and approached Ambedkar for his support. But Ambedkar, having been let down during the Kala Ram Temple Satyagraha, knew that no upper castes would willingly vote to allow Dalits into temples. Dalits had already "tested the Hindu mind" and discovered that they were not wanted, so he argued that Dalits didn't need to enter places which banned them, any more than Indians needed to enter Europeans-only places that declared "Indians and Dogs not allowed." Perhaps Ambedkar knew that, as with the Anti-Untouchability League, the Ranga Iyer Bill had little interest in removing untouchability and offered nothing beyond token temple entry to Dalits. In his statement to the press, he wrote, "To accept temple entry and be content with it is to temporize with evil and barter away the sacredness of human personality that dwells in [Dalits]."[21]

Many leaders in 1932 believed that with reserved seats for Dalits under the Poona Pact, untouchability would become a thing of the past in the next twenty years. Ambedkar, who grew up Dalit and had faced upper-caste rejection and discrimination at every step of his political career, had no such faith. He placed his faith in the law instead, which he believed was the only way to bring about real change in the Dalit condition. Gandhi, on the other hand, thought that with enough moral conditioning, upper-caste Hindus might eventually learn to put up with Dalits. But despite all these shortcomings, Gandhi's adoption of the cause brought immense visibility to Dalit issues. But ultimately it wasn't upper-caste goodwill but Ambedkar's laws banning untouchability that helped Dalits attain a measure of equality in Indian society. If Gandhi was a product of his time, Ambedkar was way ahead. Now, almost seventy years later, it is his ideas of total notional and literal equality for Dalits that need attention. Gandhi and Ambedkar faced off several times and eventually a deeply disappointed Ambedkar wrote:

> There have been many Mahatmas in India whose sole object was to remove Untouchability and to elevate and absorb the Depressed Classes; but every one of them has failed in his mission. Mahatmas have come and Mahatmas have gone. But the Untouchables have remained Untouchables.

In 1936, Ambedkar founded the Independent Labor Party, which contested elections to the central legislative assembly from Bombay. In the same year, he published his blistering takedown of the caste system in *Annihilation of Caste* that was originally written as a speech for the Jat-Pat-Todak Mandal Committee.

After Independence, Jawaharlal Nehru invited Ambedkar to become the first law minister. But it was his appointment as the head of the Constitution Drafting Committee that became the crowning achievement of Ambedkar's political career. His constitution (initially its drafting was entrusted to a small committee, but it is argued that Ambedkar ended up writing most of it himself) introduced reservation for Dalits in government jobs and educational institutions and created reforms for women and remains one of the longest and among the most detailed documents on democracy. By the time it was adopted by the constituent assembly in November 1949, and formally applied on January 26, 1950, Ambedkar was battling several health issues, including diabetes. Having openly attacked Hinduism as the cause for Dalit abuse and discrimination in *Annihilation of Caste*, Ambedkar had been looking into other religions, including Sikhism and Buddhism. After two decades of academic engagement, Ambedkar found Buddhism to be most aligned with the Dalit philosophy of absolute equality. But there were some basic tenets that he couldn't agree with. So Ambedkar radically reinterpreted Buddhism; he called the new philosophy he had come up with "Navayana," a new offshoot of Buddhism. Instead of nirvana that Buddhist philosophy aimed for, Navayana's aim was to prepare for social action against inequality.[22] On October 14, 1956, just two months before his death, Ambedkar led Dalits in his last public political act. At Deekshabhoomi in Nagpur, Ambedkar and his wife, Savita, formally rejected Hinduism and converted to Navayana Buddhism. Nearly five hundred thousand Dalits followed. On December 6, 1956, Ambedkar passed away in his home in Delhi.

Dalit social action was continued by many others over the years. It was a group of Marathi poets and writers who created one of the most radical Dalit movements in Indian history. Marathi literature has had a history of Dalit activism at least since 1966, when Dalit academic and literary critic M. N. Wankhade published "Dalits, Write Rebel Literature," a powerful essay calling for Dalits to write their own stories. It was published in *Prabuddha Bharat*, a Dalit literary magazine Ambedkar had started in the 1930s. In 1967, Wankhade's fellow academic Gangadhar Pantawane started *Asmitadarsh*, which would give rise to a new kind of literary tradition that would not only comment on its activism but also "ideologically direct the Dalit movement."[23] Since then, it is through Dalit literature, whether in online spaces like *Round Table India* or in academia, where the Dalit movement has continued to sharpen its responses and find its focus. *Asmitadarsh*'s focus on young Marathi Dalit writers and poets was so impactful that it soon led to a torrent of Dalit writing in Tamil, Telugu, Punjabi, and Hindi. Soon their work started showing references from African American literature, as many writers discovered the obvious parallels between the Black struggle against white supremacy and the Dalit struggle against upper-caste hegemony. Many took inspiration from the works of African American authors like James Baldwin and Ralph Ellison, and wrote rich, deeply painful stories and poems that attacked structural discrimination. But upper-caste authors, particularly those who wrote in Hindi and Marathi, found their work to be "inelegant" and "lacking aesthetic sophistication." Several Hindi and Marathi upper-caste authors didn't like sharing space with Dalit writers and refused to accept them as part of the literary tradition in those languages.[24]

In 1972, a collective of disillusioned Marathi writers created the Dalit Panther Party along the same lines as the Black Panther Party that actively represented African American radical politics in the United

States. Like the Black Panthers, emerging out of the American civil rights movement of the sixties, Namdeo Dhasal, Raja Dhale, J. V. Pavar, Arun Kamble and others set up the Dalit Panther Party as a militant Dalit activist organization and drew heavily from the Panthers' symbols and ideology. Dalit Panthers used similar iconography and an organizational structure, and also had a reactionary, anti-state view based on armed self-defense. The Phule–Ambedkarite philosophy that forms the basis of most Dalit activism today was initially drafted as a Dalit Panther manifesto, merging their theories with Marxism. Their ideas directly reflected in their work: as well as Dalits and Bahujans, they also stood up for economically marginalized peoples. Their radical ideas, especially the one where they asserted that Independence had not come to all Indians since Dalits were "not free," successfully mobilized several young Dalits in Maharashtra.[25] They gained more notoriety when their public meetings were often disrupted by police violence and brutality. They used *Vidroh*, their official party newspaper, to spread their ideas through articles, poems, and caricatures, which were meant to "brutalize 'upper' caste sensibility by violently opposing it."[26] The *Black Panther*, a journal that published radical artwork and literature, gained a cult following in the US; *Vidroh* also gained popularity among activist circles in India. The Dalit Panthers soon caught the eye of *Time* magazine, *The Guardian*, and the *New York Times*, who called them the "Bombay Counterparts of the Black Panthers." Even the Black Panther Party endorsed this association by acknowledging Dalit struggles against "Brahminical hegemony" in the party newspaper.[27]

After declaring their manifesto in 1973, the Dalit Panthers began to debate about what or whom the party represented, and who exactly was "Dalit." The disagreements about these concepts ultimately split the party into three factions, each representing a different version of the same ideology. By the 1980s, the ideologies became further diluted and the memberships dwindled. Yet, their impact on Dalit culture and consciousness was lasting. It presented Dalits with a new, assertive, and radical way to represent themselves. And while they inspired grassroots activism, their biggest contribution was to the still nascent Dalit literary movement. Most founders of the Dalit Panther Party were writers and poets and through *Vidroh* they created a safe space for unrestrained and radical Dalit writing. Dhasal, Dhale, and Pawar, in particular, challenged the polite, and somewhat affected discourse of Marathi literature with their gritty and direct writing. They wrote about their experiences of growing up in slums and red-light areas in a confrontational style that was abrasive, brazen, and heavy on profanities. Along with *Vidroh*, they started *Magova* and *Amahi* to tear down the upper-caste monopoly on Marathi literature and radicalize Marathi Dalits. The three continued writing individually after they split, but it was Dhasal's challenging poetry narrated through painful images of Dalit violence that got the most attention. He went on to write several books and became one of the most popular Dalit writers of all time. His books *Gophilatha* and *Moorkh Mhataryane* (By a Foolish Old Man) gained immense popularity with Dalit and non-Dalit readers and are now essential reading. For Dalits and non-Dalits alike, Dalit literature is an emblem of strength, resilience, support, and, most importantly, hope.

For some Dalits, Ambedkar is an actual prophet who changed the course of their history and future.[28] But despite his outstanding political career and invaluable contribution to Dalit rights, Ambedkar's celebrity faded fast, especially when compared to upper-caste nationalist leaders like Gandhi and Nehru. So why are political parties, especially ones like the BJP, which stand for everything Ambedkar opposed, slashing at each other now to declare him as "one of their own"? According to political theorist and Ambedkar scholar Ananya Vajpeyi, it's precisely because he opposed them. For all these years, Ambedkar was deliberately kept out of the spotlight because his blunt analyses about complex power structures were too dangerous for the upper-caste establishment, which includes not only the BJP but all political parties that have been in existence since Independence, including the Congress. Most people who read Ambedkar's original texts for the first time end up with an impressive understanding of politics, human rights, and government policy. His skill and expertise turn difficult theories into simple concepts that are accessible to anyone with a basic understanding of the language and do not require knowledge of academic theories. Generations have missed out on learning his contributions to equality and human rights. But in the past few decades, especially after the anti-Mandal protests, Dalits turned to him in a big way and actively brought his work back into the spotlight, even if it was limited to Dalit circles. The BJP, known for its astute political strategy, discovered that Ambedkar was a clear and direct path to Dalits and their votes. But they couldn't possibly risk engaging with his ideas, which directly attack their foundational principles and would not be palatable to the powerful upper-caste vote bank. So they appropriated Ambedkar but did not discuss his philosophy or his criticism of the established power structure. By aligning with Ambedkar's image, which has been a symbol for Dalit rights, they would like to project themselves as a political party that stands for equality. But most political parties want nothing to do with his ideas. Vajpeyi writes that the BJP's strategy to appropriate Ambedkar—along with Gandhi and Patel—is a "means to neutralize the ideological threat posed by these leaders."[29]

When Ambedkar was alive, and even in the decades after his death, he was attacked for his ideas and his vehement criticism of Hindu philosophy. In 1987, the posthumous release of his book *Riddles in Hinduism*, that questions the greatness of Krishna and Rama, sparked riots in Mumbai and Hindu organizations demanded its ban.[30] But only thirty years later, the Rashtriya Swayamsevak Sangh (RSS), India's largest Hindu nationalist voluntary organization, not only included him in "Hinduism's Historic Heroes" but also published books with titles like *Prakhar Rashtra Bhakt Dr. Bhimrao Ambedkar* (2014) and *Rashtra-Purush Babasaheb Dr. Bhimrao Ambedkar* (2015).[31] These books twist arguments to claim that Ambedkar did not in fact leave Hinduism since he didn't convert to Islam or Christianity. He merely converted to Buddhism, which is but a "different sect of Hinduism." Another outrageous title, *Manusmriti Aur Dr. Ambedkar* (2014), explains that since Ambedkar was not an expert in Sanskrit, his interpretation of the Manusmriti was flawed. In a stunning denial of facts, history, and well-established cultural truths, it claims that the Manusmriti was not in fact a manual that dealt with caste and gender rules.

As outrageous as the RSS's attempts to appropriate Ambedkar as a "Hindu Hero" might be, they're certainly not the only ones to do so. As I have the noted, the current BJP government that shares an ideological relationship with the RSS has also displayed an increasing allegiance to Ambedkar.[32] "[W]e have seen frequent sentimental references to Ambedkar in the PM's speeches, expensive new museums being constructed in houses where Ambedkar lived in Delhi (Civil Lines) and London (Primrose Hill), and an eruption of Ambedkar signage, statuary and memorabilia in public spaces all across the country," writes Vajpeyi, who is currently working on a project related to Ambedkar's life.[33] The Indian Left parties, which have historically not paid much attention to Ambedkar's work or ideas (at the time of discussions of the Poona Pact they claimed that reservation for Depressed Classes was taking away from the real struggle for freedom), have discovered what Vajpeyi calls a "newfound admiration" for Ambedkar. Prominent Communist leaders like Sitaram Yechury, Prakash Karat, and D. Raja have not only spoken about Ambedkar's commitment to Dalit rights but also criticized the BJP's admiration as "politically expedient and motivated by a desire to tap into the Dalit vote." Vajpeyi rightly observes that the Hindu Right ideology directly clashes with everything Ambedkar stood for and the Left's efforts to cozy up to him are also "too little, too late." "[O]ne wonders why the Left parties have allowed decades to pass before recognizing their own natural affinities with Ambedkar, especially on questions of inequality, caste and class, reservations, labor, and Ambedkar's scholarly interest in Karl Marx," she writes.

The pushback against Ambedkar (and the attempt at appropriation by various factions) has failed to stop his ideas from spreading. While the larger Dalit community has actively nourished his legacy, it is Dalit students who have even modelled themselves on his ideas, often in the face of severe discrimination and backlash. It was Rohith's adherence to Ambedkarite principles that caused him to clash with the university administration, led him to be suspended and finally take his own life.

The Ambedkarite Students' Association (ASA), which was formed on the Hyderabad University campus in 1994, is among the many active student bodies that live by and propagate Ambedkar's philosophy. Initially, it worked mainly as a support group for Dalit students, but in 2007, it also took on a political role when it decided to contest the university student elections.[34] Since then, the ASA has been a powerful player in the university's politics and has tried to steer it in a direction more aligned with Ambedkar's beliefs of equality, fraternity, and liberty. Similarly, the Birsa Ambedkar Phule Students' Association (BAPSA) at JNU and the Ambedkar–Periyar Study Circle at IIT–Madras have been actively disseminating his ideas into the mainstream. BAPSA describes itself as an independent organization that "has been consistently fighting and taking part in the Ambedkarite movement, which is striving to annihilate the caste system and Brahmanism."[35] Meanwhile, the Ambedkar–Periyar Study Circle hopes to "promote the thoughts and ideas of Ambedkar, Periyar and other progressive social thinkers and reformers," and cultivate a scientific temper. Universities being the upper-caste spaces they are, it's hardly surprising that all three of these Ambedkarite student organizations have faced pushback from their administrations. Even before the ASA became politically active, under the administration of then chief warden Appa Rao Podile (he was the vice chancellor who suspended Rohith Vemula and four other Dalit students in 2015) measures were introduced that would be detrimental to poor Dalit students.[36] In 2001, he discontinued a flexible payment system that allowed poor Dalit students to cover their food bills. When ASA members confronted him about this, he allegedly asked the guards to "throw them out." A scuffle broke out and several Dalit students were arrested and suspended for a few years. BAPSA was formed in 2016 and several of its student members were arrested and suspended months later for "physical violence." They were protesting a new UGC policy that would make in-person interviews the only criterion for admission at JNU. Similar to ASA in 2001, in this case as well, when the students began to argue, the administration called security guards to throw them out, which led to the physical struggle.[37]

Five students including Rohith Vemula were suspended in July 2015 for allegedly injuring an ABVP student.[38] Although a proctorial board found that there was no substance to this complaint, union Minister for Labor and Employment Bandaru Dattatreya wrote to the Human Resource Development (HRD) Ministry complaining that "anti-national" and "casteist" groups were operating from the university campus.[39] After this, a new committee was set up which revoked the suspension of the students, but they were expelled from the hostel and barred from using university facilities.[40] After Rohith committed suicide, students protested, demanding the resignations of Dattatreya and HRD minister Smriti Irani for their alleged role in this affair. It was somewhat puzzling that a central government ministry got directly involved in the day-to-day administration of a college.

The incidents that got these ASA students labelled as "anti-national" and even casteist were directly inspired by Ambedkar's ideology. In July 2015, the ASA, with Vemula as the organizational secretary, was labelled anti-national for protesting against the death penalty for Yakub Memon for the 1993 Bombay bomb blasts. Ambedkar was famously against capital punishment, which even today disproportionately targets Dalits, Adivasis, and Muslims.[41] While this protest didn't garner much attention at the time, it was the excuse that the political establishment used to delegitimize Rohith Vemula after his death.

Rohith was deeply inspired by Ambedkar's ideas and frequently quoted him on his Facebook page. But he didn't start out with the ASA or even with an Ambedkarite political identity. Initially, Rohith joined the Students' Federation of India, the student body of the Communist Party of India (Marxist), but quit after he noticed their apathy towards the suicides of Dalit students Pulyala Raju and Madari Venkatesh on campus. By 2015, even a few days before his death, Rohith was constantly evoking Ambedkar with his actions, particularly with the Velivada protest. Banned from entering the hostel and with nowhere else to go, the suspended students (Rohith and four others) decided to create "Velivadas" (a Telugu word that refers to Dalit ghettos) on campus to drive home the casteist discrimination they were facing. With grimy rolled up mattresses, plastic tarps, and white sheets with "Velivada" scrawled across them, they squatted in the middle of the campus, forcing people to pay attention to their pain. It was an elegant, modern, and charged form of protest similar to that of Emma Sulkowicz—the Columbia University student who carried the mattress on which she had been raped on her back throughout campus in 2014. But, more importantly, their protest directly emulated Ambedkar himself, who set Hindu holy texts on fire to force people to pay attention. Even in his death, which triggered a Dalit revolution that hasn't been seen since the anti-Mandal protests of the 1990s, Rohith brought Ambedkar's ideas to public attention.

Dr. B. R. Ambedkar is the godfather of Dalit rights in India. Many of us are hugely indebted to him and his ideas. But in following his principles, all of us Dalits are vulnerable to attacks by the upper-caste establishment. This does not deter us; it only makes us more determined. His legacy is now stronger than ever. Dalit groups in India and all over the world—some of them provided my first real brush with Ambedkar—have made sure that his work, his ideas, and his contribution to Dalit lives remains alive forever.

CHAPTER 10

MY INTRODUCTION TO AMBEDKAR

As I have mentioned in a couple of the earlier chapters, in the years before I applied to Columbia, I had become so good at pretending to be upper caste that I almost forgot I was Dalit. That was until I started writing the "identity essay" for my application to Columbia Journalism School. As I thought about how I could describe myself, the word "Bhangi" kept popping up. I kept swatting it away. Obviously, I wasn't going to tell a college board that I was Bhangi. At that time, I had no idea that it was the same college where Dr. Ambedkar had presented a thesis on caste in 1916. I spent a few days thinking about what to write in the essay and remembered the struggles of my great-grandfather when he wanted to attend school in colonial India. I soon gave up trying to come up with something else because I realized that I had no other personal story to tell, apart from the most obvious one of hiding my lower caste. So I wrote about my caste, about growing up Bhangi and learning to hide it. The shame I had carried around for twenty-seven years slowly started to vaporize with each click of the keyboard. I chose my words cautiously, running through a list of excuses and explanations in case someone I knew were to read that essay. But by writing what I had buried all these years, somehow I wasn't all that ashamed of my Bhangi caste anymore. In fact, as I read what I had written about the struggles of my grandfathers, I even felt a little proud. Maybe it wasn't so bad to be Bhangi because people in my family had not only stood up to discrimination but also somehow managed to move past it. For a few precious minutes, I felt an unfamiliar combination of triumph and self-worth. Until I realized that I might never meet the people who would read this essay. The people who knew me in my current life still didn't know anything about my caste. Despite the stirrings of pride, I wasn't ready to risk being rejected. But it was the beginning of the realization that this shame I had been carrying around might someday vanish.

Just a few days before I was to leave for New York, I was at a roof-top bar in Connaught Place with my friend and then colleague Parul. I asked her if I could tell her something, and could she not hate me for it. I wrung my hands and looked around for the exit, and Parul impatiently burst out: "Tell!" Parul and I had started out by sitting next to each other at work, comparing results on *BuzzFeed* quizzes and going to the gym together. She remains one of the least judgmental people I know, someone who gave a fair chance to everyone regardless of their behavior. She was also one of my closest friends. If there was anyone I was going to tell my secret to, it had to be her. But in those few minutes as she waited for me to tell her what it was that was making me so nervous, I was fifteen again, back in that moment when my friend's parents had asked me about my caste. I was back in that school bus where my friend who had found out my caste was refusing to look my way. I was worried: what if Parul turned away too?

Hesitantly, I told her I was from a lower caste. I still couldn't say the word "Bhangi." "This is your big secret? You sounded like you had killed someone." She called me crazy, laughing uncontrollably for a few minutes. As my shoulders relaxed and I saw that Parul's feelings towards me hadn't changed, it occurred to me that maybe not everyone was going to hate me for my caste. Perhaps I could even stop hiding it. That I could be Bhangi as well as everything else I wanted to be.

By the time I left for Columbia, I had sent my "identity essay" to other friends. It talked about things other than my caste and none of them said anything except that it was well written. I had known some of those friends, like Harsh Vardhan Sahni, for over ten years then, and perhaps for them my caste was not relevant. It didn't change what they thought of me. Some of them had even forgotten about it when I wrote the Facebook note and "came out." Those small moments of support were exactly what I needed before I was about to leave the country to study among some of the brightest journalists in the world. They made me think that despite everything that I had come to believe, I mattered, no matter my caste.

When I landed at John F. Kennedy airport at 11:30 at night, almost twenty-six hours after I had left Delhi, I had already missed one class and had nowhere to stay. Thankfully, I was saved from spending the night at the airport when a room opened up at the YMCA in Flushing, a few blocks away. The loan had been approved just a couple of weeks before the orientation date and that had severely delayed the visa process. I spent the last few days in Delhi scrambling to get last-minute shopping done and Skyping with potential roommates in New York. No housing had worked out, and I wasn't willing to take a yearlong lease, which is the norm in New York, while still in Delhi. Plans to crash at a friend's house for a few days had not materialized, and I didn't have enough foresight to arrange for a sublet, leaving me with no place to go in a city where the only people I knew worked at the scholarship assistance office at Columbia Journalism School. As I hauled my two bags and suitcase into the YMCA building, it was almost 1 a.m. I booked a double room, where I stayed alone for the next few days until I moved closer to the university in Upper Manhattan. The YMCA was a strange yet somehow perfect introduction to New York, where I saw bloody fights outside my window almost every night and shared three showers and two bathrooms with every renter on the entire floor. The months of grad school, rigorous classes, writing assignments, and working on the thesis that followed, were rough but seemed almost meditative compared to those first few bewildering days I spent at the YMCA.

I expected my course at Columbia to open a whole new world to me. My education in science had not taught me anything about how forces like capitalism, race, caste, and patriarchy worked only to benefit the few. Writing about fashion hadn't given me much perspective on that either. Even though I didn't fully understand what I would learn at an Ivy League school like Columbia, I had a sense that it would make me a better writer and well-informed journalist. But when I finally reached class, severely jet-lagged, several days late, I had no idea what was to come. Most of my classmates were more or less familiar with the coursework and had probably had the time to go over the study material that the professors had sent weeks in advance. I had been running ragged until the last minute and had not had time to go over the material. The gaps in my education and unfamiliarity with the subjects we were to study didn't help either. So the first few classes I attended were not only confusing but also made me realize that I had so much catching up to do, especially when compared to the bright international journalists around me. I threw myself into the gruelling but ultimately rewarding process of reading everything I could find and soaking up every idea I came across.

As I learned about theories of journalism, the political, racial, and social structures around the world and in the United States in particular, I began to see how that could be applied to the caste system. It was just a made-up system created by the upper-caste minority to control and exploit everyone who was deemed lower. I was still to come to terms with my newfound understanding of my own caste, when I joined a class on feminist theory in the second semester of the course. The coursework included reading arguments by leading feminist authors and breaking down the frameworks of male dominance and white superiority in movies and popular culture. Often, during the discussions, my Black, Latino, and queer classmates would talk about their experiences of racism, discrimination, and even abuse that they experienced regularly. Besides their matter-of-fact openness about their painful personal stories, what struck me was how the rest of the students responded to them. No one tried to argue, contradict, or take over their stories. They seemed to respect the courage that it took for those students to discuss their stories in that small yet public setting. After almost two months of listening to many such stories, I decided to talk about my experience with caste. I had stopped myself from doing that several times in the past because I was worried that it would seem almost insignificant compared to what the others had talked about so far. As I saw it, my lower caste and the discrimination it led to was completely routine. It was the way things were, something that I and everyone else around me grew up with. I almost felt like I would be wasting their time by talking about how I had pretended to be upper caste all this while.

But as I began talking about how the caste system affected my life and the lives of millions of others, my classmates were shocked. They did not understand how I had not seen that this was a deeply unfair system. As I spent my life trying to be as upper caste as I could, questioning why my caste was considered lower didn't even occur to me. But the horror and righteous anger of my classmates helped me see that I had been cheated—into believing that my caste was "low," that being lower caste was shameful and, most importantly, into accepting that the only way I could progress in life was by pretending to be upper caste.

In the weeks that followed this class, I seesawed between anger and sadness every time I thought about how I had gone for so long without asking why. Why had I overlooked the fact that caste was an artificial construct without logic or reason? Why hadn't I realized that what I had accepted as normal was an unfair set of practices created so that the powerful could retain their power? For many, that journey from acceptance to anger to challenging the caste system starts with Ambedkar. But for my journey to start, I had to leave India so I didn't have to worry about what would happen if people found out about my caste. In Delhi, I could not declare my lower caste because the demands of daily living and making ends meet were tough enough. Adding Dalitness to that could topple my already unstable life and threaten any opportunities that could come my way. I was too worried, too weak, too tired, to face the fallout. It was only when I moved to New York, where caste was not an issue, that I learned to accept my lower caste. And during those months in Columbia in 2015, I stopped hiding from myself.

I spent almost a year at Columbia learning about race, class, and colonialism. It gave me some context to think about my own caste and understand how the caste system worked in similar ways. And this awareness was growing in me as I was walking through the same halls that Ambedkar had walked a little over a hundred years ago, even though I was initially unaware of his legacy or even the fact that he attended the same university. Discovering Ambedkar was a journey I was going to take in my own time. But to even start, I first needed to accept myself.

Unlike those Dalits who grow up with Ambedkar's ideology and doctrine, I knew next to nothing about him. By the nineties, Ambedkar had been relegated to a "lower caste icon," someone that only the lower castes talked about. As my family continued their aspirational journey, my parents never encouraged me to find out about Ambedkar, perhaps fearing that the lower-caste subtext associated with him would rub off on me. At school, all I learned about Ambedkar was that he drafted the Constitution and was a leader of the Depressed Classes. According to the images that accompanied this information, the Depressed Classes were starving, bare-chested, stick-thin people who lived in remote villages with neither electricity nor roads. As an urban, English-speaking, educated millennial born into an educated Dalit family there was no reason for me to think that I belonged to this class. As recently as 2016, when I came out as Dalit in the Facebook note, I only had a faint idea of his contribution to our history. But once the note went viral, I started learning just how immense his role was in my story of coming to study at Columbia University in New York.

Between January, when I published the note, and April, when I attended my first ever gathering of Ambedkarites, I had filled in some of the gaps in my knowledge. But it was only when the Ambedkar Association of North America generously invited me to speak on a panel at the 125th birth anniversary celebrations of Dr. Ambedkar that I learned what he meant to the Dalit community (and to me). It had been just a few months since I wrote the note and I was still learning about what it meant to live with a very public Dalit identity, even if on a different continent. I was to present a paper on "Human Rights Violations Against Dalits" on a panel with prominent Dalit activists Thenmozhi Soundararajan and Smita Narula. In the months before I wrote the note I had silently followed Soundararajan on Twitter. Her handle @DalitDiva was the first time I had seen an educated Dalit assert their identity with pride and openness. I decided to arrive a few hours early—the celebration was at Barnard College, across the road from Columbia, where Ambedkar spent many crucial years sharpening his argument against caste. I didn't know quite what to expect, thinking that it would be somewhat like the other dry and impersonal panel discussions I had attended in the city. Instead I found a warm, vibrant, and radically smart cultural fest. As I walked to the Barnard main gate, I saw sharply dressed young couples lining up to take photos in front of the huge Ambedkar poster. That's when it finally struck me: Ambedkar was an icon, a celebrity for Dalits. The undergraduate lecture halls were filled with Indian men, women in bright saris, and children running around. People greeted one another with "Jai Bhim," the Dalit greeting based on Ambedkar's first name, Bhimrao. Knowing that almost all of them were Dalit filled me with a sense of safety I hadn't experienced so far. Upstairs, the hallways had tables at each corner, every inch covered with copies of Ambedkar's books. I grabbed my first copy of *Annihilation of Caste* before the books sold out in the next two hours. Inside, the auditorium was full. Mostly Dalit businessmen, journalists, activists, educators, academics, professionals, and Buddhist monks sat listening to the ongoing panel describe heartbreaking statistics of student suicides in universities and colleges. Seeing Rohith's portrait hanging beside a much larger portrait of Ambedkar in rich jewel tones, as presenters showed slides of how many Dalit students killed themselves in colleges, was like seeing a snapshot of Dalit history. Between the panels that were mainly about Dalit rights, atrocities, Dalit women, Ambedkar's policies on economics, Buddhism, and education, there were song and dance performances. Instead of the popular Bollywood numbers one expects at any South Asian gathering, especially in New York, these performances were based on Dalit culture and Ambedkar's legacy and life. The songs recalled his journey from Mahad in Maharashtra to New York in the United States, and the dances traced his relationship with Buddhism. There were other dances that were indigenous to Dalit culture, performed and preserved only among Dalit communities.

A month later, in May 2016, I attended another almost identical but somewhat smaller celebration close to Boston at Brandeis University, where the local Dalit community had organized a three-day event. Both in Boston and New York, I met Dalits with their roots in different parts of India. From states like Maharashtra, Telangana, Punjab, Uttar Pradesh, and Bihar, many of them shared nothing in terms of background, regional culture, or language, except Ambedkar. His life story, which children at both events recited almost like Dalit folk tales, connected them to each other more than the upper-caste culture they perhaps grew up with in India. In almost all Dalits I met at the events, Ambedkar inspired deep gratitude and pride. Gurinder

Azad, a Delhi documentary filmmaker who also attended both events, told me several times: "It is because he was, that's why we are."

Not surprisingly, Ambedkar stirs strong emotions in most Dalits. Many, like professor and activist Sujata Surepally, who identifies as an Ambedkarite and whom I also met at Barnard and Brandeis, feel like they owe him their existence. Surepally grew up with Ambedkar because of her father. But like me, there are young Dalits who only start to appreciate his ideas much later in life, often after experiencing hurtful instances of upper-caste discrimination. Noida-based IT engineer Sar Ansh who uses his Facebook account to mock the absurdities of Brahminism, grew up rejecting Ambedkar's ideas and hiding his lower caste even though his grandfather was a keen follower. "I started to drift towards it when in college I faced direct discrimination and (after) my experience with anti-reservation," he wrote to me.[1] But even beyond his ideas, Ambedkar's life choices and his academic achievements make him an ideal Dalit for many. Like Benjamin Kalia, whom we have heard from earlier, who grew up Gandhian, thinking his lower caste was a result of karma until he discovered Ambedkar's work at twenty-six, in what he calls his "born again" moment. "Being educated in Telugu medium, I couldn't speak a single correct sentence [in English] even after graduation. Dr. Ambedkar's inspiring life ignited [a] thirst for knowledge . . . I started learning English with the help of [a] dictionary and became a frequent visitor to second-hand bookshops to read on caste, Dalit, and social issues."

Dalits across India and the world mark Ambedkar's birth and death anniversaries with ceremony. April, the month of his birth, is celebrated as Dalit History Month, with monthlong panel discussions, debates, speeches, and tributes. In Delhi, every year on April 14, Dalits march to the Ambedkar statue in Parliament Street to pay their respects. But a truly unique way for Dalits to honor Ambedkar's ideology of education and social activism are the eighteen-hour study-ins that Dalit students participate in across the country. Dalit communities organize these events, which provide water and food to the students who hope to follow Ambedkar's example of studying or reading for eighteen hours on average.[2]

Dalits who have yet to discover Ambedkar's legacy or actively stay away from it have a slightly different response. I grew up with no images of Ambedkar in my house, except a small portrait in my grandfather's study that I brushed off as a political keepsake since he had been a member of the Bahujan Samaj Party. Even then I knew to stay silent whenever someone mentioned him, which in the 2000s among my mostly upper-caste friends, was practically never. In the late nineties, I came across a life-size Ambedkar portrait at a distant relative's house. As a nine-year-old doing everything to hide my caste, their assertive Dalitness and Buddhist philosophy confused and even scared me. I remember fearing being outed as Dalit if someone found out my distant relatives were Ambedkarites. That puzzling memory stayed with me till I was much older and brought back the same fears around Ambedkar's imagery. Much like Sar Ansh, who describes how some of his Dalit relatives still panic about Ambedkar's literature or his ideas. An anonymous contributor to *Documents of Dalit Discrimination* wrote that before he learned about Ambedkar, he would get upset with his father for hanging Ambedkar's photos in the living room because his upper-caste friends made fun of "slum dwellers and Ambedkarites." Most of us who reject or stay away from Ambedkar often fear being found out as Dalit. When we deny our Dalitness and our legacy of struggle, whether knowingly or not, we accept the upper-caste as the better, more superior, option. African American racial theorist Donna K. Bivens calls that internalized racism, which in the context of caste translates to internalized casteism. Bivens identifies it as an entire system that convinces people of color to "develop ideas, beliefs, actions and behaviors that support or collude with racism."[3] For thousands of years, Dalits have been abused, mistreated, discriminated against, and killed because of their lower caste. With gestures, actions, and words, they have been made to understand that the only thing that defines them is their lower caste. So it's not difficult to understand why so many Dalits hate their caste and seek "better," upper-caste identities. In her study about race, Bivens argues that individuals with both high and low self-esteem can be tricked into thinking that people born in white (or upper-caste) families are inherently better than them. These damaging ideas can last until someone actively seeks different ones, as Dalits often do with Ambedkar.

Beyond internalized casteism that forces so many of us to either reject or avoid Ambedkar, some Dalits are violently punished or abused for identifying with him. As the Dalit identity has evolved with reservation and anti-untouchability laws, casteism has also shifted shape into different but equally toxic forms. Earlier, upper castes could identify Dalits because of where they lived, how they dressed, and what they did for a living. Today Dalits, at least those in urban areas, easily blend in with the upper castes and their identifiers have changed with them. An untraceable last name that isn't Brahmin, Bania, Kshatriya, or Dalit; vague responses to the caste question; and any association with Ambedkar are generally lower-caste red flags in post-Independence India. But those Dalits who openly support Ambedkar, who joyously take to the streets to march on Ambedkar Jayanti decked in Ambedkarite silver and blue, who use "Jai Bhim" as a greeting, use his photos as their desktop images, his songs as their caller tunes—who fearlessly announce their Dalit pride and claim their equality—it's those Dalits who offend and threaten upper castes the most. When they can't call them Bhangi, Chamar, Chuda, or other lower-caste labels they think are cuss words, they call them "Jai Bhim waley." And when Dalits refuse to step gingerly, violence is used to force them into submission. In Shirdi, Maharashtra, eight upper-caste men killed a young Dalit man because he refused to silence his ringtone which announced: Tumhi kara re kitihi halla / Mazbut Bhimacha quilla (Shout all you want / Bhim's fortress is strong).[4] Chetna Kamble, who lives in Mumbai and identifies as an Ambedkarite, wrote on *Documents of Dalit Discrimination* that every year her mostly upper-caste classmates would kick up a fuss about the Ambedkar Jayanti celebrations, which she attends with her family. When Kamble would remind them of the disruptive religious celebrations that also take place annually, they would attempt to justify them with casteist excuses. Bivens includes this kind of punishment for opposing white (which is the same as upper caste) privilege and asserting African American (Dalit) pride as a part of internalized racism (casteism). It also stems from the same system where "individuals, institutions and communities of color are often unconsciously and habitually rewarded for supporting white privilege." No wonder so many of us hide our Dalitness and try to pass as upper caste.

CHAPTER 11

DALIT WOMEN'S MOVEMENTS

I am a Dalit and a woman, and am therefore doubly disadvantaged so long as the casteist and patriarchal attitudes of Indian society continue to prevail. This far I have talked mainly about how casteist attitudes have ostracized and humiliated and killed Dalits. In this chapter, I'd like to focus specifically on the treatment meted out to Dalit women.

The bodies of women, which Indian societies consider the storehouse of their bloodline's honor, don't belong to them as much as they do to their families. But for Dalit women, their bodies are also where the upper-caste societies deliver abuse and caste violence. When upper-caste men need to remind a Dalit family of their place, they attack and abuse Dalit women. But even when punishment is not the point, upper-caste men feel they are entitled to sexual and physical ownership over Dalit women. Among the five hundred (mostly rural) women that the authors of *Dalit Women Speak Out* (a study of the systemic violence that Dalit women face) interviewed, many spoke about the shocking practice of an upper-caste man raping a young Dalit bride on her wedding night. This rape and abuse continue throughout her life, where any upper-caste man can rape her any time he wants. When the husband of the woman sees the footwear of an upper-caste man outside his house, it is a sign, and he must spend the night elsewhere. The sexual abuse of Dalit women, where upper-caste men feel entitled to a Dalit woman's body, follows them into the workplace. Dalit women from Coimbatore, Tamil Nadu, told the authors that on the day an upper-caste landowner wants to rape a Dalit woman working in his field, other workers are made to leave early to let him assault her. Like caste discrimination, this rape of Dalit women is still shockingly normal in many parts of the country. Dalit women often have no choice but to accept it as a part of their lives.

Upper-caste men also use public humiliation, mutilation, and brutal violence against Dalit women to keep their families and entire Dalit communities in check. They use this violence on Dalit women to kill any pushback or dissent. It is also used to remind Dalits of their place if they are seen improving their lives by wearing good clothes, getting educated, or making money.

When it comes to rape in rural areas, it is very hard for Dalit women even to file a report. A 2001 study by Amnesty International recorded that police officers dismissed 30 percent of rape cases as false.[1] Often, even the lawyers representing the women join forces with their rapists and try to stop them from filing their case. The Amnesty study found that lawyers often accepted bribes from the accused to advise their clients to drop the case altogether.

If this doesn't stop the woman from filing a First Information Report (FIR), then the upper-caste establishment, which includes the panchayat, punishes her family, and the entire Dalit community—blocking their access to water, land, or neighborhood shops—until she is forced to withdraw her complaint. Or they try to buy her silence with an insignificant amount of money. If nothing works, then in some cases the police accept bribes to frame the Dalit survivor and her family with fake cases.[2] So in a cruel irony, instead of the rapists, the Dalit woman and her family end up in jail instead. The authors of *Dalit Women Speak Out* discovered several cases where the Dalit woman is not only raped but often imprisoned on false charges for trying to get justice.

Among the many excuses the police use to not file the report of a Dalit woman's sexual assault is to declare her "criminal" or, worse, "sexually available." It's a catch-22 situation for the woman—no matter how she reacts to her rape, she is to blame. If she resists the rape, then she is "violating" the caste order and must be punished. Two upper-caste men were convicted for gang-raping a twenty-year-old woman in Bhawani, Haryana. When they were released from jail three years later, they raped her again to punish her for complaining.[3] Men

COMING OUT AS DALIT • 147

use the "she deserved it" excuse across all castes, but Dalit women are disproportionately at the receiving end of this because of the belief that due to her caste, she is "sexually available."

There have even been cases of policemen committing rapes of Dalit and Adivasi women. In 1972, two policemen raped Mathura, a fourteen-year-old Adivasi girl in the Desaiganj police station in Maharashtra.[4] In 1989, two policemen raped Suman Rani in Haryana. More recently, several horrific reports claimed that policemen assaulted Adivasi women in conflict-ridden areas in Bastar. In early 2017, the National Human Rights Commission sent a notice to the Chhattisgarh state government, holding state police officials guilty for raping, gang-raping, and sexually assaulting at least sixteen Adivasi women in that region between October 2015 and March 2016.[5] In Bastar, Dalit women have complained that policemen squeezed women's breasts to confirm if they were lactating mothers.[6] It's not uncommon to hear about police brutality against both upper-caste and Dalit women in conflict-ridden areas as a means of punishing their partners who are evading the police.

This perception that Dalit women are "sexually available" also affects the judgment in court cases. Indian courts in general suffer from patriarchy, especially in cases of sexual assault where the accused are acquitted by placing the blame on the survivors, even when they are as young as eight. In fact, in 2016 only one out of four accused sexual harassers and rapists were convicted.[7] And when a Dalit woman is the complainant, the rates are even more skewed.

When Mathura's rape case came to trial, the Supreme Court declared that because she was "used to sex, she might have incited the cops to have intercourse with her."[8] There was a huge backlash against the Supreme Court verdict. After years of protests and petitions by women's rights organizations, in 1982, the judiciary was forced to amend the law to consider the survivor's testimony as proof that she did not consent to have sex and was, in fact, raped. But even after that amendment, similar arguments are used to acquit accused rapists. In the case of Suman Rani, the argument was made that since Rani was "used to frequent intercourse" and there were "no marks of violence or sexual assault on her body," there was no rape. The Supreme Court did not apply the minimum ten-year sentence for rape, and instead sentenced the rapists to five years. Even thirty-six years after the amendment, Indian courts continue to set upper-caste rapists free by justifying a Dalit woman's "sexual availability" as the cause for her rape. It's because of these light sentences and extremely low rates of conviction that there is a perception that raping a Dalit woman has no consequences.

Even seemingly credible agencies like the Central Bureau of Investigation (CBI) appear to side with upper-caste rapists as they did in their shocking report of the death of Dalit cousins in Badaun, Uttar Pradesh. The women were gang-raped and murdered, and their bodies were hung from trees in Katra in 2014.[9] When their families approached the police to file a report, they were turned away. After days of protests by the villagers, the postmortem report declared they were gang-raped before their death, leading to arrests of men from the upper-caste Yadav community. The state and central governments and the United Nations got involved in the investigation. Despite this, after five months of investigations under the glare of global attention, the CBI concluded that the young women had killed themselves because of their family's displeasure over one of them dating a boy.[10] The accused were not even taken to trial.

The situation only seems to have deteriorated as rapes of Dalit women increased by 500 percent in Gujarat between 2001 and 2014. The conviction rates dropped massively in sexual assault cases in Haryana in 2012, with the courts setting higher percentages of accused rapists free.[11] In fact, cases of rapes of Dalit women had a shamefully low conviction rate of 2 percent compared to the overall 24 percent rate (still disgracefully low) of conviction in 2014.[12]

This reprehensible idea that Dalit women are responsible for their rape by being "sexually available" also trickles down to the public response to their assault. It creates a damagingly false idea that Dalit women are somehow "less virtuous" and therefore less deserving of sympathy or justice.

Since 2012, the conversations that we've had around sexual assault and rape have undergone a shift. And that came from the public's reaction to the violent rape of Jyoti Singh Pandey. Jyoti was brutally gang-raped in a moving bus in Delhi in 2012 and thrown on the roadside to die. In the days following the attack, Jyoti became the symbol of protest against India's rape culture and violence against women and was dubbed Nirbhaya—one with no fear—by the mainstream media. While the information regarding her caste (Pandeys are Brahmins) was not released till much later, the media reported enough to indicate that she was "one of us." Her family was not well-off, but she lived a life that was familiar to most middle-class, upper-caste women. Even though I was not covering the attack or the protests that followed, it was clear to me that "Nirbhaya" was one of those cases of gruesome violence that would change the way we thought about women's rights to their bodies, their safety in public spaces, and why men feel entitled to this level of violence against them. Almost every newspaper, online outlet, and columnist talked about the horrific assault and why it needs to stop. Jyoti Pandey's rape and death initiated a public conversation we should have had decades ago. But since then, we have not seen the same outpouring of support for other victims of rape and sexual assault.

Jisha, a thirty-year-old Dalit woman, was also horrifically raped inside her single-room shack in Perumbavoor, Kerala, in April 2016. Jisha, like Jyoti, had overcome several hardships to continue with law school. Her single mother, Rajeshwari, worked as a daily wage laborer while Jisha saved money from her fellowships to keep her siblings in school. As a single Dalit woman living with her mother, men in her neighborhood routinely made unwanted sexual advances towards her. Even after multiple complaints, the police didn't take any serious action to stop it. In fact, Jisha and her mother were almost expecting some sort of attack.[13] In part, this was because they were isolated from the rest of the neighborhood. The neighbors swore they didn't know of the family's caste and blamed their hostility on Rajeshwari's ferociousness, but they had broken the family's water pipe and even thrown stones at their house. After a motorcycle accident, the biker, who lived in the area, reportedly threatened to kill them saying no one would care because they were "scheduled caste." Jisha and her mother already knew that in case of an attack they couldn't turn to their neighbors for help. And they were right. No help came during the attack. The neighbors reportedly assumed that the noise was a result of domestic violence and didn't want to intervene. After the attack, Rajeshwari came home to find the door locked.[14] On getting no response to her knocking, she broke down the door. Even this noise did not bring the neighbors out to help.

The police then took a full five days to cordon off the area, by which time crucial evidence was already damaged or lost. In fact, early reports in local media and the FIR carried no mention of her rape or the brutal nature of the murder.[15] Commentators and activists took to social media to condemn the slow response of authorities. The Twitter handle @DalitLivesMatter said, "Why Jisha is not Nirbhaya? . . . No State, No Center Sheds tears. No candlelight vigils. No mass rallies."

The national media only reported the incident after Dalit social media started trending it on Twitter using the hashtag #Justicefor Jisha. "The silence surrounding Jisha's murder, according to many, is linked to another evil deeply ingrained in Indian society—that of caste. Unlike Jyoti Singh . . . Jisha belongs to the dalit community. Atrocities against dalits are hardly accorded comparable media real estate," commented an article in *The Citizen*. "The comparative quiet around Jisha's murder—no less tragic a case—has been blamed on . . . her status," said *The Telegraph*. Ranjana Kumari, director of the Center for Social Research, a Delhi-based women's rights institute said, "It's a very sad reflection on the way we look at women, especially Dalit women. They are attacked on [a] regular basis."[16]

When Dalit activists and social media framed Jisha's Dalitness among the crucial factors of her rape and murder, members of the public and media protested the use of that "irrelevant detail." While Jisha wasn't raped for being Dalit, her family's life on the margins and their isolation from the upper-caste neighbors likely gave the attacker the assurance that he could get away with it. Much like Delta Megh-wal, the seventeen-year-old polytechnic student from Barmer whose upper-caste instructor not only made her clean rooms but also forced her to sign a letter saying that the sex was consensual. He perhaps knew that it would be easy to convince the school authorities that a "sexually available" Dalit girl had consensual sex with him. When her body was found floating in a water tank the day after the alleged rape, the school authorities whisked it away in the back of a truck without informing the police or her father. The abuse by her instructor and the school's attempted cover-up of her death show how easy most of the upper-caste establishment feels it is to get rid of a Dalit woman. In general, upper-caste women face less sexual assault and violence compared to Dalit women. Data from the National Family Health Survey indicated that in 2001, 11 percent of SC/ST women between the ages of fifteen and forty-nine had experienced sexual violence compared to 7.6 percent of non-SC/ST women.[17] Which is why, every time a Dalit woman is assaulted, abused, raped, or murdered, her caste matters. Even if she is not raped simply because she is Dalit, the conditions that lead to her assault are almost always affected by her status as a lower-caste woman in an upper-caste male-dominated society.

Yet, most of the upper-caste establishment refuses to see how a Dalit woman's sexual assault is nearly always linked to her caste. Even national data collection agencies don't seem to think caste has anything to do with the rape of Dalit women. Both government and nongovernment organizations report crime data either by caste or gender. As the authors of *Dalit Women Speak Out* discovered, statistics that could prove just how many lower-caste women are sexually assaulted compared to upper-caste women barely exist. So when cases like the rape and murder of Surekha Bhotmange and her children (who were viciously assaulted and killed by an upper-caste mob in Khairlanji, Maharashtra, over a land dispute) are taken to court, the judges don't charge the accused under the SC/ST Act.[18] This blind spot around how the lower caste of Dalit women puts them at greater risk for sexual assault exists even in progressive, feminist, academic, and activist circles. Both upper-caste men and women benefit from their "higher" status in the caste system, and both discriminate against Dalits, and protect their caste benefits. While upper-caste men might lay down the structures of caste differences, it is upper-caste women who—through practices like banning Dalit women from public wells, and not allowing Dalit domestic workers inside their kitchens—keep the caste system running. In the several testimonies I received for *Documents of Dalit Discrimination*, it was clear that upper-caste women were just as cruel and discriminatory against Dalit women as upper-caste men.

In the early feminist movements in India, which were rightly started to protest the systemic control and entitlement of men over women—i.e., patriarchy—upper-caste women seemed to focus on issues that directly affected them, but never acknowledged how Dalit women might have it even worse. Since these feminist movements emerged largely out of colleges and universities, they also tended to focus mainly on issues that urban and middle or upper classes were facing. Several researchers have noted that most Indian women's rights organizations often exclude poor working-class women, "since they tend to have a middle class membership."[19] But beyond overlooking class, most women's rights organizations also don't consider that lower-caste women face a lot more discrimination and sexual assault because of their caste. In fact, even urban, educated, middle-class Dalit women find that there is no space for their issues in the mainstream feminist movement. Which is why it was not surprising that some women's rights organizations protested the Mandal Commission guidelines lamenting that they wouldn't find educated upper-caste men to marry if it was implemented. They also lacked a basic understanding of how systems of caste benefits had worked against Dalits for centuries.

In the two decades since their casteist and distinctly "unfeminist" protest, not enough has changed. In 2017, after Hollywood executive Harvey Weinstein was forced to leave his company after multiple rape and sexual harassment allegations against him became public, lists of similar predatory men in media and academia began making the rounds. It turns out, women had shared these "secret lists" for years to warn each other. Soon after, US-based Dalit law student and anti-caste activist Raya Sarkar sent out a call asking students to send her names of Indian professors who might have got away with harassing them in the past. Once the submissions rolled in, Sarkar began publishing these names on her hugely followed Facebook page. The list included some well-known upper-caste academics in India. Sarkar refused to reveal the identity of the survivors or even the specifics of the assaults to protect their anonymity. Soon after the list was published, a statement criticizing it was published in *Kafila*, cosigned by thirteen feminists including academic Nivedita Menon and All India Progressive Women's Association secretary Kavita Krishnan. The statement pointed out that anonymous complaints such as these are problematic and encouraged those behind the list to withdraw it and follow due process. But the problems with due process are many: institutional indifference, red tape, and a real fear of backlash, not to mention the onus that it puts on survivors to prove the assault or harassment. The publication of the list and the response in *Kafila* showed the clear fracture in the feminist movement across class, caste, and generation. As an article in *The Wire* asked, "Would a list of Uber drivers enrage us so bitterly?"[20] Indian academia, as we have seen, is dominated by the upper castes. Therefore, they enjoy the social and cultural capital that goes with their position in society. Feminist writer Shreya Ila Anasuya pointed out in an article in *DailyO* that "the [*Kafila*] statement—as many, many people have pointed out—is patronising and dismissive."[21] She goes on to explain that the women who signed the statement did not seem to realize that they were talking from positions of power as established academics and as upper-caste women. "The letter reads like a *savarna* feminist 101 lesson to all 'other' feminists; an exercise that comes off divisive . . . discrediting the campaign and dismissing it in a rather intimidating tone," said KrantiKali in an article on *Medium*.[22] In response to the criticism of the statement, Nivedita Menon wrote a long piece in which she made some important criticisms about the list, pointing out that in many cases there was only the name of the accused and no specific allegations. But then she went on to equate criticism of "savarna" feminism from anti-caste feminists with misogynistic attacks on women by right-wing trolls.

It is somewhat bewildering that academics and activists who have spent decades studying gender theory and systems of male entitlement don't seem to understand the advantages their own caste gives them over Dalit, Bahujan, and Adivasi women.[23] And as Anasuya said, "Dalit Bahujan activists and still others who are in different locations have never bought into the idea of a singular 'feminist movement' as they have been excluded from feminist movements by upper-caste feminists."

Despite its obvious lack of understanding of caste and how it adversely affects Dalit women, I am not suggesting that the mainstream upper-caste feminist movement has not been responsible for positive change where Dalit women are concerned. Four upper-caste women lawyers challenged Mathura's rape verdict in 1972, bringing a change to the law, and the women's rights organization Vishakha led the public interest litigation against the State of Rajasthan in the Bhanwari Devi case, creating the Vishakha protection guidelines against workplace sexual harassment in 1997. However, it's precisely because of their intention to stand up for all women that the mainstream upper-caste feminist movement has failed to be more effective in safeguarding the interests of Dalit women. By ignoring how their lower caste shapes Dalit women's lives, and narrowly focusing on urban, middle-class, and upper-caste issues, the mainstream feminist movement has ignored the needs of Dalit women. Which is why after the anti-Mandal protests of the 1990s, several Dalit women got together to create groups that could finally focus on their issues.

The All India Dalit Women's Rights Forum also called the All India Dalit Mahila Adhikar Manch (AIDMAM), and the National Federation of Dalit Women (NFDW) are two of the most prominent Dalit women's rights organizations in the country. After Jyoti Pandey's 2012 rape and murder made headlines, new legal measures and fast-track courts were set up and the rate of conviction increased for the first time in Indian courts (it has since dropped back to the dismal normal).[24] Even so, in the months after the December 2012 incident, at least twenty-two cases of gang rape perpetrated on Dalit women were reported from Haryana alone, to which the national media and even the police paid no attention. These incidents only made it to the national records because members of Dalit women's rights organizations decided to document them. Members of the AIDMAM traveled to different districts in the state to record testimonies from the survivors and to collect data on the sexual assault of Dalit women.[25] It was not the first time the AIDMAM or NFDW stepped in to collect data and draw attention to the caste-based violence against Dalit women. Dalit and Adivasi women have been a part of the Indian women's rights movements since the seventies. In fact, they were largely responsible for the Shahada movement, one of the most prominent uprisings of the early 1970s, which protested the exploitation of landless Bhil laborers.

Ruth Manorama, who worked with many mainstream women's rights organizations in the seventies, says that Dalit and Adivasi women were not only overlooked in these organizations, most groups didn't even notice that the issues they faced were vastly different from those of upper-caste women.[26] Tired of finding no space for their issues or credit for the work they did, Manorama finally quit mainstream organizations and founded the NFDW in 1995. She won the Right Livelihood Award, also known as the Alternative Nobel, in 2006 for her work on Dalit women's rights. Along with AIDMAM, NFDW has managed to create a space for Dalit women in the larger feminist movement through which they can create their own identity, fight for their rights, and solve their own issues "as Dalits and as women." Upper-caste feminists though have criticized Dalit women's organizations as dealing with "narrow identity politics."[27]

Since being formed in the nineties, Dalit women's organizations have given Dalit women the chance to have their voices heard. They have shown up for advocacy work, created education programs, and assisted Dalit women with legal aid. But perhaps their most crucial contribution is doing what most mainstream women's organizations had miserably failed at so far—creating Dalit women leaders. Both AIDMAM and NFDW run several programs to create leadership skills and self-reliance among Dalit women. AIDMAM, in particular, holds regular training sessions, seminars, and workshops on human rights activism, law, gender and sexuality, digital security, direct action, and self-defense. In their 2014–15 Dalit Swabhimaan Mahila Yatra (Dalit Women's Assertion March), activists went from state to state collecting testimonies from survivors and conducted mental health and self-care training workshops to help them deal with the trauma of sexual assault. In their public meetings, street theater shows, and cultural programs where hundreds of people gathered to learn about their trauma, "Dalit women were leading [the] process," Asha Kowtal, general secretary of AIDMAM, said of the march.[28]

If casteism and caste-based discrimination is getting any attention from the global community, it's because Dalit women activists have been pushing it into the spotlight for two decades. In the historic 2001 UN World Conference against Racism, Racial Discrimination, Xenophobia and Related Intolerance in Durban, South Africa, Dalit women activists argued for casteism to be recognized as a massive injustice to millions of Indian lower-caste people. And it was mainly because of Dalit activists, and Dalit women in particular, that caste became an issue of global injustice at Durban. Since then, US-based Dalit activists like Thenmozhi Soundararajan have been building networks with Indian Dalit women's rights organizations to create a global conversation around caste-based atrocities. In 2012, Soundararajan, who is also a filmmaker and a transmedia artist, staged a "die-in" with dozens of others in New York's Times Square to call out violence on Dalits. Her public performance art received enough attention to make it to several local and national dailies in the US. More recently, Soundararajan led an extremely public fight against the American Hindu advocacy group, Hindu American Foundation.[29] The foundation wanted all mention of caste removed from textbooks for California state schools because, they argued, any mention of the caste system or the pitiable conditions of Indian women would lead to harassment of Indian students in schools. Soundararajan, along with other Dalit activists, successfully argued that American and Indian American students needed to understand the caste system.

The efforts of Dalit activists and Dalit women created a space for the Dalit Women's Assertion March to participate in the highly regarded Women of the World summit in New York City. There, activists like Kotwal and Soundararajan introduced the scale of caste-based violence against Dalit women to an audience of Hollywood celebrities, international media, and activists.[30] Attending the prestigious summit was not their only objective in the US. They held seminars, talks, and interviews with American media outlets to call attention to the state of Dalit women in India. But perhaps far more significantly, they built alliances with the group they have the most in common with—Black women.

Historically, mainstream white feminism has disappointed Black women and other women of color pretty much the same way that upper-caste feminism has often, unwittingly, let down Dalit women in India. Just like upper-caste feminists, white feminists too assumed that their experiences represented the lives of all women. With better access to education, Black women activists in particular have been able to push back against this assumption. Notable Black female academic bell hooks published *Ain't I a Woman? Black Women and Feminism* in 1981. Her groundbreaking book, which remains one of the most significant feminist texts of recent times, explained that white women shouldn't get to define the experiences of Black women which were almost always colored by their race. Since then, Black women activists, like Dalit women activists, have been building spaces to address their own issues. It was Black women (two of them are also queer) who created Black Lives Matter and #SayHerName, two of the most visible

movements of resistance against white supremacy and anti-Black police brutality since the seventies. When members of AIDMAM met
the creators of #SayHerName on their US tour, there was instant
solidarity. Both groups not only shared similar struggles, but Dalit
activists also borrowed from their highly successful framework for the
fight against casteism.

This meeting wasn't the first time that Dalit women activists were
inspired by the struggles of Black women in the US in recent times.
Soundararajan was among the activists who started Dalit History
Month along the lines of the highly popular Black History Month in
the US. Many Dalit women who don't find their issues addressed by
upper-caste feminists often turn to Black women activists and academics for inspiration. Despite their many differences, Dalit women
share a lot more with marginalized Black women than upper-caste
Indian women. Like Black women, Dalit women have not only struggled against caste-based violence and discrimination from upper-caste
men and women; they've also had to deal with Dalit men who think
of themselves as more influential and powerful than Dalit women. In
the American civil rights movement, Black women found themselves
in supporting roles to Black men. Their work was either neglected or
not taken seriously and despite their overwhelming efforts, the women
were not considered leaders of those movements. If they spoke about
their neglect or demanded equal credit, Black women were often criticized for weakening the movement by "airing dirty laundry."[31] The civil
rights movement expected the women activists to stand behind the
men and unequivocally "support" and "respect" them. In Indian societies as well, where a man, regardless of his caste, is always thought of
as more important than a woman, it's not surprising that Dalit women
activists often have similar experiences.[32] Even though Dalit activism
and the struggle against caste is firmly based on Ambedkar's idea of
equality of the genders, Dalit women activists find themselves overlooked. Savita Ali, an activist from the Dalit Mahila Adhikar Manch,
explained how she joined a Dalit women's organization after the male
activists in previous organizations ignored her contributions.[33] Even
the Dalit Panther Party lacked any visible female leadership. While
they routinely highlighted caste-based atrocities against Dalit women,
they barely had any Dalit women's voices. Like the Black Panthers,

the Dalit Panthers were also criticized for being "hypermasculine." Among the only women famously associated with the movement was non-Dalit Malika Amar Shaikh, party founder Namdeo Dhasal's ex-wife. Her contribution was pretty much absent from the narratives of the Dalit Panther Party till she addressed it herself in her memoir.[34]

Even though most Dalit male activists fully support Dalit women activist leaders, many still think of themselves as more deserving than Dalit women of those leadership roles. It indicates the larger issue within Dalit communities themselves, where Dalit women suffer from violence and abuse even from their partners and male family members. Yet several upper-caste feminists and Dalit male academics argue that Dalit men are "kinder" or "less violent" to Dalit women. That because they earn almost as much money as Dalit men, traditional, nonurban Dalit women have more "freedom" to hit back when abused. They claim that since Dalit women, unlike most upper-caste women, go out of their house to work, they are more independent. Even progressive upper-caste feminists like Sharmila Rege claimed that Dalit women didn't face the same threat of domestic abuse as upper-caste women.[35] Perhaps they forgot that it's in these public spaces that upper-caste men rape and abuse Dalit women. That when an upper-caste man rapes a Dalit woman, both upper-caste and Dalit communities feel more sympathy for her husband. Because instead of her abuse and trauma, it's his "honor" and good name that matter more.[36] Despite Dalit women working outside their homes as domestic workers, farm laborers, and manual scavengers, Dalit men violently abuse them and control their earnings. Dalit women never earn as much as Dalit men, and work both at home and outside. When it comes to abuse and violence against women, Dalit men are no different than upper-caste men. Both abuse women to make their power and authority clear. Women like my mother, who hope to pass as upper caste and are financially more stable, still face abuse from their husbands, their families, and even their own parents. Dalit women might be able to fight back, but from what I saw growing up, they are also made to "fall in line" with even greater violence.

Some things have changed. Now there are more Dalit women's organizations that amplify Dalit women's voices. With more Dalit women having access to the Internet, the feminist narrative in India isn't limited to a few upper-caste women academics and activists. They no longer get to be the gatekeepers, deciding who's allowed in and who remains excluded. The discourse is now largely democratic and Dalit women lead it from the frontlines. They are able to speak for themselves and are forcing society to give them the attention they deserve.

Even as India's #MeToo movement gained prominence with actress Tanushree Dutta opening the floodgates by alleging that Nana Patekar had assaulted her a decade ago, most upper-caste feminists could not ignore the list that Sarkar published, which did exactly that with alleged harassers in academia a year ago.[37] While the most visible feminists in India are still mainly upper caste, the movement at large is shifting, even if grudgingly, to make space for Dalit women. While some issues like the patriarchy and misogyny of Dalit men towards the women in their families and communities still remain more or less unaddressed, that Dalit women are finally getting to make changes in their own lives is a hopeful start.

CHAPTER 12

THE DANGER OF
THE SINGLE NARRATIVE

I started the *Documents of Dalit Discrimination* because all I saw in the media and popular entertainment were stories about victimized Dalits, or those undeserving of reservation. There were no stories about people like me.

Among the many messages I received after I came out as Dalit, several expressed amazement that I could speak English. It was almost as if without going through horrific violence or abuse or growing up in extreme poverty in a remote rural area, I couldn't possibly be Dalit. In her immensely popular 2009 TED Talk, Nigerian author Chimamanda Adichie recalls how as a young girl she was shocked to find out that a family member of her domestic helper made beautiful baskets. All she had heard of his family was that they were poor. The idea that they could also make something beautiful had never even occurred to her. Even though she only knew one story about the domestic helper's family—their poverty—it became the story that defined their lives. This is what Adichie calls "The Danger of a Single Story." When the rest of the country only hears of Dalits as suffering victims or reservation grabbers it becomes their single story. They never see Dalits as actual people with full lives.

When I wrote the note in which I came out as a Dalit, I was sitting in a comfortable chair in a café in Chelsea, far away from my caste roots. Even before I wrote the note, I had decided that I wasn't going to work in an Indian newsroom again. So by outing myself as Bhangi, I didn't feel like I was putting my career on the line. If some people decided I was less worthy or less qualified because of it, I didn't have to work with them. I took a risk, but only because it was a limited one. But there are many Dalit journalists who don't have that choice. To continue working in the Indian media space, Dalit journalists must either fall in line (especially while covering Dalit issues like reservation) or, like me, keep their heads down and their caste well hidden. Most media houses are brimming with upper-caste journalists, editors, and heads of departments, but they tend to think of themselves as "above caste." But this declaration falls flat anytime there is a discussion on the number of Dalit journalists in Indian media.

After the anti-Mandal protests, it took an outsider, more specifically an African American journalist who was familiar with the strength of minority voices in covering minority issues, to raise that question. Kenneth J. Cooper, then South Asia correspondent for the *Washington Post*, was looking into a story of an argument between Bahujan Samaj Party leader Kanshi Ram and his workers and some journalists. (Kanshi Ram famously mistrusted the media, calling it "Manuwadi" and biased.) Cooper wanted to get a Dalit journalist's opinion to fill him in on the context and background of the argument. But he couldn't find one. So he turned to senior journalist B. N. Uniyal, who worked at *The Pioneer*. Uniyal couldn't find a Dalit journalist either. "Suddenly, I realized that in all the 30 years I had worked as a journalist I had never met a fellow journalist who was a Dalit; no, not one," Uniyal wrote in his column for the newspaper.[1] He checked with editors in other newsrooms. Instead of supporting his quest, many editors turned on him for dividing the journalistic community. One accused Uniyal of showing off that he was the only one who was not casteist. An editor at a Hindi newspaper complained that Cooper knew nothing about "Indian history" and was simply trying to malign the country by asking that question. Another editor suggested that journalists shouldn't be screened based on their caste.

The truth is that in the job market, journalists *are* screened based on their caste. Academic J. Balasubramaniam spoke to a Dalit journalist who reported that at his interview with a Tamil daily he was first asked about his hometown, and then if he was one of the upper-caste

Pillamars who were the dominant community there. When he admitted that he was, in fact, from one of the lower castes, the journalist was turned down for the job.[2] Uniyal even tried to investigate the number of Dalit journalists by checking the Accreditation Index of the Press Bureau of India. Out of the 686 names listed, 454 were upper caste. Of the remaining 232, he called 47 at random and discovered that none were Dalit (or admitted to being Dalit).

One would expect that Uniyal's groundbreaking column, which was the first of its kind on Indian media, would lead to some sort of change. But nothing much came of it. Two Dalit intellectuals, Chandra Bhan Prasad and Sheoraj Singh Bechain, even requested the two leading Indian media watchdogs, the Press Council of India and Editors Guild of India, to address the situation. The Press Council replied that it had no control over the organization of newsrooms, while the Editors Guild didn't even respond. But *The Pioneer*, which had published Uniyal's column, asked Prasad to write a weekly column on Dalit issues, making him one of the lone Dalit voices in Indian media for a long time. A few years later, in 2000, Uniyal wrote about the disappointing response to his previous column, adding that "None felt aghast or alarmed at the situation described in the article . . . No one felt that there was a need for making special efforts to draw qualified Dalits into the media."[3]

Several reports since Uniyal's article appeared have confirmed the bias against hiring or promoting Dalit journalists. In *India's Newspaper Revolution* (2009), media historian Robin Jeffrey went to "20 towns, visited dozens of newspapers and interviewed more than 250 people" over ten years and didn't find a single Dalit journalist on the payroll. Soon after, in 2006, a Center for the Study of Developing Societies survey found that out of 315 heads in over thirty-seven Delhi-based English and Hindi publications and TV channels, 90 percent of the decision makers in English-language print media and 79 percent in English TV channels were upper caste. Six years after Jeffrey's book was published not a single Dalit was in the top ten positions at these organizations.[4] In 2013, media watchdog *Hoot* commissioned Delhi-based journalist Ajaz Ashraf to investigate if the situation had changed, after almost seventeen years since Uniyal's column. Ashraf contacted the government-funded Indian Institute of Mass Communication, one of the most popular mass communication colleges in the country, to seek a list of a hundred SC/ST students in the reserved category. Out of the twenty-one who agreed to go on the record, almost every single one complained about discrimination and harassment on campus. Like any other government college and university with reservation, seniors and professors would abuse the "quota" students with casteist slurs and challenge their "merit." In their jobs, senior colleagues and editors would often try to find out their caste. The only difference, Ashraf noted, was that in the English-language media the discrimination was more subtle compared to most vernacular publications where journalists were blatantly asked their caste, which would determine if they were to be promoted or even hired.

But even English newsrooms, which, from my experience, stick to a "don't ask, don't tell" policy, are no less of a minefield for a Dalit journalist. Ashraf discovered that an otherwise neutral journalist would be "accused" of being lower caste if they stood up for Kumari Mayawati or protested the media's decades-long sexist coverage of her haircuts, outfits, or "lack of style." Or, conversely, a Dalit journalist who was open about their caste would be called "biased" for covering caste issues or criticized of colonizing a particular beat.

Jeffrey found most English-media editors assume that Dalit journalists cannot write or communicate in English and use that as a reason for not hiring them. English-language journalists and reporters with a poor grasp of the language isn't a Dalit problem. It's an Indian journalism problem. Reporters across publications, regardless of their caste, often file badly written copy, which the subeditors work on for hours so it is fit to print. The *News Minute* was able to get its hands on examples of unedited copy filed by upper-caste reporters, which they labelled "devoid of grammar and sometimes bordering on gibberish."[5] Dalit journalist Sudipto Mondal wrote that to judge the writing skills of even popular upper-caste journalists all one needs to do is "watch them live on TV news or social media, where there is no subeditor to refashion their dispatches into English."[6] Ashraf pointed out that in his interactions with Dalit journalists for the story, many of which took place over email, he found that their "skills in the English language [were] better than many whose pre-published copies I have read over the years in the profession."

Lack of diversity in newsrooms is not limited to India, but is, in fact, a global concern. Especially in countries like the United States, which have racially diverse populations, newsrooms have been making a serious effort so they don't look like an "endless parade of white men."[7] But it wasn't always that way. In fact, the racist bias was palpably visible in newsrooms until 1968, when the National Advisory Commission on Civil Disorders in America called out newsrooms for reporting stories that only showed African Americans as either criminals or victims. It was "as if they [African Americans] don't read the newspaper, marry, die, and attend PTA meetings," their statement read.[8] Just like with Indian newsrooms on Dalits, there was an easy answer to why the mostly white male journalists of the time had a narrow frame of reference for the entire African American population. It was because there were hardly any Black journalists in mainstream American newsrooms who could tell their own stories beyond the criminal-victim combination. Before the civil rights movement, which had ended the same year, the Commission on Civil Disorders stated that there were almost no Black journalists in mainstream newsrooms in America. But even as they reluctantly opened their gates to journalists of color, it took a full ten years for the American Society of News Editors (ASNE)—the US counterpart to our Editors Guild—to include diversity within newsrooms as one of its banner issues. In 1978, ASNE conducted its first annual newsroom employment census and called out newsrooms for not hiring journalists of color in proportion to their population in the country. They gave newsrooms until the year 2000 to meet those numbers and suggested several ways that it could be done. Along with affirmative action measures, like creating special scholarships for journalists of color and organizing minority-specific job fairs, they started special departments that focused exclusively on increasing newsroom diversity. Later, ASNE even started an institute to provide low-cost training to minority journalists.

Going by these examples, there are clearly many ways that Dalit and tribal journalists can be included in Indian newsrooms. But there are no clear guidelines on how this can be done effectively. Guidelines alone can't make up for decades of apathy towards Dalits in Indian journalism. Even ASNE's guidelines have fallen short of making

American newsrooms truly diverse. While they greatly helped in creating accountability, there has been only a marginal increase in the actual numbers. From a depressing 3.8 percent in 1978, the numbers grew to 12.4 percent in American newsrooms in 2014.[9] And the initial deadline for newsrooms to create more diversity had to be extended from the year 2000 to 2025. Yet it's probably because of the measures that were undertaken so far that the American media landscape now has African American, Latino, Hispanic, and Asian American narratives that go beyond their limited stereotyping. Even the *New York Times* (despite being criticized for doing "too little, too late") announced a special department to cover gender and racial issues in 2016.

Meanwhile, the Indian media is only now beginning to wake up to not having enough Dalit perspectives. There are still only a small number of openly Dalit journalists in English and vernacular media. Mondal wrote in his column that the fact that my "coming out" as Dalit was hailed as some sort of a hallmark of diversity only goes to prove how few Dalits work in our newsrooms. Among English-language publications, so far only *Caravan* and the *News Minute* have separate positions for Dalit and Adivasi writers. Both announced these positions soon after Rohith's death, when the Indian media wasn't just covering the chain of events that followed but also other narratives of caste surrounding it. In terms of training, apart from the Indian Institute of Mass Communication, which has a constitutional reservation for Dalits, Asian College of Journalism (ACJ) is the only private journalism institute that has made an effort to include Dalits in its student body. While it doesn't have a reservation as such, it does offer scholarships that cover tuition and residence costs for Dalit students, and English-language classes for students who need them. But few Dalit students have managed to benefit so far. For a few years after they were announced in 2007, these scholarships barely got any applications, in large part because the institute wanted to keep the "diversity project" secret to avoid any backlash.[10] It was only in 2010–11, when the institute started reaching out to candidates through lectures, emails, texts, and even personal calls that these scholarships became known. The next year, 107 Dalits applied to the four SC/ST scholarships available.[11] Despite that, the seats went empty year after year, because many Dalit students with rural or economically weaker backgrounds never stood a chance against the urban, English-speaking students that form the bulk of applicants each year. Mondal wrote in his column that after word about these special scholarships got out, upper-caste students launched a "whisper campaign" condemning the "reverse racism" of the institute. Since the names of the recipients of the scholarships are kept secret, every year the students try to discover the identities of the SC/ST scholarship recipients. However, the institute, perhaps by now used to handling what Mondal calls "caste vigilantes," is always quick to shut down any such investigations. But even when the students' identities don't become known, they still have to deal with the stress of hiding their caste. Even in a seemingly progressive space like ACJ, the only way Dalits can avoid harassment, bullying, and challenges to their legitimacy is by lying about their identities. These scholarships, while offering Dalit students career-building skills also demand their silence. Understandably, this compromise is perhaps the only way for the institute to help the students while withstanding casteist attacks, but it is yet another example of the distress and difficulty Dalits face to survive in public spaces in India, even the seemingly progressive ones. Mondal writes that it's because of this discrimination that several activists and student leaders often discourage Dalit students from applying to these scholarships, and even push them towards academia or the civil services instead. This could explain why, despite the institute's efforts, Dalit ACJ graduates between 2010 and 2013 only increased by a disgraceful 1.5 percent.[12]

For many decades since Independence the only news media outlets were the state-controlled Doordarshan and AIR. But by the 2000s, with the entry of many private media organizations and the arrival of online outlets, that monopoly began to crumble. With the arrival of the Internet, traditional news organizations took a hit as their readership reduced. Online media spaces were more open and democratic and allowed anyone with access to the Internet to have a voice, regardless of their journalism training (or caste). What began as personal blogs turned into fully functional websites, new narratives emerged, among which one of the strongest was the Dalit side of the story. Dalit bloggers started telling the stories that mainstream media often ignored and found a huge audience among Indian and global Dalit communities. Casteism in Indian societies, especially the urban ones, might not always be staring you in the face, but it's never too far from the surface. Dalits across the world were angry. Online, they could be angry together and turn that fury into something potent.

The biggest threat to the upper-caste media stranglehold came when Dalit academics, bloggers, and activists took to Twitter and Facebook to highlight issues of casteism in nearly all aspects of Indian society. These platforms help to spread ideas beyond the Dalit communities to a larger upper-caste audience. So stories that would have flown under the radar or been tucked into the back pages of newspapers were catching the attention of thousands.

It was through these platforms that Dalit writers reported on the events that led up to and followed Rohith's suicide. News of his death broke first on Facebook and it was almost immediately picked up by *Round Table India* (*RTI*), *Dalit Camera* (*DC*), and other Dalit-run websites. Almost all of them released up-to-the-minute updates of the campus protests that broke out in Telangana, Mumbai, Delhi, and Hyderabad soon after his death. But while Rohith's eloquent last letter was going viral on Facebook and Twitter, most traditional media outlets (including the *Times of India, Hindustan Times, The Hindu,* and *Indian Express*) either ignored the incident and the protests that followed or squeezed them into a tiny column.[13] Only on January 19, when TV news channels had broadcast images of the violent clashes between the protesters and the police all day, did the news make it to print. But more than the circumstances of his death, or the reasons that led to it, most outlets, both online and print, focused on what they seemed to think was the most unexpected detail of the event—a Dalit's elegant prose in English. Rohith's letter was perhaps the obvious focus for print since it was already viral on social media, but it was many days before traditional media outlets examined the backstory that led to his death.

What followed was wall-to-wall coverage of his death and the protests that followed and the deeper investigative stories of casteism on campus that had been unheard of in the Indian media. Dalits and their issues dominated the Indian media for weeks in a way that hadn't happened before. Almost every outlet, online, television, or print, was forced to pay attention and talk about the discrimination and harassment that exists in Indian universities. But this coverage wasn't due to the editors undergoing a sudden change of heart. It was the students who went out on the streets, the people who kept the conversation alive, and, most importantly, the Dalit writers, activists, and editors who worked day and night to feed the news cycle with updates and made the narrative too big to ignore. Large numbers of people now started following *RTI*, *Ambedkar's Caravan*, *Savari*, *Velivada*, and *Dalit Camera* for updates they couldn't find elsewhere.

Other stories too were given focus and in-depth coverage by these outlets: the rapes and murders of Jisha and Delta Meghwal and the assault on teenaged Dalit tanners by cow protectors. These stories also got picked up by most traditional media outlets. So did the video that showed cow protectors brutally assaulting teen Dalit tanners for transporting dead cows in Una, Gujarat. The response to this assault grew into a huge rally and an important protest against social injustice (as we saw in chapter 5). A significant rally such as the Azadi Kooch March to protest the lynchings and demand the upholding of Dalit rights should have been big news. But despite its radical thrust and historic context, most media outlets didn't find it worth covering. NDTV covered the last two days of the march; most news channels gave it no coverage at all.[14] And when they did cover them, most news channels focused on how the marching Dalits would "inconvenience" the political parties in the upcoming elections. While there were screaming debates on TV about which political party would benefit from Dalits taking to the streets in the Uttar Pradesh and Gujarat elections, they brazenly ignored the Dalits themselves and the issues that they were raising. The large gathering of Dalits in Una received attention only when a national political leader made the rounds, dragging TV cameras along. This was their narrative, a story that the Dalits were writing by putting themselves and their bodies at risk, by coming out on the streets and demanding what they had been denied.

"It was as if 200 million people had no mind or intellect of their own," wrote Dhrubo Jyoti, a queer Dalit journalist for Dalit-owned *RTI*. Jyoti pointed out that many TV channels didn't invite any Dalit activists or leaders on their panels, and had upper-caste commentators deliver the verdict on a historic Dalit uprising and its impact on the state elections. The print publications fared only marginally better. They covered the march but only as a footnote to the more convenient narrative of the rise of Jignesh Mevani and his charismatic leadership. A former journalist, Mevani has a background in law, activism, and academia and has been a grassroots organizer for several years. His fiery and articulate speeches leading the protests instantly seduced the print and online media, which couldn't stop writing about how the Dalit movement had found a new leader. But with the next cycle, he too was old news.

Even by ignoring the marching Dalits, the media couldn't silence them, because they didn't need traditional print and TV news outlets to leave their mark on history. While most media outlets limited their reporting to the first and the last day of the march, Dalit publications like *DC* reported the ongoing developments in detail for the entire ten days. Since 2008, when Ravichandran Bathran started it as a You-Tube channel to upload videos from Dalit events that most media outlets ignored, *DC* has consistently reported breaking news about Dalit atrocities and assertion. Along with *RTI*, it was among the few publications that provided exhaustive coverage on the events that led to Rohith's suicide. It also reported the events in the aftermath of his death, with updates on the student protests and Radhika Vemula's Velivada style sit-in. A year later, when Radhika and Rohith's brother, Raja, were arrested for entering the campus to honor Rohith's statue, *DC* once again broke the news. Bathran, a former student leader, started *DC* because when ABVP students assaulted him on the Hyderabad University campus, not one media outlet covered it. Now a fully functional and rather prominent website that is among the most reliable sources of information on Dalit issues, *DC* has volunteers across Delhi, Mumbai, and Hyderabad. They are known to arrive on the scene as soon as they are contacted to shoot video, record audio, and take detailed photographs of unfolding events. Beyond original reporting, the site also hosts documents and data on crimes against Dalits in free-to-download PDFs and Word documents along with well-researched opinion pieces on current events. Over the years, *DC*'s relentless and detailed reporting of discrimination and violence against Dalits has made these incidents that much harder to ignore.

DC thrives as part of a hyperconnected information system of Dalit news, opinions, and voices. The outlets, websites, and portals that are a part of this network boost each other by hosting articles, trading writers, and directing traffic to each other. The most visible and widely read among them is *RTI*, an in-depth website of Dalit, Bahujan, and a few upper-caste voices and opinions. It is not only one of the largest websites on Dalit and Bahujan perspectives but also among the oldest. In the aftermath of the 2006 anti-reservation protests, anti-caste blogger Kuffir Nalgundwar, academic Anu Ramdas, and entrepreneur Bhanu Pratap Singh started *RTI* in 2007 to host "Dalit history and anti-caste history." In addition to the voices of Dalit-Bahujan writers, they started including "Ambedkar's writings and philosophy . . . Dalit poetry, women's poetry, anti-caste poetry across religions."[15] Soon, Dalit writers, academics, researchers, and activists turned it into a platform for incisive analysis, critiques, and passionate and personal interpretations of the Phule-Ambedkar ideology. And with no other outlets for Dalit news, *RTI* also became the site for breaking news, reporting, and coverage of events and well-informed commentary on Dalit-Bahujan-Adivasi issues. Currently, the site has nearly three hundred writers who post regularly with no specific agenda or editorial direction aside from giving an open, judgment-free, and visible space to Dalit-Bahujan ideas. In its early years, *RTI* largely had a Dalit-Bahujan readership, and even though it was soon discovered by upper-caste academics, the site remained largely under the radar. But with Dalit websites like *Savari*, *Velivada*, and *Ambedkar's Caravan*, along with the support of a highly vocal Dalit social media, *RTI* and its smart, articulate, and fierce Dalit perspective soon went mainstream. Even nonacademic upper-caste readers started visiting the website for Dalit news and opinions. *RTI* started out in English for Dalits and Bahujans in all parts of India and the world to access it easily. But with an increase in upper-caste (and Dalit-Bahujan) readership from the Hindi-speaking belts of the north, it launched a Hindi edition in 2016.

In the years that followed the 2006 protests, many Dalit blogs and portals started in quick succession. Among these was UK-based Pardeep Attri's *Ambedkar's Caravan*, started in 2009 to collect resources on Ambedkar and Dalit history. Now *Ambedkar's Caravan* also publishes breaking news and opinion pieces on Dalit issues. It's also among the few sites to publish short articles on Dalit leaders and how they shaped Dalit history. During the Dalit History Month in April,

Ambedkar's Caravan often runs a series on Ambedkar, Phule, Periyar, and Savitribai, celebrating their achievements. The publication is also a valuable resource on Ambedkar's books, writings, and speeches. Attri started the website under a pseudonym (to avoid the threats and backlash that are the usual responses) and runs the site himself. He later revealed his identity, at which point @ambedkarscaravan's (he retained this handle) followers jumped to more than 44,000 on Twitter and the Facebook page gathered over 189,000 likes. Attri has often spoken about the urgent need for Dalits to have their own media—in early 2017 he started *Velivada*, and *Ambedkar's Caravan* became an exclusive portal for his own writing. Named after Rohith's protest, in just a few months, Velivada.com became yet another reliable source for Dalit news and opinions. Designed in a clean, minimalist, millennial friendly, *BuzzFeed*-style format, its articles have eye-catching photographs and graphics, lists, and videos. Like *RTI*, Attri launched a Hindi version of the site—the stories on it are passionate and opinionated, and cover a 360-degree take on Dalit issues.

Even though the founders of these portals, save for Ramdas, are all men, the space isn't overtly male dominated. While all these websites do focus on Dalit women and their issues, *Savari*, founded by Dalit women, covers caste entirely from a woman's perspective. Besides articles, *Savari* regularly uploads papers by female academics. But what makes it spectacularly unique is its focus on Dalit food history, which is so intricately linked to the history of Dalit women. There is a separate section for recipes and their origins that trace the cultural evolution of the community associated with that type of food.

Together, these websites are building new ways for Dalits to think, discuss, and share information. They have created, controlled, and taken over the Dalit narrative so persuasively that it's no longer easy to dismiss them as Dalits agreeing with other Dalits. These sites not only support each other but are also incredibly open with their resources. All papers, data, and research are accessible without paywalls and anyone can use and share them. Attri even puts up articles and posts on *Ambedkar's Caravan* without claiming copyright. Unlike other publications, which are understandably selective about their writers, they are open to submissions from any Dalit-Bahujan person, regardless of their academic, linguistic, or literary capability. But this openness also leaves them vulnerable to appropriation, most often by upper-caste academics and media. After years of research, Dalit websites have collected reams of crucial data about caste in India, often with few resources and little funding. Many activists have spent years going door-to-door to gather this data. While the mainstream media and to a large extent even academia has more or less ignored caste issues for years, the sudden prominence of these websites has forced them to acknowledge these issues. But rather than invest in research, most media outlets find it convenient to use their work without permission or even credit. Almost all Dalit-owned websites face blatant plagiarism, and find their work paraphrased without context mostly by upper-caste authors and academics. While they try to highlight this issue through their social media channels, ultimately these websites are no match for the media giants they are up against. Nalgundwar says that while plagiarism is a huge issue, what is essential is that these are spaces for democratic debates for "the educated Dalit-Bahujan public."[16]

Dalit-owned publications that started after 2006 managed to make it because of the popularity they achieved through the Internet. Earlier Dalit publications had no way to achieve that reach nor did they have the large educated Dalit readership that pushed the current crop into the mainstream. As early as 1920, Ambedkar started *Mooknayak*, a Marathi newspaper with which he hoped to contest the casteist view of Dalits. In 1927, he followed that with *Bahishkrit Bharat* and a few years later started the Bharat Bhushan Press. This last was printing till 2016, when the Ambedkar Bhavan where it was located was demolished to build a seventeen-storey building to honor Ambedkar, destroying valuable handwritten manuscripts and records of the Buddhist Society of India in the process.[17] Ambedkar used both the publications and the press to create a space for Dalit narratives that didn't exist at the time in the mainstream media. Ambedkar's publications didn't receive much support either from the mainstream press or advertisers who gladly supported Gandhi's *Harijan*, which started much later in 1933. Notably, African American publications like *Jet*—it published the graphic photographs of Emmett Till, a Black teenager killed by white Americans, that catalyzed the civil rights movement—and lifestyle magazines *Ebony* and *Essence* also encountered similar exclusion from white-owned media in the United States. But they were able to overcome that with the support of the politically influential Black churches and an educated Black middle class, something that Ambedkar's Dalit publications didn't have.[18] In the years that followed Ambedkar's publications, several Dalit publications started up and shut down because of lack of funding and support.

Over time, Dalit social media and Dalit-owned websites built such an intensely vocal narrative between Dalit and upper-caste followers that mainstream media outlets had no choice but to cover it. Academic K. Satyanarayana calls this a Dalit "subaltern counter public" where Dalits are creating spaces to organize strategic activism against the upper-caste establishment.[19] A few months after Rohith's death, this network once again sprang into action. They covered the rapes and deaths of Jisha and Delta Meghwal with hashtags like #JusticeforDelta and #JusticeforJisha, forcing mainstream media to take these crimes seriously.[20] Many print and online outlets were now not only following Dalit influencers but also using them as sources and experts for stories.

It was in this changed atmosphere that *The Doctor and the Saint* was published in 2014. The essay, by the same name, was written by Man Booker-winning upper-caste author Arundhati Roy as an introduction to *Annihilation of Caste*, the seminal text on caste by that giant of the Dalit movement, Dr. Ambedkar. This angered a large number of Dalits. To understand this anger, we have to understand the context in which Ambedkar wrote *Annihilation of Caste* and what it has come to mean to Dalits.

As we have seen, after years of attempting to negotiate with caste Hindus—especially during the 1927 Mahad Satyagraha and the Nasik Temple Entry, and his ongoing clashes with Gandhi—Ambedkar was no longer willing to work with them on the issue of caste. So when the caste Hindu reformers of the Jat-Pat-Todak Mandal, an organization whose "one and only aim was to eradicate caste," invited him to give a keynote address, Ambedkar decided to tell them what he thought was the best way to go about it.[21] In the speech (which he was asked to send to the organization before the event) he suggested that the only way to get rid of caste was to reject the foundation of the entire caste system: Hinduism. Even though the Chaturvarna system is what divides people into four castes on the basis of their professions, it is also the founding principle of the Hindu religion. So Ambedkar questioned why Dalits should remain part of a religion that would always consider them as inferior. When Ambedkar sent this speech to the organizers, they balked and asked him to "remove the section" about leaving Hinduism. Ambedkar replied that since his entire argument was that Hinduism is the "central cause for Dalit suffering" he couldn't make the speech without it. The Mandal then withdrew their invitation. So Ambedkar decided to publish his original speech and aptly named it *Annihilation of Caste*. This has since become a sacred text for Dalits.

When *The Doctor and the Saint* was published by Navayana, Dalit activists and academics criticized this introduction to the text on a number of points. A big point of contention for many Dalits was the comparison between Gandhi and Ambedkar. In the introduction to Ambedkar's most radical and significant work, Roy positions Gandhi front and center. "Her introduction, in fact, barely references the original text and mainly focuses on comparing Gandhi with Ambedkar, which seems to be the real purpose of the book," says Murali Shanmugavelan in his review in the *Independent*. Roy spends most of her essay picking apart Gandhi's position on the caste system and his conversations with Ambedkar. She astutely and patiently unpacks the sainthood of India's most famous leader by rationally examining his actions in the current political and social context. And she does that with Ambedkar too. But Omvedt points out that Roy makes no real attempt to "grapple with the question of erasing caste under the rather different conditions of the caste system today" and calls her out for not seeing the "importance of the central theme which she is supposed to be introducing—the annihilation of caste."[22] In reducing Ambedkar to a side note in his own story, Roy, in the view of many Dalits (and I include myself in their number) was exposing her own biases, which led her to treat upper-caste subjects and opinions as more important. This is part of a larger issue in academia. Often, it is upper-caste academics and writers who are lauded for their engagement with Dalit history and Dalit studies, ignoring the important work that Dalit intellectuals are doing. Ilaiah concurs: "It's not just the Right-wing, even Left and liberal academics have biases against PhD scholars from Dalit and Bahujan communities." A close look at the bibliography to the introduction by Roy reveals that "out of the 120 references, half of them are by Savarna authors and less than 15 are by Dalits."

As the protests and criticism grew stronger, Navayana and several upper-caste journalists, activists, and authors retorted that Dalits were angry for the sake of being angry and that "Ambedkar belonged to everyone."[23] They did not seem to understand or empathize with the intensity of the debt several thousand Dalits feel they owe Ambedkar.

While a few groups did ask for a ban on Roy's book, almost all Dalit intellectuals, academics, and writers collectively dismissed that demand. Many posted on Facebook, Twitter, or Dalit-owned outlets to explain that they were only criticizing Roy's introduction to *Annihilation of Caste*, and not asking for the book to be taken off the shelves. Yet, not many mainstream outlets defended or even tried to understand the Dalit side of the argument except for *Live Mint*, which published a thoughtful piece on why Ambedkar did in fact belong to Dalits. Journalist G. Sampath pointed out in his article in *Live Mint* that it was the Dalits and not Savarnas who for decades had kept Ambedkar's legacy alive. And while the upper-caste S. Anand, the publisher of Navayana, and Roy could discuss and write about Ambedkar whenever they wanted, we still lived in a society where Dalits could be assaulted and even killed for even using his name or imagery. What Roy and Anand failed to understand was that Ambedkar was also a source of "spiritual succour and moral support for Dalits whose lives have been questioned on a routine basis," as Sampath noted.[24]

As a lifelong activist, it's not unreasonable to expect that Roy would have read Ambedkar before writing this introduction. When questioned on this, she responded that "unlike many people, including many Dalits," she had at least taken "the trouble to read him." Roy missed the crucial point unlike for her and other upper castes, it's not lack of will or interest but often poverty, illiteracy, and such other scourges of the Dalit condition that have prevented Dalits from reading Ambedkar. In her defense against criticism of the privileged space she occupied, Roy challenged the privilege of Dalit authors themselves. She turned their argument around and asked if Dalit writers were "fighting against Brahmanism or strengthening it."[25]

In all this, it's worth noting that *Annihilation of Caste* has been in print for decades, published by many Dalit and government presses but has largely been unread by upper-caste readers. The fact that it needed an introduction from a celebrity upper-caste author for upper-caste readers to notice it is telling in itself.

It's not that white or upper-caste authors have not written on race or caste. Americans Eleanor Zelliot and Omvedt and French-origin Christophe Jaffrelot have written on and even criticized Ambedkar's ideas, Bhandari upper-caste Dhananjay Keer's biography of Ambedkar published in 1954 is still popular among Dalits, and Pratap Bhanu Mehta's work on him is shared widely on Dalit social media.[26] Almost all of these writers have written with an understanding of their position as outsiders to the Dalit community. However, in the charged political and social setting of our world today, upper-caste authors like Roy will be called out, repeatedly, if they fail to acknowledge their own privileged place in the system. Moreover, no matter how masterful their storytelling and deep their understanding of the subject, for a richer, more authentic narrative, it's the voices of the Dalits themselves that need to be heard.

Apart from representation in the media, one of the biggest reasons why the rest of the country sees Dalits as abused victims living in poverty in the villages of the country is because that's how Indian cinema portrays us on screen. Even the reformist films of the thirties and forties inspired by Ambedkar's ideology and Gandhi's upliftment programs that featured Dalit characters showed their discrimination and abuse but offered no resolution. According to many of these movies, including the massively popular Ashok Kumar and Devika Rani-starrer *Achhut Kanya* (1936), the only way to end discrimination was by killing the Dalit character. Over the decades, as the stories evolved and the mostly upper-caste lead pairs found different scenarios to fall in love, the Dalit character has remained the same. In the 1959 film *Sujata* starring Sunil Dutt and Nutan, the Dalit female lead is just as tortured and abused as the ones from a few decades ago. While she doesn't need to die this time, the filmmakers do make sure that her sacrifices are painful enough for her to be accepted. Later, in art house cinema, filmmakers like Satyajit Ray, Mrinal Sen, and Shyam Benegal focused extensively on the injustices of the caste system.[27] But almost all of their Dalit characters went through intense abuse and trauma to the extent of resembling poverty porn—gory and violent depictions of death and rape—to elicit sympathy.[28] Ray's *Sadgati* (1981) has Om Puri playing Dukhi, a character whose life is filled with such intense gut-wrenching trauma that his name almost falls short to describe his sadness. In the caste-infested societies of our country, where real people often have worse fates than even the most tragic Dalit characters on screen, these depictions are crucial. But in the absence of any other stories on Dalits, these tragic characters become the only way to see and understand us.

Just like Black characters in Hollywood movies, Dalits in Indian movies somehow remain deserving of their abuse and discrimination. In *Lagaan* (2001), the Oscar-nominated film based on an early nineteenth-century cricket match between a team of British officers and Indian farmers, the Dalit bowler was accepted in the team only because he was exceptional. While the rest of the upper-caste team were able-bodied and sufficiently decent at the game, the Dalit bowler was not only handicapped, but because of his disability threw spin curve balls that could rival the most experienced and well-trained cricket players of current times. Without that exceptional ability, Aamir Khan's Bhuvan perhaps would never have considered him for the team. And even with his talent, his story revolves around how other upper-caste players still refused to play with him because of his caste. Somehow a movie made in 2001 still needed a Dalit character to be exceptional to consider him worthy. Arguably, a film based in the 1800s might have no choice but to showcase the extreme discrimination Dalits faced in that time. But by creating him as an awkward teen with no background or traits except his bowling and literally naming him garbage—Kachra—director Ashutosh Gowariker ultimately threw up the same movie stereotypes for Dalits that had existed twenty years before Independence.

The stereotyping of Dalit characters as inferior, pitiable victims is seen in pretty much every language Indian movies are made in. And it goes without saying that the lead characters are almost never anything other than upper caste. In the thousands of movies made in Bollywood in the past few years, almost every popular character that comes to mind is upper caste, with last names like Malhotra, Oberoi,

Chauhan, Pandey, or Singh. In movies released between 2014 and 2015 only six lead characters out of three hundred were not upper-caste Hindus and barely any were Dalits.[29] Even Tamil cinema, which has relatively more non-upper-caste characters, is obsessed with casting extremely fair, typically upper-caste female actors against somewhat darker, hypermasculine male actors. The only movie to buck that trend was Prakash Jha's *Aarakshan* (2011). In his accurate and sympathetic portrayal of reservation, Jha had Saif Ali Khan play a Dalit professor who faces discrimination at his workplace, while Amitabh Bachchan plays a college principal who loses his job for supporting caste-based reservation. While the film had several narrative flaws and abruptly abandoned the reservation plot mid-story, it was among the rare pro-reservation films to come out in recent times.

It's crucial for Dalits to have somewhat realistic if not always positive stories in popular culture.[30] Since most of what we study in school talks about caste as though it only exists in the past, television, cinema, and pop culture shape our opinions about this topic. If Dalits are only seen as victims or undeserving college students, then that will always be the "normal" for non-Dalits watching us. Unless we are also represented on screen as regular people—twenty-something middle-class college kids, forty-something neighbors, Internet-savvy parents, or successful entrepreneurs, just like we are in real life, upper-caste folks might never see us for who we are. Lately, the threat of high-quality content from other countries and even our own Facebook and YouTube channels has since pushed (a part of) Indian cinema to explore original and authentic stories. In the past few years, several filmmakers have managed to create Dalit characters that do more than serve as plot points. Films like *Court* (2014) and *Chauranga* (2016) attempted to show Dalits as real people. But even they shied away from going into what makes us Dalits and how caste actually affects us.

Thankfully, Dalit directors do exist. Nagraj Manjule, Neeraj Ghaywan, and Pa. Ranjith grew up experiencing caste discrimination and they use this experience to tell their stories. Manjule's *Fandry* (2013) and the hugely successful *Sairat* (2016) which even inspired a Karan Johar-directed Hindi remake had layered and nuanced Dalit leads who were neither victims nor "magically" exceptional.[31] *Sairat*'s Parshya was neither Kachra nor Dukhi but a bright teen who is the star of the cricket team. He is not only charming but also doesn't care for traditional gender roles. Parshya sits pillion behind his upper-caste girlfriend and she rescues him when he gets arrested. In Ghaywan's *Masaan*, Deepak looks up his upper-caste girlfriend on Facebook and notices her last name before anything else.[32] The scenes where he worries about his girlfriend's reaction to his caste were among rare moments of recognition for all Dalits. Pa. Ranjith's *Kabali* (2016), on the other hand, moved away from romance and was all-out radical. Ranjith had Rajnikanth, arguably India's biggest superstar actor, playing a Dalit don who casually quotes Ambedkar and reads revolutionary Dalit authors. *Kabali*, named after the caste whose characters usually appear as punch lines in Tamil cinema, is not coy about embracing its Ambedkarite roots either. In fact, the Ambedkar-blue color palette, Rajnikanth's three-piece suits as an obvious nod to the Dalit leader, and having a production crew that was almost entirely Dalit turn the entire movie into an anthem of Dalit pride.[33] Each of these Dalit directors wrote stories that show Dalits as complex people with rich inner lives who eat, breathe, and feel pain in the same way that upper-caste characters have done for decades. Their Dalit characters not only told their different stories well but also helped upper-caste cinemagoers understand why telling them matters.

In other forms of entertainment, too, creators are focusing on Dalit stories. Ginni Mahi, the eighteen-year-old queen of Chamar Pop has turned "Chamar" from a term of abuse into a badge of pride with her music. In the videos of her Punjabi pop songs with titles such as "Danger Chamar" and "Main Fan Babasaheb Di," Ginni flexes her wrists, crosses her arms, and stares into the camera as she sings about being Chamar. Her videos, each of which have millions of YouTube views, have not only turned her into a music celebrity but have also given Dalits a "fight song" against casteism. Along with Mahi's Chamar Pop, Ambedkarite Buddhist Gospel from Mumbai's Dhamma Angels, and Thenmozhi Soundararajan's Dalit Blues, Dalit artists have started to create art that tells our stories. As more Dalit creators join them, there is some hope that we can move beyond the "single story" that the upper castes have written for us so far.

CHAPTER 13

SILICON VALLEY, MODEL MINORITY, AND THE MYTH OF CASTE-LESSNESS

They came, they saw, they conquered. That's how most Indian Americans think of their remarkable success in Silicon Valley. Indian Americans comprise around 1 percent[1] of the total United States population and close to 6 percent[2] of the total Silicon Valley workforce. In 1999, just before the burst of the dot-com bubble, an unprecedented study by the University of California, Berkeley, revealed that between 1980 and 1998, Indian immigrants founded 7 percent of Silicon Valley startups.[3] In 2007, an updated survey confirmed that this number had shot up by nearly 100 percent—India-born entrepreneurs founded 13.4 percent of the Valley's startups and 6.5 percent of the total startups nationwide,[4] the highest among any immigrant group. A more recent claim by India's current finance minister, Nirmala Sitharaman, from 2022, states that this number might be closer to a whopping 25 percent of Silicon Valley startups having Indian-origin founders,[5] although that might be due for a fact-check.

A number of articles, most written by Indians, credit India's unique pastiche of living conditions as the reason behind this remarkable success. A piece in the *Los Angeles Times* suggests that Alphabet (Google's parent company) CEO Sundar Pichai and Microsoft head Satya Nadella are successful because they belong to a generation that's raised on "humility, close-knit family ties and respect for all walks of life."[6] "Indians learn to be resilient, battle endless obstacles, and make the most of what they have," outlines a piece in *Fortune*.[7] The author hints at their innate "entrepreneurship," "creativity," and "resourcefulness" as the likely reasons Indian Americans successfully make it out of a "land of more than a billion people, most of whom are hampered by rampant corruption, weak infrastructure, and limited opportunities, [where] it takes a lot to simply survive, let alone to get ahead,"[8] effectively painting a picture of a debilitated socialist economy, which these tycoons-in-making had the foresight to "escape from," before landing in the outstretched arms of a "first world" savior with its permissive capitalist freedoms—like refugees of a different breed. (Ajantha Subramaniam also writes about this in *The Caste of Merit*: "Several characterized the India they left behind as one where the IITs were islands of possibility within a sea of socialist constraint. Compared to India, the United States for them is a capitalist land of opportunity where merit finds its due. Nevertheless, it, too, is not a uniform cartography.") Meanwhile, *Forbes* chalks it up to their English language skills and science education, and a knack for being frugal.[9]

Rarely, however, do any such pieces mention the extremely powerful, tight-knit, and dependable networks that have shored up connections between India and the United States, between fresh graduates from India's engineering colleges and postgraduate programs there, and between job seekers and American tech companies for over forty years. Nor do they reveal how these networks, almost always, are overwhelmingly woven around the exclusion of those who belong to a "lower" or oppressed caste. Ajantha Subramanian, a professor of anthropology and South Asian studies at Harvard University, explains in detail in her book *The Caste of Merit* just how extensively these networks functioned as an "upper"-caste-only club, where graduates from India's prestigious Indian Institutes of Technology (IITs) operated as a collective to coordinately ensure that their applications to American colleges in the early nineties were successful, and that almost everyone who applied got a seat, if not at their first choice, then at least at a "safety school."[10] "That was one of the reasons why the IITs had a much higher percentage of students going abroad—not because the universities preferred them. It was the network. It was the way the IIT students coordinated amongst themselves," recalled one of the graduates of the IIT–Madras 1992 batch that Subramanian interviewed.[11] In days predating the Internet, students would actively encourage their "juniors," going as far as drawing up manuals and giving them "inside information" to apply to the same university as them. "It wasn't totally organized but it was more in these informal ways that the very powerful IIT alumni network worked," observed another IIT graduate from 1990, who moved to the United States for a graduate degree at MIT.[12]

Immigrant networks between international students that are used to exchange information to facilitate admissions into foreign universities are neither new nor unique. But these IIT networks stood out for an exceptional trait: their sense of superiority undergirded by their status of being "upper" caste.[13] "IITians think they're born intellectually superior, that other castes just don't have the ability to compete with us," the '92 IIT–Madras graduate told Subramanian. "I think some of the same biases that we carry in IIT are even more reinforced here because in the U.S. we don't even get to see other kinds of students. The only students you see from India are pretty much ninety-nine percent upper caste. IIT itself is a filtering mechanism. Migration to the U.S. is one more level of filtering," he continued.[14] While the Indian diaspora reflected in Silicon Valley includes graduates from other Indian universities, Subramanian asserts that IIT graduates have worked especially hard at elevating their visibility and inventing a brand out of their university system, one that clearly stonewalls and excludes not only Dalits and OBCs but sometimes even "upper"-caste graduates from other universities. Subramanian explains that IIT graduates she interviewed from Harvard, Duke, MIT, and Stanford universities were "explicit about their goal of admitting and hiring their own." (The announcement of Satya Nadella—unlike Sundar Pichai and Parag Agarwal, he is not from an IIT—as Microsoft CEO sparked a fierce debate on the Indian Internet, with many questioning the American tech firm's decision to choose "a non IIT-ian" to lead the company).[15]

The "upper"-caste IIT network has worked hard for decades to position and elevate its cohorts as among the best and brightest minds of the world (articles in the early 2000s casually described IITs as harder to get into than Harvard, MIT, and Stanford universities combined[16]) while simultaneously gatekeeping Dalit and Adivasi workers, often and especially if they too belonged to an IIT. Dalit graduates from IITs are routinely harassed about their ranks in the institute's entrance exams, mostly as a way to suss out whether they availed reservation, India's large-scale affirmative action program, and therefore, belong to a "lower" caste. Once discovered, they are actively discriminated against and often told how they don't belong in these spaces. Case in point, the now-famous Cisco case where a Dalit engineer was withheld from promotions and targeted for his "lower" caste origins, despite his having attended an IIT like his Brahmin managers.[17] However, today the IIT "upper"-caste network is more than a listserv about which American universities are ripe for attending. Now, it has coalesced and expanded into a much larger "upper"-caste identity that can also dictate hiring within American tech companies and decide the fate of South Asian entrepreneurial hopefuls trying to make it big within Silicon Valley. "The IIT network has become more powerful than the HBS [Harvard Business School] network. IITians help each other like I have never seen in any other network," Subramanian quotes another prominent Indian American entrepreneur as saying.[18]

The Indus Entrepreneurs (TiE) hosts a gathering that is currently billed as the world's largest tech conference "designed by Silicon Valley leaders for entrepreneurs, executives, and investors," and the organization has a footprint of sixty-one chapters in fourteen countries.[19] It was started as a networking group for South Asian tech entrepreneurs in 1992 by several former IIT graduates, including some who were by then among the biggest and most recognizable names in Silicon Valley: Suhas Patil, the founder of an early semiconductor company, Cirrus Logic; Prabhu Goel, who founded Gateway Design Automation; and Kanwal Rekhi, who was the first Indian American CEO to take his venture-backed company public on the Nasdaq stock exchange.[20] Subramanian notes that while Silicon Valley success was not limited to IIT graduates, they "made up some of the early successes." Because the TiE founders had faced a fair amount of resistance while setting up their companies in the eighties, they decided to come together with other Indian founders to create an organization that would help newer entrepreneurs with advice, connections, and even capital. In an interview with Subramanian in *The Caste of Merit*, one of TiE's early founders openly admitted to being "biased towards IITians"[21] in the practice of company founders and angel investors selecting a limited number of entrepreneurs, who, as Subramanian notes, "typically were IITians," to back. TiE's tendency to pick the "upper"-caste IIT candidates over the rest might be less egregious if TiE weren't also the biggest South Asian networking organization in Silicon Valley, playing a massive role in the current success and visibility of Indian American entrepreneurs.

In the thirty years since its inception, TiE is reported to have created a value of over a trillion dollars in the startup ecosystem.[22] A 2012 study discovered that Indian American founders had set up nearly 15.5 percent of all startups in Silicon Valley, a proportion higher than that of any other immigrant community. Many of them are likely funded by TiE and its affiliates.[23] According to AnnaLee Saxenian, the former dean of Berkeley's School of Information who was among the first researchers to study Indian Americans in Silicon Valley, TiE along with another group, Silicon Valley Indian Professionals Association (SIPA), helped "break the glass ceiling" for Indian entrepreneurs and established their credibility in the region. She also notes how the groups were, implicitly if not otherwise, based around caste. Saxenian quotes Vinod Khosla, a Silicon Valley heavyweight from IIT–Delhi and the founder of Sun Microsystems, describing how "ethnic networks" (often a code for caste) play a major role in who gets their foot through this door.[24] "People talk to each other . . . they suggest other people they know, who are likely to be of the same ethnicity," Saxenian notes in a 1999 paper.[25] Meanwhile, Satish Gupta, another early TiE member, is less discerning. "Networks work primarily with trust . . . [which] has to do with the believability of the person, body language, mannerisms, behavior, cultural background, . . . caste may play a role, financial status may play a role," he declared.

TiE's casteist leanings hardly come as a surprise, especially when its founders have spent years trying to deregulate IITs and repeal the reservation policy, which is often the only chance for low-income Dalit and Adivasi students to enter these institutes.[26] In 2001, TiE's cofounder Kanwal Rekhi told the *Times of India* that he was "completely against [. . .] caste-based reservation," in a piece titled "Reservation Is Useless."[27] Subramanian, who uses aliases in her interviews, quotes a suspiciously similar-sounding former TiE founder, who also was the first Indian American CEO to take his company to Nasdaq, saying "Reservations take us back to socialism."[28] But one doesn't have to go far to discover how most Indian American networking groups, including TiE, openly champion casteist rhetoric. The Ambedkar King Study Circle (AKSC), a US-based Dalit group, collected several testimonies from Dalit tech workers that point to the discrimination they have experienced in these spaces. "In a TiEcon Bay Area meet attended by 20,000 people, a VC's announced 'All Tambrams [Tamil Brahmins] in the house make some noise,'" reads a tweet by AKSC, quoting a California-based Dalit worker who was present.[29] TiE didn't respond to a comment about its elevating "upper"-caste groups over others.

Caste in American tech spaces often shows up as bald and brazen discrimination, but mostly it works as a system of exclusion, always present but rarely seen to the naked eye. As a system of exclusion, it is invisible, however, it is very effective in perpetuating discrimination. "Upper"-caste networks, whether made of IIT graduates or otherwise, actively shut out Dalits, Adivasis, and often even "lower" caste OBCs (Other Backward Castes that are not considered untouchable) from access to information, opportunities, and even job listings. The networks that helped alumni access college applications and insider information also carried into tech companies that were wooing Indian tech graduates to join them. Facing a massive shortfall of tech workers in the late nineties, the US allowed an increasing influx of highly coveted Indian tech graduates, who had headhunters, dubbed as "body shoppers," trailing them all the way to India.[30] Needless to say, the body shoppers were likely hitting up the already visible and successful Indian Americans, who were almost always "upper" caste and more often than not from an IIT.

"Given the focus on 'merit' based technical education from the IITs and other prestigious Indian institutions in hiring practices in the US, you are correct in assuming that US corporations have attracted the privileged (upper) castes. The privileged caste employees then hire other privileged caste employees," affirms Marilyn Fernandez, professor emerita at Santa Clara University in California, who has expertise in researching caste in the IT sector.[31] "Given that Americans (white and other non-Indians) do not know much about caste relations, particularly the insidious kinds, they often defer to their senior Indian colleagues for judgement on the merits of lower-caste applicants or employees. The privileged caste members use names, location of birth, education, communities as easy, even if discriminatory, filters to keep the oppressed castes out of jobs, promotions, etc.," she says in an interview with the Indian magazine *Open*.[32] This bias-infused hiring evidently creates a chain-link of "upper"-caste IIT graduates to work in the US. "When Vijay Vashee joined Microsoft in 1982, he was just one of two Indians at the 160-person company. It added several more recruits from India, mostly IITians, over the years," reads a piece from 2014 somewhat glibly titled "Indian Americans Will Rule Silicon Valley; They Help Each Other Regardless of Caste or Religion."[33]

Connections that show up as favorable reviews, insider tips, promotions, and better opportunities in the workplace are forged over food, parties, and temple visits outside of it. In her 2002 follow up study, Saxenian describes how Indian Americans socialize over dinner, and at other family-oriented events where support is also provided for technical and professional advancements.[34] Ajantha Subramanian, in *The Caste of Merit*, quotes a Tamil Brahmin IIT graduate from the sixties, who says, "My closest friends are IITians: I socialize with them, their families, I hike with them, we help each other's kids in their professional careers. My business partners in all my startups are IITians."[35] These spaces of socialization, be they familial, religious, or communal, are also notoriously caste coded; invitations could be rescinded over matters as small as eating meat (Brahmins and other "upper" castes are often vegetarian) or as large as not celebrating traditional Hindu festivals, like Holi and Diwali. In other words, when a Dalit person's "lower" caste origins are discovered, they are ostracized and abandoned, with no access to crucial networks of support.

Studies often point to Indian tech spaces adopting subtle Brahminical norms, like vegetarianism, in a way that goes beyond a preference for not eating meat and instead acts as an exclusionary tactic, segregating groups from "lower" castes.[36] Creating barriers for Dalits and Adivasis to thrive at their "vegetarian-only" team lunches and weekend picnics with "upper"-caste colleagues might seem discriminatory, but still fairly benign, until events congeal into hardened caste-specific communities, where those outside of the caste cannot participate. Many such communities exist not only in Silicon Valley but all across the United States. For instance, Brahmin Samaj of North America (BSNA), a caste-based group whose entry is restricted to Brahmins (the highest caste in the system), has been written about extensively and covered by publications like the *New York Times*, which problematically likened Brahmins to the original Pilgrim descendants.[37] "Just as descendants of the Pilgrims use the Mayflower Society as a social outlet to mingle with people of congenial backgrounds, a few castes have formed societies like the Brahmin Samaj of North America, where meditation and yoga are practiced and caste traditions like vegetarianism and periodic fasting are explained to the young," reported an uncritical yet widely circulated article published in the *New York Times* in 2004.[38] The truth, however, is much less varnished and far more treacherous.

The Brahmin Samaj of North America, which was formed in Boston in 1994, does more than provide a space for Brahmins to congregate.[39] By limiting its membership to the highest Indian castes (the website says for "Brahmins only"), it not only excludes members of every other caste, including Dalits, but also solidifies the segregation that is necessary for the caste system to thrive. In addition to hosting community gatherings, BSNA has a networking section, where fellow Brahmins (who form a large chunk of the Indian American population but represent only 4 percent in India[40]) can connect with other Brahmins and help advance their careers, in tech and beyond, effectively securing the collective status and visibility of their high caste in the United States. Although the website makes a bold attempt at saving its own hide by mentioning that "BSNA strongly disapproves the evils of the Hindu caste system," likely as a response to the growing anti-caste resistance in the United States, it also brazenly lists matrimony among Brahmins as one of its key missions.[41] In his 1916 Columbia University thesis on caste, Dalit iconoclast and trailblazing civil rights leader Dr. B. R. Ambedkar called out endogamy (the practice of marrying within one's own caste) as one of the principal ways of maintaining and propagating the caste system.[42] Not only BSNA but dozens of caste groups actively engage in the practice in the United States. BSNA has chapters in eighteen American states, out of which two are in New York and four in California, and there is one chapter specifically dedicated to the Silicon Valley Bay Area.[43]

Agrawals of Washington, a Seattle-based caste group for Agrawals (members of various business castes), declares itself made up of the descendants of Maharaja Agrasen and provides a list of gotras (subcastes) a person must belong to, to become a member.[44] "If we are unable to ascertain your connections to Washington state and/or having an Agrawal heritage based on the information provided, your request 'will' be rejected," states its website. Like BSNA, it too focuses on matrimony and professional networking among members of its own caste. In Washington State, where the population of South Asian Americans is over 167,000, a majority of whom work in Seattle's tech companies, caste-based professional networking points to an inherent caste bias in hiring practices, which is especially exclusionary for Dalits, Adivasis, and "lower" castes.[45] In 2023, the city of Seattle passed a law banning discrimination based on caste and cited the presence of caste-based groups to point out how caste works within Indian communities.[46] Similar warnings of exclusion are pasted over the websites of several other caste-based groups, many of which, like the Agrawal Samaj Dallas Fort Worth (ASDFW), actively prohibit the members from posting any evidence of its existence on social media.[47] "ASDFW discourages public posting of event photos on social media networks, except on the private ASDFW Facebook group," reads its website, making it that much harder to discover the presence of such groups unless a member of the community invites you.[48] After weeks of research, I was able to ascertain that in the United States there are at least twenty different groups catering to different castes.

Indian Americans in the US are considered a "model minority." They are the second-largest immigrant group, with incomes higher than any other Asian American populations—almost double that of the national average (according to the Migration Policy Institute). Eighty percent of Indians in the US are college graduates, and they are more likely to be proficient in English compared to other foreign-born populations. They are CEOs, entrepreneurs, politicians, academics, and vice presidents. They are also casteless, race agnostic, and a "meritorious" community who pulled themselves up entirely by their own bootstraps, minting their success out of nothing, without any "help" or "charity." Or so we would have you think. Professor Ajantha Subramanian describes this branding of Indian Americans as a result of years of hard work by Indian Americans themselves, especially alumni from the IITs in the more recent decades. As we have seen in the previous chapters, during the centuries of British rule, the "upper"-caste minority fashioned themselves into de facto managers of the nation. When this population began to migrate out of India, especially into the United States as early as the 1880s, their sleight of hand and obfuscation of caste markers created a notion that they were also leaving caste behind.

This became even more significant starting in 1965, when the US Immigration and Nationality Act allowed more Indians to move to the US.[49] Almost all of them were "upper" caste, with the exception of 2 to 3 percent of migrants being Dalits and Adivasis.[50] Among these new migrants, the largest group were IIT graduates, thanks to the Cold War era policies of the United States that favored "scientists, engineers and businesspeople" as immigrants. According to Subramanian, this reinforced the links between their alleged "merit" and their higher caste, while ensuring its muted visibility to anyone unfamiliar with the intricate workings of this dense and rigid system. That almost all members of the Indian American diaspora at the time were "upper" caste helped conceal the existence and stratifications of different castes, even as, clearly, caste-based gatherings were taking place long before they segmented into formal groups in the late eighties and early nineties. The aggressive branding of the IITs as "temples of merit" largely untouched by the "undeserving" and "unmeritorious" "lower" castes, while also being eternal fountainheads of geniuses who were changing tech, Silicon Valley, and, by extension, America, was envisioned by the IIT networks who were working overtime to create this image. Subramaniam describes the deliberate and premeditated process through which the building of this brand unfolded in multiple stages. From asking successful graduates to prominently highlight their IIT college in their résumés, consolidating an expansive pan-IIT kinship to bring the disparate colleges under a single umbrella, to, finally, cementing these talking points as accepted truisms through news pieces like a *60 Minutes* segment by Lesley Stahl on CBS, Silicon Valley IITians ensured that America bought the story they were selling.[51]

The IIT success story of the early 2000s, however, purposefully left out caste, even as everything about it was driven by the order of birth and the status it granted people. Focusing on reservations, obsessing over merit, and promoting a narrow idea of deservedness while simultaneously denying the existence of caste, simply because they refused to call it by that name, allowed the "upper"-caste Indian American diaspora members to claim caste-lessness. In the *60 Minutes* episode, from 2003—which Subramanian asserts became the tipping point for the popular recognition of IITs in the United States—Lesley Stahl travels to India to report directly from IIT–Bombay. Her voiceover tells us how getting into the quiet and uncrowded gates of this institution, away from the "slums, chaos and congestion of Bombay," is the "fervent dream of every schoolboy." She talks about the intensely competitive exam and how only less than 2 percent of those who apply get accepted each year, compared to the inflated 10 percent acceptance rate at Harvard. But the final salvo that ossifies IITs as the fecund terrain for "upper"-caste merit comes when Stahl states, "Unlike so many other institutions in India, they [IIT students] all know they're here because they deserve to be here." Compared to the other Indian schools and universities where Dalits and Adivasi students undeservedly occupied seats that "didn't belong to them" was, however, left unsaid. (Subramanian notes that, until 2006, IITs were mostly unaffected by India's reservation policies.)

The *60 Minutes* segment opened the floodgates to more media coverage solidifying the claim of IITians as being the flagbearers of "upper"-caste merit, while allowing them to dismiss any discussions of caste rights as a "parochial—even regressive—endeavor," notes Subramanian. *Forbes*, the *Wall Street Journal*, *Time*, and *Business Week* came out with their own Indian-merit-asserting pieces.[52] CNN published a lengthy profile of venture capitalist and noted anti-reservationist Kanwal Rekhi titled "The Hidden Geniuses of Tech Revolution," identifying him as "Don Corleone who turned Gandhi," likely due to his propensity to advocate for deregulation of the socialist-leaning Indian economy, often at the cost of the most marginalized and vulnerable Indians, including Dalits and Adivasis.[53] Two decades later, this revisionist media history has given way to an elevated if not entirely new parable: Indian American CEOs rise to the top because they are just *that good*. No explanation necessary. Indians in Silicon Valley are majority "upper"-caste caste. They are also mostly men. It is hardly a coincidence that this conversation centers on Indian "upper"-caste men who make up a massive chunk of Indian Americans in tech. Historically, Indian women have been severely underrepresented in tech spaces, with their enrollment in the IITs only now reaching 20 percent,[54] while women make up barely 30 percent[55] of the total workforce in Indian tech industries. Even though this is higher than the overall representation of women in tech in the US, these numbers hardly reflect the reality of Indian American female tech workers. While female Indian workers and entrepreneurs might have heightened visibility in tech spaces—especially when compared to Black and Latina women, who, out of the total 26.7 percent[56] of positions held by women in tech, make up only 3 percent and 2 percent respectively[57]—their numbers are still miniscule, especially when compared to Indian men. Only four people on *Forbes* magazine's latest "Top 50 Women in Tech" list[58] were of Indian origin, while almost 93 percent of current holders of H-4 dependent visas are South Asian women,[59] indicating that many Indian female tech workers who move to the United States with their male spouses are forced to sit out of the workforce due to immigration restrictions.

However, when it comes to practicing exclusion and discrimination against Dalits and Adivasis on the basis of caste, gender makes no difference. As we have seen in earlier chapters, casteism is espoused as easily by women as it is by men. "Upper"-caste women led the charge against reservation in 1990 and 2006, the two big events in India's affirmative action history, and are ritualistic flagbearers for practicing endogamy both in India and the United States. Ajantha Subramanian maintains that among the IIT graduates she interviewed for her book *The Caste of Merit*, the women students, alumni, and faculty held the same discriminatory views on caste as their male counterparts. Indian women in US tech might not have the power in numbers to execute the caste-based discrimination and exclusion Indian men practice. But as evident from the board members and founding committees of caste-based communities, where they are abundantly represented, "upper"-caste women certainly fortify these segregations in spaces of networking and socialization outside the workplace.

If the construction of the "model minority" myth for Indian Americans rides on the back of their alleged caste-lessness, then their anti-Blackness, or at least a deliberate effort to separate themselves from marginalized Black Americans and other "less desirable" Indian immigrants, has also played a massive part in its edifice. Even as Indian

Americans prefer to assert their model behavior by touting their selectively handpicked IT professionals, tech workers, and entrepreneurs, forgotten is the swelling population of undocumented Indians, which according to the Migration Policy Institute as of 2019 is approximately 553,000[60] (5 percent) of the estimated 11 million unauthorized immigrants in the United States. Nor included are the working-class Indians,[61] some of whom moved to the United States in the late 1800s and continue to form a significant population of Indians, especially in areas like New York City and Philadelphia, and parts of California. Bengali Muslim peddlers and Punjabis from rural immigrant communities in the nineteenth century experienced and responded differently to discrimination from the largely "upper"-caste educated professionals during the time and were among the most targeted by the "yellow peril" racist American policies of that era. "While those who came to work the land, work in lumberyards, or work on the railroads bore the brunt of physical attacks, educated professionals who did not confront such direct hostility began crafting a racial politics that would distinguish them from their poorer compatriots, from other nonwhite immigrants, and from Black Americans," notes Subramanian.[62]

The notorious case of Bhagat Singh Thind—an Indian immigrant who, in 1923, argued to be considered white, since he was a "high caste Aryan full of Indian blood"—is a remarkable insight into the period's eugenics-flavored "upper"-caste ideology, by which several "upper"-caste Indians considered themselves genetically superior to Dalits and Adivasis, and instead more aligned with white Caucasians.[63] As Thind lost the case (ultimately leading to scores of Indians having their citizenships neutralized by 1926), equating "upper" casteness to whiteness became a losing strategy.[64] However, by the 1960s, around the second big wave of Indian "upper"-caste immigration, identifying as "not Black" was quickly becoming a go-to for Indian Americans. "There was a common thread of understanding that emerged: the path to social and financial security was to avoid the taint of blackness. While professional Indians no longer did so through recourse to whiteness, as had earlier elite migrants, they now leveraged class, nationality, and, most importantly, educational achievement, to fashion themselves as members of a model minority," writes Subramanian in *The Caste of Merit*.[65]

Regardless, Indian Americans who moved to the US over the last century were treated with racism, with many of them still considered "Black" regardless of their effortful delineations. During her interviews with IIT graduates from the sixties, Subramanian discovered the tactics which several immigrant Indians employed to distinguish themselves as "not black," especially in the South, which was still in its Jim Crow era. Men started wearing a turban, whether or not they wore one back home in India, while women were encouraged to wear a sari to identify themselves as distinctly Indian. "I got the impression that the South was embarrassed to be mistreating foreign visitors," one of the interviewees told Subramanian. "They had no problem discriminating against U.S. blacks, but they went to lengths to ensure that we were fine." This disposition, although prevalent in the "upper"-caste Indian immigrant professionals of the time, more or less ignored the efforts of the Black civil rights movement that, after decades of exclusion, made Indian immigrants' reentry in the US possible with the changes in the 1965 US immigration laws.

"Immigrants from India, armed with degrees, arrived after the height of the civil-rights movement, and benefited from a struggle that they had not participated in or even witnessed. They made their way not only to cities but to suburbs, and broadly speaking were accepted more easily than other nonwhite groups have been," reads an *Atlantic* piece titled "The Truth Behind Indian American Exceptionalism."[66] Mindsets towards those who were "lower" than them on the hierarchy of caste among "upper"-caste Indian Americans easily transferred to those who they saw as now being "lower" on the hierarchy of race. By not treating Indian "foreigners" with the same disdain and disgust they did Black folks who had helped build their country, white Southerners, among others, inscribed a racial hierarchy, where Indians—neither the highest but not the lowest either—found themselves squarely in the middle. This new racial marker perfectly aligned with the self-ordained myths of "upper"-caste Indian tech graduates who, according to Subramanian, already equated their middle-class identity with a constructed idea of "upper"-caste merit, and further propelled this notion leading them to define themselves as different if not "better" than Black Americans. In her interview with the famous angel investor who launched the first Indian American company on

Nasdaq, Subramanian finds him saying that Indians in Silicon Valley were "seen differently, as people who engaged in self-help, not asking for handouts," echoing an anti-welfarist rhetoric targeted against Black and Brown Americans that is also often used against Dalits and Adivasis who avail reservations.[67]

The model minority ideal, created by "upper"-caste Indians with more than a little help from white Americans who first coined the term to describe Japanese immigrants, suffocates all other modes of existence and helps Indian Americans deny the existence of caste-based distinctions in the United States.[68] There has been a long history of Black and South Asian solidarity, including the relationship between Ambedkar and W. E. B. Du Bois; the Dalit Panther Party; the early relationships between Black civil rights leaders and the Gandhian movement (including Martin Luther King and Bayard Rustin);[69] and the rich tapestry of Bengali Muslim and Punjabi immigrants who settled in New York's East Harlem and in Baltimore, New Orleans, and Detroit, and married and partnered with Black and Caribbean women since the early 1900s. Yet, they are rarely heard, recounted, or remembered. "It was the more prosperous sector of South Asians, the post-1965 professionals, who had the means to represent the community as a whole, so it was their image that came to dominate the image of South Asian-Americans," says documentary filmmaker, historian, and MIT professor Vivek Bald, who painstakingly traced the narratives of Bengali immigrants in Bengali Harlem and the lost histories of South Asian America.[70]

The lid has been held tight for too long. Breaking free from this mold will allow the Indian American community to not only reckon with their denial of caste but also allow more vulnerable members, Dalit, Adivasi, and otherwise, to get the attention, care, and justice they deserve. Caste has successfully escaped our attention for far too long, not in small part as a result of the concerted efforts by the Indian American "upper"-caste majority who have willfully erased, denied, and blurred its existence while continuing to benefit from the privileges their higher status provides them. It's time to stop accepting wafer-thin excuses on why we should not pay greater attention to this damaging segregation and discrimination of people on the basis of their birth. And it's time to start rethinking our models.

CHAPTER 14

THE RECKONING OF CASTE IN TECH

The history of caste in the United States is written in two parts: BC (Before Cisco case) and AC (After Cisco case). Starting from the 1700s, when immigrants from the Indian subcontinent first came to this country, until 2020, caste as it existed among South Asians was coded as an "ancient" relic from a remote country that sometimes made the headlines but was often dismissed as an intracommunity microdynamic not especially relevant to everyday Americans. However, a single case of workplace discrimination changed that when California's Department of Fair Employment and Housing sued Silicon Valley giant and $51.6 billion company Cisco Systems for failing to prevent discrimination against its Dalit employee by dominant-caste Brahmin managers.[1] This was different from earlier cases of discrimination of "lower" caste individuals by dominant-caste perpetrators, like the stomach-churning case of Lakireddy Bali Reddy, who was arrested in the year 2000 for sexual slavery and human trafficking of Dalit girls—some of them as young as nine years old—from the state of Andhra Pradesh in India.

Reddy, one of Berkeley's richest landlords, who owned close to a thousand properties in the city and was known for his extensive philanthropy, exploited and enslaved young Dalit girls after bringing them over from his home state in India on false pretenses of employment.[2] He forced them into "sexual servitude" and into cleaning and maintenance of his restaurants and rental properties. The case broke in November 1999, when a seventeen-year-old girl, Chanti Pratipatti, died from carbon monoxide poisoning at one of his apartments.[3] This led directly to California's first law setting higher criminal penalties for human trafficking and grabbed national headlines for months, as American reporters descended into Velvadam, his native village in Andhra Pradesh, to cover the story. However, lost in this conversation were the brutal dynamics of caste that not only allowed the abuse of Dalit girls to continue for close to fourteen years (between 1986 and 2000), but also led to the inhabitants of Velvadam defending Reddy even after the abuse was discovered.

The 2020 case, however, was another story. Caste awareness, thanks to the collective effort of Dalit organizations over the last several decades, was at an all-time high when the news broke that a Dalit engineer had taken his Brahmin managers to court for denying him professional opportunities, promotions, and bonuses, simply for being from a "lower" caste. Earlier, the violent outcomes of these incidents held greater focus, while caste, which perpetuated the imbalances in power that allowed this violence to happen (like in Bali Reddy's episode) was pushed to the sidelines. But with caste at the heart of this high-profile case, it became impossible to ignore. Unlike in the past, this time caste *was* the conversation, and it was happening at the center of Silicon Valley, exposed to the world. Finally the stories of marginalization against Dalits, Adivasis, and lower-caste people in the US began to cascade. After the news of the Cisco case broke, reports emerged that a similar lawsuit had been filed by a former employee against HCL America, the US unit of the Indian IT giant HCL Technologies, for wrongful caste-based termination.[4] Although the HCL lawsuit was filed three months earlier, in March 2020, it was recognized widely only after the Cisco case attracted global attention. Soon after, a group of thirty Dalit women engineers anonymously issued a collective statement in the *Washington Post* about how dominant-caste "boys clubs" operate in Silicon Valley and influence hiring, referrals, and peer-review processes in their workplaces; the group called working under Indian managers a "living hell."[5] The testimony revealed a range of treatment, from subtle to heinous—they reported managers leaving them out of important meetings, underestimating their skills, and overlooking valid Dalit candidates in order to hire their "caste friends," and even harassing employees sexually.

Since the summer of 2020, which also saw a parallel racial uprising with the George Floyd protests, countless incidents of harassment and discrimination of Dalit employees in tech workspaces have come to light. However, none of the complaints have been officially registered, mainly due to the enormously complex and taxing process of dealing with the American legal system, especially as an immigrant, but also because of the condition of forced anonymity that comes as a given with being Dalit in America. The Dalit engineer who took his multibillion-dollar corporate employer, Cisco, to court showed immense fortitude and resolve, seemingly to the detriment of his personal safety, potential employment, and well-being. But that singular act of courage remains rare precisely because of the exceptional circumstances that are required to hold caste offenders accountable. For John Doe of the Cisco case, keeping his identity from being made public during the trial was a vital safety measure. But ironically for Dalits—including for the Cisco Dalit engineer who experienced it from his Brahmin colleagues—in the United States, having caste identity stripped bare without consent is an extraordinary form of violence that has emerged as a leading form of caste discrimination.

A significant number of Dalits in the US, especially those who work in tech, hide their caste origins, and they live with the fear of being found out. Of the Dalit engineer from the Cisco case, the thirty women Dalit engineers who released their statement, the Dalits who have come forward in the multiple media stories that have been published since, and the dozens of Dalit folks I have interviewed in the past few years, none (with few exceptions) have felt safe to assert their caste—and in turn their political identity or religion—or to openly talk about the discrimination they have experienced during their time in the United States. It is undeniable that this forced anonymity among Dalits exists as a response to a chilling culture of fear, shame, and bullying that has covertly emerged in American tech spaces. The threat of being "discovered" or, even worse, "outed" by a dominant-caste colleague, and subsequently subjected to unfair assessments, unwarranted negative feedback, blocked promotions, and loss of employment—which for Dalit immigrants can easily turn into a loss of a work visa—forces Dalit tech workers into self-imposed silence around their cultural and religious expressions. Unencumbered by laws or even a basic wider understanding of caste to rein them in, dominant-caste Indian tech workers openly discriminate against colleagues they perceive as a threat to their cultural and caste order.

Maya Kamble, who moved to the United States over two decades ago and works for a FAANG company (the industry-wide acronym for Facebook, Apple, Amazon, Netflix, and Google), has been careful throughout her career to not reveal her lower caste.[6] Yet while at a previous company, an Indian dominant-caste manager discovered her caste origins through the educational videos for Dalit kids that she had posted on YouTube. Nothing was said directly, no caste slurs were exchanged. "Looks like you're a very popular person. I saw your videos," the manager said to Kamble, before he started ignoring all her suggestions and behaving "like I did not exist in meetings," as she told me over the phone in the summer of 2022. "It was so apparent that my colleagues started to notice, and they started to back me up in these conversations because my suggestions were valid," she continued. The stonewalling came to a head when Kamble offered to participate in a project the manager was heading, and he bluntly refused. "No, no, no. I don't even want you to touch this project because you're ill-fated. You, you're ill-fated," she told me, recollecting the incident and noting how instead of communicating in English, he had used a Hindi word, which is a widely recognized casteist slur in India: *manhoos*.

Loosely translated to "someone whose shadow/touch can bring bad luck," this insult, which is casually used to invoke Dalits and their place in the caste hierarchy, would likely slip through the cracks for most non-South Asians and even some Indians who are not versed in specific cultural cues. But Kamble knew what was happening, and that it was only going to get worse. "I went in a shock; I didn't know how to . . . what to tell and what to expect . . . I could never imagine that this is the way caste could manifest after me. You know, [I came] all the way from India to . . . make my whole career here," she shared. Kamble recalled there were other Indian colleagues at the meeting who called out the manager's behavior and who took the matter seriously when the dominant-caste manager tried to pass it off as a joke. Kamble considered reporting it, but in the absence of laws she decided it wasn't worth risking her job and losing the H-1B visa. When she finally confronted him, he told her, "I'm sorry if you felt hurt, it was just a joke." Kamble left that job soon after. After moving to a new position at one of the FAANG companies, she said she wished that big tech companies would set a precedent by implementing caste protections, which would force smaller companies to follow them.

A few months after our conversation, reports emerged that Apple had become the first big tech company to include caste protections in its official policy, and that it had added trainings for its staff that mentioned caste.[7] Despite some minor changes in their global policies (Amazon amended its supply chain standards and global human rights principles to add caste protections;[8] IBM added caste trainings for Indian managers) none of the other major tech companies have caste in their official policies. Before Kamble left her previous company, she removed the videos from YouTube to prevent a repeat of the incident. "For me, the question is, do I want to have a toxic environment near me, or do I want to grow in my career? You know, do I want to work eight hours being in a toxic environment or not? That's the question," she told me. While she believes that her colleagues at her current company don't know her caste, it's only a matter of time before they find out. At the smaller company where she worked, other dominant-caste colleagues would invite her for Hindu religious ceremonies, temple visits, and festivals like Diwali. As a Buddhist, she did not feel the need to accept their invites, but she didn't want to turn them down either. "I come from a Buddhist background and Buddhist is also a red flag," she said about the religion, which continues to be a haven for many Dalits, at the behest of Dr. B. R. Ambedkar, who adopted Buddhism in 1956.[9] After months of being questioned for not showing up, Kamble finally relented and revealed her religion, and she immediately noticed the exclusion beginning. "The lunch conversations that we used to have, the desk conversations or the kitchen conversations that we used to have at the office, they all were reduced. So, you're alienated every time and not just by your manager but also by other colleagues," she said. Now Kamble is careful about separating her private life from her work and has no intention of revealing her caste any time soon. "The main reason why I hide is because [if they know it] . . . I'm not [going to be] able to thrive at my workplace, rather . . . I'm just surviving every single day, . . . I don't want that kind of life."

The fear of dominant-caste managers sabotaging their careers is a common theme among Dalit tech workers, and most find themselves getting their due and thriving only when the people they are reporting to are "not Indian." In the statement that the Dalit women engineers gave to the *Washington Post*, they also talked about the difficulties they faced working with dominant-caste managers who repeatedly undermined their skills, and whose caste and gender politics, they said, "left a lot to be desired." Mismanagement of Dalit workers by dominant-caste managers came under some scrutiny with the Cisco case, but it is hardly an isolated incident. Satya, who has been working in tech for more than two decades and now works with Microsoft, has dealt with his fair share of dominant-caste managers. As one of the rare Dalit tech workers who openly embraces his caste identity, he found the experience of working with non-South Asian managers has always been vastly different and favorable. At a company he previously worked for, Satya had a record of receiving positive reviews, until he was placed under a Brahmin manager from South India. "All my previous managers gave [me a] good review, and he was my supervisor for about three months or four months, and he put me under insufficient results criteria and totally zeroed out my bonus," he told me over the phone. Not willing to back down, Satya reported this to the company's human resources department, which reassigned him to a non-South Asian American manager but did little else. "Next year, my new manager came in and he knew about [the previous review]. He's an American and I was given 130 percent [positive performance review], meaning I met the expectations, I crossed the expectations in terms of my performance," he said.

Unlike most Dalits whose exact caste origins often remain nebulous (not that it stops dominant-caste colleagues from dredging them up anyway), Satya never made a secret of his caste identity, and in fact openly discussed it with the Brahmin manager who was invited to his house for dinner. "He saw the surroundings [which had Ambedkar's photographs]. We openly talked about me going to farms [in his ancestral village] and eating the meat and everything . . . [We had] conversations about reservations and he expressed that India is backward because of it . . . That is when I noticed he felt uncomfortable," Satya recalled, while adding that he assumed it wouldn't make a difference, since this was an informal conversation and at that time his manager remained friendly. "Until he did this thing [the negative performance review], I could all connect to [this], Oh, okay, he didn't like my lifestyle," he said. His company fired the manager soon after for reasons that were not directly related to this incident and never addressed it again.

In their paper on merit and navigating caste in the "casteless" world of computing, "Interrupting Merit, Subverting Legibility," Palashi Vaghela, Steven J. Jackson, and Phoebe Sengers address the harm inflicted on Dalit, Adivasi, and lower-caste workers by their dominant-caste managers and reference an interview where a non-lower-caste worker witnessed a colleague go on a casteist tirade assuming that it would remain unchecked.[10] "In a meeting to discuss revenue strategies for meeting the projected numbers that quarter, one of the managers addressed Prakash (a tech worker at an American MNC), saying, 'I will onboard *yaar* (Hindi expression of exasperation) . . . I will . . . kisi Bhangi ko bhi daal dunga (I will hire anybody, even a Bhangi),'" the report reads. Bhangi, which also happens to be the caste I was born in, remains among the most reviled subgroups in Indian communities, with even the name of the caste hurled as an insult. The report states that when Prakash called him out for saying "this word" and told him it was offensive, the manager reneged and stated that he was also from a backward caste.

For Dalits, Adivasis, and lower-caste people, especially women, who work in American tech spaces, hiding their caste or passing as higher caste is their only bulwark against routine humiliation, systemic bias, and prejudice in the workspace. However, building a life around hiding the most crucial parts of one's cultural and social life comes at a deep loss of identity and well-being, as well as the truest expression of oneself. Dalits in America experience the same lack of freedom that minorities in this country's past have endured and fought against. The suppression of one's values and beliefs, and the punitive outcomes for Dalits when discovered, especially call to mind the hateful workplace discrimination in the last few decades against LGBTQ+ folks, who had no choice but to conceal their true, authentic selves in their places of employment. The nuances of the discrimination that both experience are vastly different, but systemic biases occurring in a smaller control group, like within the South Asian American population, can create similarly traumatizing losses of identity and expression. Even without their dominant-caste managers getting in the way, Dalit tech workers experience discrimination from their colleagues, where common sites of interactions, like the water coolers, the lunch tables, and the get-togethers, turn into minefields of caste hatred and prejudice.

Vinita Gopi, a tech worker from Michigan, told me that, similar to Maya Kamble, her dominant-caste coworker berated her in front of other colleagues for utilizing reservation in her university, when the coworker found out Gopi's religion and place of origin.[11] "I said I'm from Nagpur and I practice Buddhism and you know . . . instantly she was so upset, and she said because of you people, my sister did not get an admission in medical college . . . they know that Nagpur is famous for a couple of things, and one is [there are] a lot of [people from the] community who live there," she said. Gopi, who did not in fact avail herself of affirmative action in India, left that job soon after, but remains scarred by these interactions. "I don't want to get embarrassed because I am capable. I know I work hard. Just like my other colleagues. I don't want people to judge [me] based on my background, because that's not me," she said adding that while she was somewhat used to facing this discrimination back home, having her caste scrutinized in the US was unexpected. "I came here all across the borders and I thought I will never face [this] . . . But coming to the US, and facing that thing was shocking for me." Like Kamble, she hides her caste, even though it's difficult, since she lives in a majority South Asian neighborhood, but feels like this strategy helps prevent being discriminated against.

For New York-based Brinda, who works for one of the FAANG companies and hides her caste, navigating tech spaces as a Dalit woman is treacherous and forces her into hypervigilance about her surroundings. At a team-focused icebreaker, when people started to ask each other's middle names, her anxiety about being "found out" triggered a trauma response. "So much curiosity about my full name is jarring," she told me. However, the wider conversations in the last few years have led her to reflect about her relationship with her caste. Spurred by the newfound enthusiasm on this subject, she reached out to her company's human resources department to ask if they had any materials on caste sensitivity for her colleagues who had expressed interest in learning more about it, similar to information they had received on racial and gender diversity in the past. "The very first question they asked me was, Why are you interested? Who are you?" she recalled. She revealed to them she was Dalit and was interested in educating her team in light of the Cisco case. While the HR person did get back to her saying that they did not have anything related to caste at the moment, they also made it a point to caution her to not "push this conversation on anyone." "Make sure that this is with people who are actually interested . . . no mass emails. And it was just like so restrictive. If [it was] a Black person asking for such resources that . . . sort of response . . . would be so openly discriminatory," she said.

In 2022, when Google cancelled a talk with Equality Labs founder Thenmozhi Soundararajan in response to the casteist backlash from its dominant-caste employees, Brinda was glad to see a dominant-caste person and organizer of Google's 2018 MeToo walkout, Tanuja Gupta, taking a stand against casteist bigotry. Gupta was a Google employee who had invited Soundararajan for a talk in 2021 for Dalit History Month in April 2022. She revealed in a company-wide letter that has since been made public that two employees privately reached out to her in September 2021 about the caste discrimination they had witnessed in the company earlier, and about how they were struggling to organize a talk on caste equity, which Gupta, as the head of the Google News team, agreed to host as part of the "News DEI Program."[12] Sources revealed that two days before the talk was to take place, seven Google employees began sending emails to Gupta and senior Google leadership "with inflammatory language about how they felt harmed and how they felt their lives were at risk by the discussion of caste equity," according to emails that were sent by Gupta and have since been published in the *Washington Post*.[13] Soundararajan, who frequently attends panels and has given multiple talks at other tech companies, including Microsoft, Adobe, Airbnb, and Netflix, has been an active target of Hindu right-wing groups for her work around caste in the United States. The backlash got especially intense when, in 2018, Twitter founder Jack Dorsey was photographed holding a poster that read "Smash Brahminical Patriarchy" on his trip to India. The poster's origins were linked to Equality Labs. Prominent Indian right-wing accounts outraged against Dorsey's apparent endorsement of anti-caste politics compared it to "antisemitism," forcing Twitter to apologize and claim that it was not a reflection of its values or official policy.[14]

Since then, Soundararajan has remained in the crosshairs of organizations and individuals that oppose caste awareness, and that often characterize any conversations around caste as a grand conspiracy to spread hatred against Hindus by calling proponents "Hinduphobic." When news of her talk spread on internal Google channels in April 2022, dominant-caste employees echoed the same accusations of Hinduphobia that had been making the rounds on Indian right-wing Twitter and Hindu fundamentalist propaganda websites, like OpIndia, for years at that time.[15] Unsurprisingly, Google, which had officially asked its employees to scale back on political debates in 2019, "pumped the brakes" on the talk on caste equity and asked Gupta to "debunk the misinformation in the emails from a handful of Googlers."[16] Meanwhile, Soundararajan was rigorously vetted and made to submit multiple reference letters (which was later admitted to be a rare occurrence within the company) with assurance that, even though April as Dalit History Month had by then passed, the talk could resume in May, which was also Asian American and Pacific Islander History Month. Honoring Dalit History Month however, Gupta hosted two separate talks with Soundararajan, which were "off-Corp" and open to the public. At the same time, witnessing silence from Google as the days passed, Gupta, a senior Google employee who had been with the organization for eleven years and is known for her work around diversity at the company, posted on an internal South Asian employees' email group of eight thousand people, seeking support from those who were interested in attending the conversation.[17] Her call received over four hundred responses the next day.[18]

In January that year, California State University became the first state university system to add caste as a protected category, which created a heated backlash from dominant-caste South Asians who deemed caste visibility as a threat to their world order.[19] (Later in October, two dominant-caste professors from the university even sued their employer for "unfairly targeting Hindus.")[20] Earlier, caste protections at University of California, Davis, and at Colby College in 2012 and Brandeis

University in 2019 had instigated a momentum towards greater awareness in the United States.[21] In the backdrop of this burgeoning caste awareness, the talk about caste at Google became the inflection point of a clash between caste deniers, who were keen to maintain the status quo through their supremacy in the cultural hierarchy, and those who understood the urgency of caste justice. Dominant-caste Google employees who opposed the talk not only appealed the highest of company leadership, including Alphabet CEO Sundar Pichai, to get what was ultimately a relatively low-level talk (the talk was initially intended for sixty or so employees who worked in product and engineering at Google News and Google Search) cancelled; they did so through echoing the tactics of the Hindu Right in India, where dissenters, activists, academics, and journalists are met with a punitive approach, both online and in real life. Reflecting a nearly identical approach, a 2021 academic conference in the United States titled "Dismantling Global Hindutva" that was supported by fifty-three universities, including Harvard, Berkeley, Columbia, Princeton, and Stanford, faced similar resistance from US-based Hindu right-wing groups.[22] In a maneuver that has now become the norm to silence any dissenting ideas against Indian mainstream politics and culture, the organizers and speakers were doxed online, subjected to death threats, and forced to go into hiding. The notoriously vocal Hindu right-wing group Hindu American Foundation famously sent close to a million emails to forty US universities to protest the conference.[23]

In April, as the pressure on Google management to arrive at a decision on the talk heightened, some of the dominant-caste employees from Google helped leak on Twitter the personal details of another Google employee, Gupta's direct report, who was helping her organize the talk. In addition, personal details of Gupta and Soundararajan, including phone numbers and addresses, were leaked online, putting the three women in the crosshairs of a seemingly coordinated online campaign of dangerous threats of violence, rape, and death. Soon after, Soundararajan started receiving calls on her personal cell phone threatening her safety and that of her elderly parents, forcing her to move into a safe house for several months.[24] Meanwhile, sources have revealed that Gupta was called into a meeting by company HR for what she thought was a conversation to address the dangerous situation that had developed around the safety of her subordinate employee, but instead turned out to be a "retaliatory investigation" into her conduct, which ultimately forced her into resigning from the company. "Retaliation is a normalized Google practice to handle internal criticism, and women take the hit," Gupta revealed in her company-wide resignation letter.

This incident at Google and the subsequent threats to the organizers and the speakers made headlines in the US, UK, Australia, India, and beyond, and, perhaps for the first time, ensured that caste received the kind of focused mainstream attention that its deniers were hoping to avoid all along. Even the *New Yorker* magazine, which had more or less stayed away from covering caste in the past few years (it has extensively focused on the rise of the Hindu Right in India), published an interview with Gupta discussing the incident, titled "Google's Caste-Bias Problem."[25] The Alphabet Workers Union came out in support of Gupta and Soundararajan and demanded caste protections be formally included in global company policies. Google was forced to issue a statement that caste discrimination had no place in its workplace. "We also made the decision to not move forward with the proposed talk which—rather than bringing our community together and raising awareness—was creating division and rancor," Google spokesperson Shannon Newberry wrote in an email when I reached out to the company in June 2022.[26] "We have long hosted a variety of constructive conversations with external guests on these sorts of topics to build awareness and understanding. In this instance, there was specific conduct, and internal posts, that made employees feel targeted and retaliated against for raising concerns about a proposed talk," she added in the email.

Dominant-caste Google employees who had opposed the talk, likely the ones whom Newberry had referenced in her email, responded to Gupta's petition to reinstate the talk with stunningly candid and hateful admissions of casteist rhetoric that is widely used to undermine and attack Dalits, Adivasis, and lower-caste people in India. In claims that I was able to access through multiple sources, and which were also verified in the *Washington Post*, employees expressed the opinion that increased caste consciousness will lead to more conflict, while other internal posts mentioned that giving the official sanction from Google to a talk on caste will "damage the fabric of this community" and Google's mission, adding it would also make Hindus feel unwelcome at the company.[27] Some posts mentioned that caste awareness was simply manufactured and divisive hate, and called for a panel that expressed "all points of view," and added that oppressed-caste people did not have the religious education to interpret scriptures that defined the dynamics around caste in Hindu societies. A post called the content of the talk biased and labelled it a systemic attempt to promote "Hinduphobia." And unsurprisingly, there were several remarks about reservation leading to "reverse discrimination" against dominant-caste people due to affirmative action, and, despite their actions specifically proving otherwise, claimed that caste did not exist in the US. After the talk was effectively cancelled, Hindu right-wing groups in the US, like the Hindu American Foundation, lauded Google for taking a brave stance and showing "moral courage against caste" and expressed the hope that other organizations would follow suit.[28]

Google's inability to separate casteist hate speech and claims from dominant-caste employees who allegedly "feared for their lives" from a seemingly benign talk (a version of the talk Soundararajan was set to deliver at Google was posted later on YouTube[29]), from the active and ongoing discrimination against Dalit workers and the climate of intimidation they are forced to survive at their workplaces is telling of the vulnerability Dalits experience in tech. Even outside Google, dominant-caste employees influence and exercise control over South Asian workers who are not only from "lower" castes but also could presumably be Muslim or Buddhist, or simply hold liberal political beliefs that don't fall in line with a dominant-caste person's parochial and fundamentalist "Hindu-first" worldview. It needs to be acknowledged that dominant-caste Hindus with liberal beliefs rarely stand to lose as much as Dalits or Muslims, whose performance at work is repeatedly called into question. Satya, the Dalit employee who was open about his caste identity and faced discrimination from his Brahmin manager, went to Jawaharlal Nehru University (JNU) in Delhi, which has historically been the seat of justice-oriented liberal movements in India and has been targeted by Hindu fundamentalist political structures in recent years for advocating a culture of dissent.

He said that, among other things, his conversations about his time in JNU and its current "state of degradation" also considerably irked his manager and contributed to the negative review of his performance.

In their paper on navigating caste in the "casteless" world of computing, the authors interview a Dalit tech worker who hid his caste but took "pro-Muslim stances against Islamophobia" and was chastised for his "anti-national' tendencies as a result.[30] "When asked about his plans for celebrating Diwali, Priyam responded that he doesn't celebrate it. He didn't reveal that he was Buddhist, but one of the coworkers remarked to the group present at that moment, 'You know mujhe pataa hai yeh konse festival celebrate karta hai . . . yeh anti-national festivals celebrate karta hai . . . (I know what kind of festivals he celebrates; he celebrates anti-national festivals),'" the authors report, referring to a somewhat recent but depressingly common way to describe Islamic, Buddhist, and Ambedkarite festivals in India. Priyam knew he could have complained to HR and the coworker would have been spoken to, but he worried his friends might stop talking to him, "so there's this peer pressure" that can make it difficult to take action. My conversations with dozens of Dalit workers revealed similar instances of bullying for their cultural and political beliefs and the widespread withdrawal into silence to survive the casteist minefields that they described as their workplaces.

Resistance to addressing caste discrimination does not always fall into a tidy correlation matrix with the rise of Hindu fundamentalism, both in India and by extension within the Indian American diaspora in the United States. However, there are serious overlaps. Even though the silence around the existence of caste, and attempts to eliminate and suppress narratives which challenge that, predate the current rise of fundamentalism in India, the rise of violence and aggression as a corollary to these actions is somewhat new. Efforts to highlight caste discrimination in the United States and other parts of the world are perceived as not only a threat to hierarchical caste order, but also a blot on the narrative of India's global ascension, or an attempt to "malign the country's image worldwide." For a majority of dominant-caste South Asians, particularly Indians, who have never had to confront their inherent casteist beliefs, let alone be answerable for them to their American employers, a spotlight on caste can come across as a threat to their success and as a retaliation to their visibility as high-income "model" Americans. It's hardly surprising then, that this perceived threat, especially in light of a 2021 survey[31] that revealed how a majority of Indian Americans vote Democrat yet support the policies of Prime Minister Narendra Modi, manifests as a culture of conformity, homogeneity, and repression in tech spaces, where there is little tolerance for anti-caste discourse or the presence of Dalits and Adivasis in general.

The irony of dominant-caste Indians denying the existence of caste while actively and intentionally restricting Dalits, Adivasis, and lower-caste people from even discussing caste—an aspect that inarguably defines our entire lives—is profoundly disheartening, but not new. It is cultural behavior that has been fine-tuned and passed down over generations of dominant-caste people's steadfast beliefs in their own supremacy. Kamal, a Dalit tech worker who lives in Michigan and moved to the United States after spending a few years in Japan, recalls how he and his family were reprimanded for putting up booths exhibiting anti-caste literature, including works by Ambedkar, at an Indian Independence Day celebration in Chicago a few years ago.[32] "Some people [came up to us] at our booth and said, 'We don't do this kind of discrimination [here]'. How come you guys are saying that the discrimination is still happening?" he told me. These interactions with dominant-caste coworkers and industry colleagues, in and outside of workspaces, especially at events like India Day celebrations, where narratives of nationhood are created, are often hostile to Dalits and Adivasis, particularly if those Dalits and Adivasis display anti-caste symbols like Ambedkar's portraits or "Jai Bhim," the anti-caste slogan woven around his name.

The culture around the denial of caste that is built on the gaslighting and bullying of Dalit, Adivasi, and lower-caste workers is perpetuated by questioning and attacking their validity in tech spaces or their skills in the workplace. In a stunning display of what could only be called a guilty conscience, dominant-caste South Asians, such as those at Google, hijack the language of racial equity and justice—equating caste discrimination couched as Hinduphobia to antisemitism takes not only a serious reach but also a willful misunderstanding of facts—to deny or silence the conversations around caste. However, they perhaps fail to understand that preventing Dalits from engaging in their culture, speaking out about their experiences, or expressing their authentic selves by forcing them to hide their caste identities is in itself an act of prejudice, hate, and discrimination. Engaging in this widespread suppression of conversations around caste while also denying that caste exists not only strikes a match to their threadbare narratives but ultimately ends up unmasking the deception behind these claims.

This pervasive sense of anxiety and fear that Dalits are forced to survive in tech spaces and which tech giants like Google seemingly actively foster in their midst can only be countered through legislation. Dalits, similar to queer folks from LGBTQ+ communities, cannot remain vulnerable while they continue waiting for a change of heart from the majority. Protections against caste that allow Dalits and Adivasis to report their discrimination without censure or rebuke to an HR person who understands the basics of caste are vital and necessary. In February 2023, Seattle became the first[33] city in the United States to ban caste discrimination, a step that might lead tech companies like Amazon that have headquarters in the city to come into its fold and likely be forced to add caste protections to their American and possibly global policies. A similar law proposed in the state of California could affect the entirety of the Silicon Valley and the Bay Area tech spaces.[34] Clearly, the march for caste protections in the United States has just begun, and with Dalits, Adivasis, and lower-caste people finally finding our voices, the day is not far when caste will be fully recognized and protected in the United States and across the world.

EPILOGUE

Coming Out as Dalit is primarily an act of bearing witness to what it means to be Dalit in a grossly unfair society. A memoir, it details my own experiences and those of my family and goes deep into the areas of Indian society I am familiar with, as well as those aspects of Dalit society and living that I have been interested in and studied. What it is not is a comprehensive history of Dalits in India and it should not be taken as such. There are many aspects of the Dalit experience that lie outside the scope of this book. For example, I have not written in detail about the atrocities that are routinely inflicted on Dalits even today. I have also only referred in passing to Dalits in politics, where they are now a significant force. India has had two Dalit presidents, the tenth president of India, K. R. Narayanan (1992–1997), and the current president of the country, Ram Nath Kovind. These leaders and others like them are powerful role models and have significantly advanced the cause of Dalits. I have touched upon successful Dalits in business and there are stories of hope and progress in many other areas of endeavor. However, this book does not go into great detail about the overall Dalit condition except as it pertains to my own life and those aspects of being Dalit that are necessary to provide context.

Having said that, what does it mean to be Dalit in the second decade of the new century? As for any other group of over two hundred million people, it obviously means a range of things. For some of us being Dalit means a lifetime of discrimination and abuse. For others, it means being able to use constitutional reservation to better our lot. What saves us from a dire fate ultimately boils down to one thing: luck.

But to escape discrimination and become part of society, which is still mostly upper caste, we have to leave some of our Dalitness behind. We leave behind our food, our songs, our culture, and our last names, so we can be "better" and "purer," more upper caste and less Dalit. We don't leave our Dalitness behind just so that we can blend in more easily. We do it because sometimes that's our only option. We change our last names so we can get jobs and rent houses. We lie about our caste so our friends, classmates, and teachers don't think we are lesser than them. We learn their habits so no one can use our Dalitness to make fun of us.

Some of us protest, organize, and write. We study Ambedkar and try to live by his values; but many of us don't. We go to school, raise children, have jobs, run businesses, experience joy and success, and that in itself is our biggest challenge to caste. That despite the extreme violence, injustice, and discrimination that still happens to us daily, we persist. We remember what our families have endured and hope to fare better. Because just living our best lives is a challenge to the caste system.

To end, I'd like to tell a poignant story that accurately sums up what it means to be Dalit in India.

In 1892, seventeen-year-old Palwankar Baloo was hired by the Poona cricket club.[1] His job was to erect nets and roll and mark the pitch. He had had the same job at the Parsi club. But at the Poona club, he had one additional duty: bowling to the British batsmen at the nets.

Baloo was born in the Chamar caste but his father was in the army. Along with his brothers Vithal, Shivaram, and Ganpat, he had learned to play cricket by using the equipment discarded by army officers in Pune.[2] Hundreds of hours of practice turned Baloo into a left-arm spinner, "one of modern India's greatest cricketers." Cricket at that time was organized along the lines of religion and caste, with teams of Hindus, Parsis, Britons, and Muslims. When word reached the Hindu Deccan Gymkhana club about this new talent, they (hesitantly) recruited him. "The Hindu team was otherwise weak. Baloo helped them match the British," said Sadanand More, a Marathi historian. A few years later, he was admitted to the Bombay Hindu Gymkhana.

As the cricket matches were played against the backdrop of the independence movement, each victory of the Hindu team against the British was cheered by the Indian crowd. The team went on to tour England in 1911. Although the Indian side was thoroughly trounced, Baloo saw great success and was celebrated on the team's return. He was "the only sliver of hope in an otherwise depressing tour of England in 1911—the first by an all-Indian team—taking 114 wickets at an average of 18.84 with a best haul of 8/103 against Cambridge."[3]

And while the rest of the team played with him on the field, in the pavilion, it was a different story. Baloo wasn't allowed to eat or drink with the other upper-caste members of the team.[4] In fact, during the game's ritual "tea interval," he was made to stand outside the pavilion at a distance from his teammates and served tea in a disposable cup. When caste barriers were finally lifted, Baloo is believed to be "the first public Dalit figure to inter-dine with upper-castes," according to Raosaheb Kasbe, who was a professor of philosophy at Pune University.

But despite talent, Baloo and his brothers Vithal, Shivaram, and Ganpat remained the "token Dalits" of Indian cricket. Baloo's successes were "heralded as a great moment for Hindu unity and cricket," but he and his brothers were ignored when it came to giving them the captaincy. For ten years between 1910 and 1920 there were several unsuccessful campaigns to make Baloo captain. When M. D. Pai was made captain in 1913, he agreed, saying, "The honor of captainship should have been given to my friend Mr. Baloo for he was the senior and more experienced player in the team."[5] In 1920, Baloo was dropped from the team and his brother Vithal, an ace batsman, was passed over for captaincy. Baloo's brothers withdrew from their teams in protest. Finally, Baloo was made vice captain. It was only much later, in 1923, that his brother Vithal was made captain and remained one till 1926. Baloo later went on to become a political figure and even contested elections against Ambedkar.[6] Ambedkar was frank about his admiration for the cricketer. As a political figure, Baloo confronted Ambedkar on several issues, including that of separate electorates and converting out of Hinduism.

But since then, Dalits have been mostly missing from cricket. Even the Palwankar brothers are largely forgotten, mainly because upper-caste history deliberately ignores Dalit heroes. Vinod Kambli, the only Dalit cricketer in recent memory, has been a rare exception. But unlike Baloo, Kambli did not enjoy the support of the fans. In fact, it was quite the opposite. A talented player "who burst on the scene with Tendulkar when the pair made a world record partnership of 664 as schoolboys," Kambli was constantly booed on the field.[7] He believed that it was because of his caste. As a result, he rarely talked about or even acknowledged[8] his caste and eventually converted to Christianity in 2010.[9] Kambli aside, the Indian cricket team has been mostly upper caste for decades, a fact not lost even on the international media. In 2008, the *Sydney Morning Herald* noted, "The Brahmin caste, which forms only a tiny fraction of India's population, has always dominated the national cricket side."[10]

As I said at the beginning of the book, the caste system is an invisible and powerful aspect that is present in every part of the lives of Indians. It is unfair and treats some people as inherently inferior to others. While many privileged people will not necessarily see its influence in their lives, it is a harsh reality for those who are disadvantaged in this system. I hope that by hearing the voices of those who have to bear its brunt, and those who are putting their lives and livelihoods on the line to fight against it, we can all begin to understand this unequal system and work towards becoming truly post-caste.

ACKNOWLEDGMENTS

Close to three years ago, when I saw some of my Columbia University batchmates applying for a coveted book writing course, I couldn't understand why they would want to put themselves through something that, for nearly everyone who attempts it, is described as torture. I was convinced that I was never going to write a book. Now having written one, I can tell you it was worse than I imagined. The fact that you hold this book in your hands today is proof that there are some things that will unfold in ways you have no control over. I probably started on the journey to writing this book long before I came out as Dalit or even came to Columbia.

I have many people to thank: My editors Neena Haridas and Poonam Saxena showed immense faith in my writing and trained me at a time when I probably had no business calling myself a writer. Vir Sanghvi, who generously made it possible for me to come to Columbia. My friends Harsh Vardhan Sahni and Aditi Surie who never once asked me to stop complaining about how difficult it was to write a book in my first few years in a foreign country—they had more faith in me than I did in myself. Parul Khanna who gave me unwavering emotional support. Saudamini Jain for being my "book friend." Leandro Oliva, Carmen Graciela Díaz, Mei and Michael Regan, Gabrielle Bruney, Ankur Paliwal, and Esha Dey for being my people in New York.

Columbia professors Alisa Solomon and David Hajdu for taking a chance on me and, in effect, making this book possible. Professor Nicholas Lemann, who patiently helped with my frantic pitch and offered invaluable advice on how to write that first sentence. Julia

Fierro and Michele Filgate of Sackett Street for helping me unpack my story for the first time in their writing workshop.

The incredibly generous and constantly supportive members of the Dalit community who helped me shape my ideas on caste through hundreds of messages on Facebook and Twitter DMs. They have been the biggest champions of my work. Kuffir Nalgundwar and Chittibabu Padavala for their valuable advice and the hundreds of talented writers on *RTI*, without whose groundwork and research the analysis in this book would have not been possible. Sudipto Mondal and Thenmozhi Soundararajan for leading the way and encouraging me every time I needed it. Dalit writers and academics who created crucially rich resources I could lean on for research. Everyone who sent me their story for *Documents of Dalit Discrimination*.

My agents Gloria Loomis and Julia Masnik who, in particular, never let me forget that it was supposed to be this hard to write this book over multiple hour-long phone conversations. My publishers, Aleph Book Company, for putting their faith in my work. My editor, Pujitha Krishnan, who practically held my hand throughout and painstakingly helped me realize my vision for this book, even when I kept making the changes she asked me not to. I thank you for sharing my ambition for my writing.

And, lastly, my therapist. You helped me become the person I needed to be to tell the world my story.

NOTES

PROLOGUE

1. Sanjana Agnihotri, "Online Outrage Against Delhi Jazz Club for Insulting Dalit Community, Outlet Cancels Event," *India Today*, June 5, 2017.

2. Sanjay Paswan and Pramanshi Jaideva, eds., *Encyclopaedia of Dalits in India: Movements*, vol. 3 (Delhi: Kalpaz, 2002), 26. For how this belief still affects Dalits, see Press Trust of India (PTI), "Dalit Girl Thrashed After Her Shadow Falls on Upper Caste Man," *India Today*, June 16, 2015.

3. Express Web Desk, "My Birth Is My Fatal Accident: Full Text of Dalit Student Rohith's Suicide Letter," *Indian Express*, January 19, 2016.

4. Sudipto Mondal, "Rohith Vemula: An Unfinished Portrait," *Hindustan Times*, accessed May 22, 2023.

5. First published as a note on the author's Facebook page, "Today, I'm Coming Out as Dalit," January 19, 2016, reproduced on author's Tumblr page, January 19, 2016, https://www.tumblr.com/dalitdiscrimination/137659894302/today-im -coming-out-as-dalit.

CHAPTER 1: THE EARLY YEARS

1. "SC, ST and OBC Reservation Percentage for Central Government Jobs," *GovtStaff News*, accessed May 22, 2023; "With Reservations," *The Economist*, October 4, 2007.

2. Brajesh Kumar, "Policy Pariahs: Why There Are So Few SC/ST Officers in Top Echelons," *Governance Now*, October 15, 2013.

3. "With a Dalit Yet to Make It to the Top of Civil Service, Can Tina Dabi Break the Glass Ceiling?," *Firstpost*, May 24, 2016.

4. Rahila Gupta and Kavita Krishnan, "Women Demand Freedom, Not Surveillance," *Open Democracy*, October 21, 2013.

5. According to Christophe Jaffrelot, B. R. Ambedkar describes something similar in "Castes in India: Their Mechanism, Genesis and Development." Jaffelot says "while the term was coined by Srinivas, the process itself had been described by colonial administrators such as E. T. Atkinson in his *Himalayan Gazetteer* and Alfred Lyall, in whose works Ambedkar might well have encountered it." *Dr Ambedkar and Untouchability: Analysing and Fighting Caste* (London: C. Hurst & Co., 2005), 33.

CHAPTER 2: THE CASTE SYSTEM

1. G. Aloysius, "Caste In and Above History," *Sociological Bulletin* 48, nos. 1–2 (March–September 1999): 160.

2. Aloysius, "Caste In and Above History," 161.

3. Gail Omvedt, "Towards a Historical Materialist Analysis of the Origins and Development of Caste," chap. 1 in *Dalits and the Democratic Revolution: Dr. Ambedkar and the Dalit Movement in Colonial India* (New Delhi: SAGE, 1994).

4. Omvedt, *Dalits and the Democratic Revolution*, 23.

5. Tony Joseph, "How Genetics Is Settling the Aryan Migration Debate," *The Hindu*, June 16, 2017.

6. Devdutt Pattanaik, "What Exactly Is the Manusmriti?" *DailyO*, February 1, 2017.

7. B. R. Ambedkar, *The Untouchables: Who Were They and Why They Became Untouchables* (New Delhi: Amrit Book Co., 1948).

8. B. R. Ambedkar, "Castes in India: Their Mechanism, Genesis and Development," *Indian Antiquary* 41 (1917).

9. Aloysius, "Caste In and Above History."

10. Jyotirao Phule, *Collected Works of Mahatma Jyotirao Phule*, vol. 1, *Slavery* (Bombay: Education Department, 1991).

11. Aloysius, "Caste In and Above History," 162.

12. Aloysius, "Caste In and Above History," 162.

13. Chinniah Jangam, "Dilemmas of Dalit Agendas: Political Subjugation and Self-Emancipation in Telugu Country, 1910–50," in *Dalit Studies*, ed. Ramnarayan S. Rawat and K. Satyanarayana (Durham, NC: Duke University Press, 2016).

14. "East Indian Immigration (1838–1917)," *Guyana Chronicle*, May 5, 2014.

15. P. Sanal Mohan, "Social Space, Civil Society, and Dalit Agency in Twentieth-Century Kerala," in Rawat and Satyanarayana, *Dalit Studies*.

16. T. A. Ameerudheen, "Is the Caste System Deep-Rooted Among Christians in India? A Kerala Bishop Stirs Up a Hornet's Nest," *Scroll.in*, April 20, 2018.

17. Mohan, "Social Space, Civil Society, and Dalit Agency in Twentieth-Century Kerala."

18. Liz Mathew, "First Time, Church Says: Dalit Christians Face Untouchability," *Indian Express*, December 19, 2016.

19. "Supreme Court to Examine Quota Benefit to Dalit Converts," *The Hindu*, January 21, 2011.

CHAPTER 3: EDUCATION AND FINANCIAL STRIFE

1. Sanjay Pandey, "Female Foeticide, India's '"Ticking Bomb,"'" *Al Jazeera*, July 6, 2015.

2. Hakim Adi, "Africa and the Transatlantic Slave Trade," BBC, October 5, 2012.

3. David Hume, "Of National Characters," http://graduate.engl.virginia.edu/enec981/dictionary/o3humeK1.html (URL defunct), accessed December 27, 2018.

4. John Philip Jenkins, "White Supremacy," *Encyclopedia Britannica*, accessed December 27, 2018.

5. Radhika Parameswaran, "Radhika Parameswaran on 'Colorism' in India," *Asia Experts Forum*, https://asiaexpertsforum.org/radhika-parameswaran-colorism-india, accessed July 21, 2023.

6. Tabish Khair, "The Roots of Indian Racism," *The Hindu*, April 16, 2017.

CHAPTER 5: THE REALITY OF UNTOUCHABILITY

1. *Cleaning Human Waste: "Manual Scavenging," Caste and Discrimination in India*, Human Rights Watch, August 25, 2014, https://www.hrw.org/report/2014/08/25/cleaning-human-waste/manual-scavenging-caste-and-discrimination-india, accessed December 28, 2018.

2. Utkarsh Anand, "HC Takes Railways to Task for Employing Manual Scavengers," *Indian Express*, April 7, 2011.

3. Anand, "HC Takes Railways to Task for Employing Manual Scavengers."

4. Debobrat Ghose, "Magsaysay Awardee Bezwada Wilson: Manual Scavengers' Deaths Are Political Murders by Governments," *Firstpost*, July 30, 2016.

5. Kainat Sarfaraz, "Manual Scavenging in Meerut: Why Are Women Made to Carry Excreta on Their Head for Two Stale Rotis a Day?" *Indian Express*, June 13, 2017.

6. Apoorva Sripathi, "How Public Apathy Continues to Keep Manual Scavengers Invisible and in the Margins," *The Wire*, March 18, 2017.

7. Sarfaraz, "Manual Scavenging in Meerut."

8. Shweta Sengar, "Sewer Story: Death of Sanitation Workers in Delhi Exposes the Hypocrisy & Failure of Govt," *India Times*, October 18, 2017.

9. Parth M. N., "India's Sewer Cleaners Keep Working Despite Ban on Job," *Los Angeles Times*, July 4, 2014.

10. Agrima Bhasin, "No Exits from These Tunnels of Death," *The Hindu*, July 29, 2013.

11. Theja Ram, "The Mother of All 'Solutions': Karnataka Wants to Legalise Manual Scavenging to Avoid Deaths," *News Minute*, March 14, 2017.

12. Sachin Unhalekar, "'BMC Playing with Lives of Manhole Cleaners,' Claims Workers Union," *Mid-Day*, March 18, 2015.

13. Sripathi, "How Public Apathy Continues to Keep Manual Scavengers Invisible and in the Margins."

14. Nilesh Vijaykumar, "Story of Hyderabad Sewer Workers: A Tale Which No One Knows," *New Indian Express*, March 14, 2017.

15. Kancha Ilaiah, "Beef, BJP and Food Rights of People," *Economic and Political Weekly* 31, no. 24 (1996): 1444–45.

16. "Una, Alwar and Delhi Cow Vigilantism: A List of 'Gau Rakshak' Attacks Since 2015 Dadri Lynching," *Firstpost*, June 3, 2017.

17. Dhrubaa Mukherjee, "What the Hindu Scriptures Really Say About Cow Worship," *Huffington Post*, October 7, 2015.

18. B. R. Ambedkar, *The Untouchables: Who Were They and Why They Became Untouchables* (New Delhi: Amrit Book Co., 1948).

19. Mahatma Gandhi, "Cow Protection," http://www.mkgandhi.org/momgandhi/chap81.htm, accessed December 27, 2018.

20. Prabhash K. Dutta, "Long Before Yogi Adityanath, a Congress CM Banned Cow Slaughter in UP Against Nehru's Wishes," *India Today*, March 26, 2017.

21. "Congress Was the First in Banning Cow Slaughter, Will Consider Backing Central Law on Ban: Digvijay Singh," *Economic Times*, October 6, 2015.

22. "India Supreme Court Suspends Cattle Slaughter Ban," BBC, July 11, 2017.

23. K. Balchand, "Modi Fears a 'Pink Revolution,'" *The Hindu*, April 3, 2014.

24. Deepshikha Ghosh, "PM Modi Hits Out at Cow Vigilantes, Says 'Gau Rakshak Business Makes Me Angry,'" NDTV, August 7, 2017.

25. Danish Raza, "'We Can't Trust Anyone': 8 Months After Junaid's Killing, His Family Fights On," *Hindustan Times*, March 20, 2018.

26. Pratap Bhanu Mehta, "May the Silent Be Damned," *Indian Express*, June 27, 2017.

27. Michael Safi, "Muslim Man Dies in India After Attack by Hindu 'Cow Protectors,'" *The Guardian*, April 5, 2017.

28. Associated Press, "Modi Condemns Rise in Mob Violence Against Beef-Eaters in India," *The Guardian*, June 29, 2017.

29. Delna Abraham and Ojaswi Rao, "86% Killed in Cow-Related Violence Since 2010 Are Muslim, 97% Attacks After Modi Govt Came to Power," *Hindustan Times*, July 16, 2017.

30. Zeba Siddiqui, Krishna N. Das, Tommy Wilkes, and Tom Lasseter, "Emboldened by Modi's Ascent, India's Cow Vigilantes Deny Muslims Their Livelihood," Reuters, November 6, 2017.

31. Aarefa Johari, "An Assault on Dalits May Have Triggered the Biggest Lower-Caste Uprising in Gujarat in 30 Years," *Scroll.in*, July 20, 2016.

32. Shoaib Daniyal, "'Your Mother, You Take Care of It': Meet the Dalits Behind Gujarat's Stirring Cow Carcass Protests," *Scroll.in*, July 23, 2016.

33. "Dalit Sammelan Gets Nod from Police, to Be Held in Sabarmati Area Today," *Indian Express*, July 31, 2016.

34. Johari, "An Assault on Dalits May Have Triggered the Biggest Lower-Caste Uprising in Gujarat in 30 Years"; Mahesh Langa, "Chalo Una," *The Hindu*, August 21, 2016.

35. Aarefa Johari, "'What Justice Can We Expect?': Gujarat Dalits Returning from Una Rally Are Beaten, Vehicles Attacked," *Scroll.in*, August 16, 2016.

CHAPTER 6: THE LONG ROAD TO ST. STEPHEN'S

1. "Minimum Wage for Unskilled Workers Increased by Rs 42 in Tier III Cities," *Indian Express*, July 14, 2014.

2. Prachi Salve, "How India's Construction Workers Get Gypped of Their Due," *IndiaSpend*, September 5, 2013; Akhil Kumar, "Watch: How Bad Is the Gender Pay Gap in the Indian Labour Market?" *The Wire*, August 19, 2017; "India Labour Market Update," http://www.ilo.org/wcmsp5/groups/public/—asia/—ro-bangkok/—sro-new_delhi/documents/publication/wcms_496510.pdf.

3. Gulam Jeelani, "Gurgaon Woman Who Owns Rs 3cr House, Suvs Sells Chole-Kulche on Road," *Hindustan Times*, August 20, 2016.

4. Abhishek Dey, "In Noida, a Riot-Like Situation over a Domestic Worker Puts the Focus on India's Bitter Class Chasm," *Scroll.in*, July 13, 2017.

5. Amrit Dhillon, "Routine Abuse of Delhi's Maids Laid Bare as Class Divide Spills into Violence," *The Guardian*, July 21, 2017.

6. George Monbiot, "The Flight to India," *The Guardian*, October 20, 2003.

CHAPTER 7: THE ARGUMENT FOR RESERVATION

1. Niharika Lal and Riya Sharma, "Campus Elections Drama: DU—Flashy, Muscle Power, Student Issues. JNU—Hype, Ideology, National Issues," *Times of India*, September 13, 2016.

2. Pallavi Rebbapragada, "Delhi University Gears Up for Student Polls: Caste, Money Factors Rob Campus Politics of Level Playing Field," *Firstpost*, September 8, 2018.

3. Anasuya Basu, "Dalit Voices from Delhi University on How They Battle Caste Every Day," *DailyO*, January 25, 2016.

4. TNM Staff, "Kerala Student Suspended After Complaining Against Professor Who Abused His Caste Status," *News Minute*, December 22, 2016.

5. "Special Story (AIIMS): The Suicide of Anil Meena," *HardNews*, April 2, 2012; Sheela Bhatt, "Reservations: The Other Side of the Story," *Rediff*, May 27, 2006.

6. Jayati Ghosh, "Case for Caste-Based Quotas in Higher Education," *Economic and Political Weekly* 41, no. 24 (June 17, 2006).

7. *Report of the Committee to Enquire into the Allegation of Differential Treatment of SC/ST Students*, All India Institute of Medical Science, Delhi, http://www.nlhmb.in/Reports%20AIIMS.pdf, accessed May 22, 2023.

8. "A Girl in Fourth Grade Said, 'Your Caste People Are at Lower Level Than Even Gutter Pigs,'" *Documents of Dalit Discrimination*, http://dalitdiscrimination.tumblr.com/post/138490950647/a-girl-in-fourth-grade-said-your-caste-people?is_related_post=1, accessed December 27, 2018.

9. Sukhadeo Thorat, "Discrimination on the Campus," *The Hindu*, January 26, 2016.

10. Vikram Chukka, "Scholar's Suicide: Discrimination in Higher Education Reflects the Violence of a Casteist Culture," *The Wire*, January 18, 2016.

11. Aarti Dhar, "AIIMS Rejects Thorat Report," *The Hindu*, September 20, 2007.

12. Harish S. Wankhede, "Two Years Later, Rohith Vemula's Soul Still Haunts Us for Failing Him," *The Wire*, January 17, 2018; Shubham Rath, "Manusmritized Nation: Institutional Murder of Rohith Vemula & the Atrocities That Followed," *India Resists*, March 24, 2016; PTI, "Vemula's Suicide an 'Institutional Murder': Satchidanandan," *The Hindu*, January 23, 2016.

13. Praveen Donthi, "'We Will Fight till the End': On the Protests Against Appa Rao Podile's Return to the University of Hyderabad," *The Caravan*, June 14, 2016; Kalpana Kannabiran, "Sunkanna's Refusal to Accept His PhD from Appa Rao Is a Historic Act of Resistance," *The Wire*, October 4, 2016.

14. Praveen Donthi, "From Shadows to the Stars," *The Caravan*, May 1, 2016.

15. "Suicides of Dalit Students Not New in Hyderabad University," *Hindustan Times*, January 20, 2016; K. P. Girija, "On Suicides, Caste and Higher Education," *Insight Young Voices*, April 26, 2011, https://thedeathofmeritinindia.wordpress.com/2011/04/26/84, accessed December 27, 2018.

16. Indulekha Aravind and K. P. Narayana Kumar, "Dalit Suicide Case: Why Rohith Vemula's Death Is the Tipping Point in Caste Bias on Campus," *Economic Times*, January 24, 2016.

17. Apurva, "Caste Came Up in 3 Suicide Probes at Hyderabad University," *Indian Express*, February 8, 2016.

18. Thorat, "Discrimination on the Campus."

19. Chukka, "Scholar's Suicide."

20. Sonali Acharjee, "The Kota System: Rs 600 Crore Coaching Industry," *Open*, July 17, 2015.

21. G. Pramod Kumar, "90% IIT-Roorkee Dropouts Are Backward Caste: A Case Against Affirmative Action?" *Firstpost*, August 6, 2015.

22. D. Karthikeyan, "Suicide by Dalit Students in 4 Years," *The Hindu*, September 5, 2011.

23. Ajantha Subramanian, "An Anatomy of the Caste Culture at IIT-Madras," *Open*, June 12, 2015.

24. Samson Ovichegan, "'Being a Dalit Female': Exploring the Experiences of Students at One Elite Indian University," Centre for Public Policy Research, Working Papers Series, Paper No. 7, King's College London (2017), https://www.kcl.ac.uk/sspp/departments/education/research/Research-Centres/cppr/working papers/Paper-7.pdf (URL defunct), accessed December 27, 2018.

25. B. V. Shivashankar, "University of Hyderabad's 'Brahmin Well' in Spotlight Again," *Times of India*, January 28, 2016.

26. Professor Vasant Tarade at an Ambedkar conference in New York.

27. Thorat, "Discrimination on the Campus."

28. "Storm Created by Mandal Commission Poses Serious Threat to V. P. Singh's Political Survival," *India Today*, October 15, 1990.

29. Pragya Kaushika, "25 Years of Mandal Protests—His Struggle Changed India's Politics: Rajeev Goswami's Daughter," *Indian Express*, October 6, 2015.

30. Dinkar Sakrikar, "The Mandal Commission Report," *PUCL Bulletin*, August 1994, http://www.pucl.org/from-archives/Dalit-tribal/mandal-2.htm (URL defunct), accessed December 27, 2018.

31. Irena Akbar, "25 Years of Mandal Protests—I Had No Idea What Reservation Was: Self-Immolation Survivor Atul Aggarwal," *Indian Express*, October 4, 2015.

32. Satish Deshpande, "Exclusive Inequalities: Merit, Caste and Discrimination in Indian Higher Education Today," *Economic and Political Weekly* 41, no. 24 (June 17, 2006).

33. K. Balagopal, "The Anti-Mandal Mania," *Economic and Political Weekly* 25, no. 40 (October 6, 1990).

34. Pankaj Pachauri, "Mandal Commission: The Great Debate," *India Today*, September 30, 1990.

35. Sakrikar, "The Mandal Commission Report."

36. Jyotirao Phule, *Collected Works of Mahatma Jyotirao Phule*, vol. 1, Slavery (Bombay: Education Department, 1991).

37. Described in B. R. Ambedkar, *What Gandhi and the Congress Have Done to the Untouchables* (Delhi: Gautam Book Center, 1945).

38. Kancha Ilaiah Shepherd, *Why I Am Not a Hindu: A Sudra Critique of Hindutva Philosophy, Culture, and Political Economy* (Calcutta: SAMYA, 1996).

39. Sukhadeo Thorat, "Paying the Social Debt," *Economic and Political Weekly* 41, no. 24 (June 17, 2006); "UPSC Interviewers Biased Against SC/ST Candidates, Says Dalit Outfit," *The Hindu*, June 4, 2016.

40. "Why UP and Bihar Are India's Top Two IAS Churners," http://upsccoaching inahmedabad.com/upsc-topper-2016-scored-less-than-59-others-in-personality-test -half-a-million-young-men-and-women-give-their-all-in-an-examination-that -offers-less-t/b292 (URL defunct), accessed December 27, 2018.

41. "Domestic Credit to Private Sector (% of GDP)—India," The World Bank, https://data.worldbank.org/indicator/FS.AST.PRVT.GD.ZS?locations=IN, accessed December 27, 2018.

42. Aurangzeb Naqshbandi, "Govt. Body Wants OBC Quotas in Private Sector," *Hindustan Times*, February 9, 2016.

43. Sukhadeo Thorat, "The Legacy of Social Exclusion: A Correspondence Study of Job Discrimination in India," *Economic and Political Weekly* 42, no. 41 (October 13, 2007).

44. Adarsh Kumar, "India Journal: Combating Caste Bias in the Private Sector," *India Journal* (blog), *Wall Street Journal*, July 12, 2011, https://blogs.wsj.com /indiarealtime/2011/07/12/india-journal-combatting-caste-bias-in-the-private-sector.

45. Arindam Mukherjee, "Skill on Skid Row," *Outlook*, June 21, 2004.

46. Syed Firdaus Ashraf, "Why I Support 27% Reservation in Private Sector Jobs," *Rediff*, February 11, 2016.

47. P. Vaidyanathan Iyer, "India Inc's Caste Census Finds ST, SCs Missing," *Financial Express*, January 20, 2011, https://www.financialexpress.com/archive/india -incs-caste-census-finds-st-scs-missing/739803/, accessed July 21, 2023.

48. Press Trust of India, "Nilekani Opposes Over Regulation of Private Sector," *Business Standard*, March 19, 2014.

49. Ashish Gupta, "Caste: Why It's Still an Issue for India Inc.," *Fortune India*, October 14, 2016.

50. Press Trust of India, "Centre to Introduce Equal Opportunities Commission Bill," *Business Standard*, January 20, 2013.

51. "There Is Valid Ground for Reservation in Private Sector: BJP," *Firstpost*, February 10, 2016.

52. Gupta, "Caste: Why It's Still an Issue for India Inc."

53. Infosys, "Infosys Foundation Launches Spark-IT to Enhance Employability of Engineering Graduates," press release, September 15, 2014.; Shivasundar, "Why the Private Sector Is Immune to the Constitutional Goal of Social Justice," *The Wire*, December 25, 2022, https://thewire.in/rights/why-is-the-private-sector -immune-to-the-constitutional-goal-of-social-justice

54. Surinder S. Jodhka, "Dalits in Business: Self-Employed Scheduled Castes in Northwest India," *Economic and Political Weekly* 45, no. 11 (March 13, 2010).

55. Thorat, "Paying the Social Debt."

56. Chandra Bhan Prasad, "Myths About Private Sector Reservation," *The Pioneer*, June 14, 2004.

57. Shikha Dalmia, "Perhaps India Shouldn't Get Too Excited About Reparations," *Time*, August 3, 2015.

58. Thorat, "Paying the Social Debt."

59. Peggy McIntosh, "White Privilege: Unpacking the Invisible Knapsack," in *Re-Visioning Family Therapy: Race, Culture, and Gender in Clinical Practice*, ed. Monica McGoldrick (New York: Guilford Press, 1998), 147–52.

60. Susan Chanderbhan-Forde, "Asian Indian Mothers' Involvement in Their Children's Schooling: An Analysis of Social and Cultural Capital," PhD diss., University of South Florida, 2010, http://scholarcommons.usf.edu/etd/1596.

CHAPTER 9: DALIT MOVEMENTS AND AMBEDKAR'S LEGACY

1. Karthik Venkatesh, "Education for Liberation: Exploring Mahatma Phule's Work in Education," *Contemporary Education Dialogue* 13, no. 1 (December 14, 2015), http://journals.sagepub.com/doi/pdf/10.1177/0973184915603176, accessed December 27, 2018.

2. Sanjana Agnihotri, "Who Is Savitribai Phule? What Did She Do for Women's Rights in India?," *India Today*, January 3, 2016.

3. Gail Omvedt writes in *Dalits and the Democratic Revolution: Dr. Ambedkar and the Dalit Movement in Colonial India* (New Delhi: SAGE, 1994), that while this theory was popularly used to legitimize the "superiority" of upper castes, Brahmin elites like Bal Gangadhar Tilak used it to establish "ethnic kinship between European 'Orientalists' and ancient Vedic peoples."

4. Paramita Ghosh, "From Mahad to Mumbai to Hyderabad, the Story of India's Caste Blues," *Hindustan Times*, March 28, 2016.

5. B. R. Ambedkar, *Dr. Babasaheb R. Ambedkar: Writings and Speeches*, vol. 17, part 1, Education Department: Government of Maharashtra (2003) (New Delhi: Dr Ambedkar Foundation, 2014, reprint).

6. Anand Teltumbde, *Mahad: The Making of the First Dalit Revolt* (Delhi: Aakar Books, 2016); Ambedkar, *Dr. Babasaheb Ambedkar: Writings and Speeches*, vol. 17, part 1.

7. Ghosh, "From Mahad to Mumbai."

8. Ambedkar, *Dr. Babasaheb Ambedkar: Writings and Speeches*, vol. 17, part 1.

9. *The Diary of Mahadeo Desai*, trans. and ed. Valji Govindji Desai, vol. 1 (Ahmedabad: Navajivan Publishing House, 1953).

10. Dhananjay Keer, *Dr. Ambedkar: Life and Mission* (Mumbai: Popular Prakashan, 1954).

11. *Times of India*, October 12, 1931; Laxman Dhoble, preface to Ambedkar, *Dr. Babasaheb Ambedkar's Writings and Speeches*, vol. 17, part 1, xvii.

12. Gail Omvedt, *Dalits and the Democratic Revolution: Dr. Ambedkar and the Dalit Movement in Colonial India* (India: SAGE, 1994).

13. Abhirup Dam, "Fast unto Vote: Gandhi, Ambedkar & Separate Electorates for Dalits," *The Quint*, April 14, 2017.

14. *Subodh Patrika*, November 15, 1931; Ambedkar, *Dr. Babasaheb Ambedkar: Writings and Speeches*, vol. 17, part 1.

15. B. R. Ambedkar, *What Congress and Gandhi Have Done to the Untouchables* (Bombay: Thacker & Co., 1945).

16. Ambedkar, *What Congress and Gandhi Have Done to the Untouchables*.

17. Rupa Viswanath, "Dalits/Ex-Untouchables," in *Brill's Encyclopedia of Hinduism* (Brill, 2018); Ambedkar, *Dr. Babasaheb Ambedkar: Writings and Speeches*, vol. 17, part 1.

18. Gail Omvedt, "A Part That Parted," *Outlook*, August 20, 2012.

19. Omvedt, "A Part That Parted."

20. Ramanathan S., "Labeling Dalits 'Harijans': How We Remain Ignorant and Insensitive to Dalit Identity," *News Minute*, October 27, 2015.

21. Ambedkar, *Dr. Babasaheb Ambedkar: Writings and Speeches*, vol. 4.

22. Anne M. Blackburn, "Religion, Kinship and Buddhism: Ambedkar's Vision of a Moral Community," *Journal of the International Association of Buddhist Studies* 16, no. 1 (1993): 1–22.

23. Manan Desai, "Caste in Black and White: Dalit Identity and the Translation of African American Literature," *Comparative Literature* 67, no. 1 (March 1, 2015).

24. Martand Kaushik, "Dalit Literature Goes Global," *Times of India*, April 5, 2015.

25. Nico Slate, ed., *The Dalit Panthers: Race, Caste, and Black Power in India*, *Black Power Beyond Borders: The Global Dimensions of the Black Power Movement* (New York: Palgrave Macmillan, 2012).

26. Mantra Roy, "'Speaking' Subalterns: A Comparative Study of African American and Dalit/Indian Literatures," PhD diss., University of South Florida, 2010.

27. Desai, *Caste in Black and White*.

28. Anand Teltumbde, *Dalits Past, Present and Future* (Delhi: Routledge, 2016).

29. Ananya Vajpeyi, "Appropriating Ambedkar," *The Hindu*, April 21, 2016.

30. S. V. Raju, "Ambedkar, Hinduism and the 'Riddles' Controversy," *Live Mint*, May 21, 2016.

31. Tapan Basu, "For the RSS, Denouncing and Appropriating Ambedkar Go Hand in Hand," *The Wire*, December 12, 2016, https://thewire.in/politics/ambedkar-appropriating-rss-bjp.

32. Gyan Verma, "BJP and RSS Renew Ties," *Live Mint*, September 11, 2016.

33. Vajpeyi, "Appropriating Ambedkar."

34. Praveen Donthi, "From Shadows to the Stars," *The Caravan*, May 1, 2016.

35. Ramanathan S., "In JNU, an Ambedkarite Student Union, BAPSA, Finds an Ally in Kabali," *News Minute*, September 9, 2016.

36. Donthi, "From Shadows to the Stars."

37. Mohammad Ibrar, "JNU Students Protest Suspension," *Times of India*, December 29, 2016.

38. Vikram Chukka, "The Chain of Events Leading to Rohith Vemula's Suicide," *The Wire*, January 19, 2016.

39. Chukka, "The Chain of Events Leading to Rohith Vemula's Suicide."

40. Chukka, "The Chain of Events Leading to Rohith Vemula's Suicide."

41. Amrith Lal, "Most on Death Row Are Poor, from Backward Caste Groups, Minorities: Law University Report," *Indian Express*, May 7, 2016.

CHAPTER 10: MY INTRODUCTION TO AMBEDKAR

1. From a private message to author on Facebook.

2. Rishi Iyengar, "At This Eighteen-Hour Study Session, Concentration Was the Name of the Game," *Indian Express*, May 4, 2010.

3. Donna K. Bivens, "What Is Internalized Racism?" CAPD & MP Associates, http://www.racialequitytools.org/resourcefiles/What_is_Internalized_Racism.pdf, accessed December 27, 2018.

4. PTI, "Dalit Man Killed in Maharashtra for Allegedly Keeping Ambedkar Song as Ringtone," NDTV, May 22, 2015.

CHAPTER 11: DALIT WOMEN'S MOVEMENTS

1. Luke Harding, "Sex Hell of Dalit Women Exposed," *The Guardian*, May 8, 2001.

2. Aloysius Irudayam S. J., Jayshree P. Mangubhai, and Joel G. Lee, eds., *Dalit Women Speak Out: Caste, Class and Gender Violence in India* (New Delhi: Zubaan Books, 2014).

3. Betwa Sharma, "When A Woman Is Gang-Raped Twice by the Same Men, What Does That Make This Country?," *Huffington Post*, July 18, 2016.

4. Human Rights Watch, "Attacks on Dalit Women: A Pattern of Impunity," in *Broken People: Caste Violence Against India's "Untouchables,"* March 1999, https://www.hrw.org/reports/1999/india/India994-11.htm, accessed December 27, 2018.

5. Ajoy Ashirwad Mahaprashasta, "Chhattisgarh Government Under Fire as NHRC Faults Failure to Act on Mass Sexual Assault by Police," *The Wire*, January 8, 2017.

6. Chitrangada Choudhury, "In Two Districts of Bastar, Adivasi Women Report Sexual Assaults by Security Forces During Military Operations; Police Delay and Resist Filing FIRs," *The Caravan*, January 24, 2016.

7. Chaitanya Mallapur, "Only One in Four Rape Cases in India Ended in Conviction in 2016," *Hindustan Times*, August 28, 2017.

8. "The Evolution of Anti-Rape Laws in India Since 1860," *Youth Ki Awaaz*, September 2018.

9. Express News Service, "Badaun Gangrape and Murder: How the Incident Unfolded," *Indian Express*, June 2, 2014.

10. Rose Troup Buchanan, "India Mango Tree Rape Case: Cousins Found Hanging 'Committed Suicide' and Were Not 'Sexually Assaulted' Claim Indian Authorities," *The Independent*, November 27, 2014.

11. Varinder Bhatia, "In Haryana, More and More Rapes Every Year, Few Convictions for Crimes Against Dalits," *Indian Express*, October 9, 2012; Parimal A. Dabhi, "Rape of Dalit Women Registers 500% Increase Since 2001, RTI Reveals," *Indian Express*, March 8, 2015.

12. Rahila Gupta, "How India's Dalit Women Are Being Empowered to Fight Endemic Sexual Violence," *New Statesman America*, December 16, 2014.

13. Shahla Khan, "The Brutal Rape and Murder of Jisha Shows That Life for India's Women Is as Savage as Ever," *The Telegraph*, May 4, 2016.

14. Betwa Sharma, "Why Jisha Is Not Just 'Kerala's Nirbhaya,'" *Huffington Post*, May 5, 2016.

15. Shahina KK, "The Life and Death of Jisha," *Open*, May 13, 2016.

16. Khan, "The Brutal Rape and Murder of Jisha Shows That Life for India's Women Is as Savage as Ever."

17. Irudayam, Mangubhai, and Lee, *Dalit Women Speak Out*.

18. S. Viswanathan, "Khairlanji: The Crime and Punishment," *The Hindu*, August 23, 2010.

19. Mantra Roy, "'Speaking' Subalterns: A Comparative Study of African American and Dalit/Indian Literatures," PhD diss., University of South Florida, 2010.

20. Vidhya Raveendranathan and Nitin Sinha, "The Name and Shame List Asks Unsettling Questions About Our Familiar World," *The Wire*, November 9, 2017.

21. Shreya Ila Anusuya, "Why the Response to a List of Sexual Harassers Has Splintered India's Feminist Movement," *DailyO*, October 29, 2017.

22. KrantiKali, "Raya Sarkar and All the List's Men," *Medium*, October 24, 2017.

23. Bhanuj Kappal, "Breaking the 'Savarna Feminism' Rules—How Raya Sarkar's List of Alleged Harassers Divided Opinion in India," *New Statesman*, November 20, 2017.

24. Prawesh Lama, "Four Years After Dec 16: Number of Rape Cases in Delhi Have Increased," *Hindustan Times*, December 16, 2016.

25. Rucha Chitnis, "Meet the Indian Women Trying to Take Down 'Caste Apartheid,'" *Yes!*, October 23, 2015.

26. Tamalapakula Sowjanya, "Understanding Dalit Feminism," *The Philosopher: A Research Journal* 2, no. 2 (2014): 145–56, accessed May 22, 2023.

27. Sharmila Rege, "Dalit Women Talk Differently: A Critique of Difference and Towards a Dalit Feminist Standpoint Position," *Economic and Political Weekly* 33, no. 44 (October 31, 1998): 39–46.

28. Chitnis, "Meet the Indian Women Trying to Take Down 'Caste Apartheid.'"

29. Seema Sirohi, "Whose Hinduism Is It Anyway? The Right's 'Improved' Version or the Left's 'Warts-And-All' One?" *The Wire*, November 24, 2017.

30. "Dalit Women Ignite the Audience at the Women in the World Summit in New York," International Dalit Solidarity Network, April 9, 2014, http://idsn .org/dalit-women-ignite-the-audience-at-the-women-in-the-world-summit-in -new-york, accessed December 27, 2018.

31. Cherise Charleswell, "HerStory: The Origins and Continued Relevancy of Black Feminist Thought in the United States," HamptonThink.org, February 27, 2014.

32. Charleswell, "HerStory."

33. Amit Kumar, "Savita Ali: Raising Her Voice to Highlight Atrocities Against Dalit and Muslim Women," TwoCircles.net, September 9, 2016.

34. Malika Amar Sheikh, *I Want to Destroy Myself*, trans. Jerry Pinto (New Delhi: Speaking Tiger, 2016); Roy, "'Speaking' Subalterns."

35. Rege, "Dalit Women Talk Differently"; she proposed "'Masculinization' of Dalithood" and "'Sarvanization' of Womanhood" to point out how, in public opinion, to be Dalit meant you were a man, and to be a woman meant you were upper caste; Ashwaq Masoodi, "In Pune, Dalit Women Get a Platform to Speak Up," *Live Mint*, November 16, 2017.

36. Sowjanya, "Understanding Dalit Feminism."

37. Reuters, "Tanushree Dutta, Who Helped Trigger India's #MeToo Movement, Says She Was Not Going to Back Down the Second Time," *Hindustan Times*, October 16, 2018.

CHAPTER 12: THE DANGER OF THE SINGLE NARRATIVE

1. B. N. Uniyal, "In Search of a Dalit Journalist," *The Pioneer*, November 16, 1996.

2. J. Balasubramaniam, "Dalits and Lack of Diversity in the Newsroom," *Economic and Political Weekly* 46, no. 11 (March 12, 2011).

3. Ajaz Ashraf, "The Untold Story of Dalit Journalists," *The Hoot*, August 12, 2013.

4. Balasubramaniam, "Dalits and Lack of Diversity in the Newsroom."

5. Anisha Sheth, "The Death of a Dalit Journalist and the Question of Casteism in the Indian Media," *News Minute*, April 27, 2015.

6. Sudipto Mondal, "Indian Media Wants Dalit News but Not Dalit Reporters," *Al Jazeera*, June 2, 2017.

7. Mondal, "Indian Media Wants Dalit News but Not Dalit Reporters."

8. Pamela Newkirk, "The Not-So-Great Migration," *Columbia Journalism Review*, May/June 2011.

9. Martand Kaushik, "Lessons for Indian Journalism from Dalit Mobilisation Online," *The Caravan*, March 1, 2016.

10. Mondal, "Indian Media Wants Dalit News but Not Dalit Reporters."

11. Balasubramaniam, "Dalits and Lack of Diversity in the Newsroom."

12. Shivnarayan Rajpurohit, "Dalit Students and Journalists—from Classroom to Newsroom," *Kafila*, March 27, 2014.

13. Kaushik, "Lessons for Indian Journalism from Dalit Mobilisation Online."

14. Sandeep Bhushan, "Why Gujarat Appears to Have Fallen Off the News Map over the Last Two Years," *Scroll.in*, August 23, 2016.

15. Panthukala Srinivas and Prudhvi Raj Duddu, "Interview with Kuffir," Anveshi.org.in, Broadsheet on Contemporary Politics, no. 13, 2020.

16. Srinivas and Duddu, "Interview with Kuffir."

17. Special Correspondent, "Historic Ambedkar Bhavan Demolished, Grandson Files FIR Against Trust," *The Hindu*, June 26, 2016.

18. Robin Jeffrey, "Missing from the Indian Newsroom," *The Hindu*, April 9, 2012.

19. K. Satyanarayana, *Dalit Studies*, ed. Ramnarayan S. Rawat and K. Satyanarayana (Durham, NC: Duke University Press, 2016).

20. PTI, "Congress Leader Describes HRD Minister as 'Manu Smriti Irani,'" *Indian Express*, April 13, 2016.

21. B. R. Ambedkar, *Annihilation of Caste*, 1936.

22. Gail Omvedt, "Ambedkar Needs No Introduction," *Indian Express*, May 17, 2014.

23. Shivam Vij, "Why Dalit Radicals Don't Want Arundhati Roy to Write About Ambedkar," *Scroll.in*, March 12, 2014, https://scroll.in/article/658279/why -dalit-radicals-dont-want-arundhati-roy-to-write-about-ambedkar.

24. G. Sampath, "BR Ambedkar, Arundhati Roy, and the Politics of Appropriation," *Live Mint*, March 19, 2014, https://www.livemint.com/Opinion /dl8AvXg2PYchgE9qGogzJL/BR-Ambedkar-Arundhati-Roy-and-the-politics -of-appropriatio.html.

25. Arundhati Roy, "Arundhati Roy Replies to Dalit Camera," *Round Table India*, March 15, 2014.

26. Shivam Vij, "Why Dalit Radicals Don't Want Arundhati Roy to Write About Ambedkar," *Scroll.in*, March 12, 2014.

27. Meenakshi Shedde, "Can Cinema Break the Caste Barrier in Society?" *Forbes India*, April 12, 2016.

28. Glendora Meikle, "Poverty Porn: Is Sensationalism Justified If It Helps Those in Need?" *The Guardian*, July 5, 2013.

29. Rukmini S. and Udhav Naig, "In Bollywood, Storylines Remain Backward on Caste," *The Hindu*, June 28, 2015.

30. Sara Boboltz and Kimberly Yam, "Why On-Screen Representation Actually Matters," *Huffington Post*, February 24, 2012.

31. Matt Zoller Seitz, "The Offensive Movie Cliche That Won't Die," *Salon*, September 14, 2014.

32. Aakshi Magazine, "How Masaan Lights Up the Pyre of India's Caste and Gender Barriers," *DailyO*, July 15, 2015.

33. Karthikeyan Damodaran, "Kabali Destabilises the Established Idioms of Tamil Cinema," *The Wire*, July 26, 2016.

CHAPTER 13: SILICON VALLEY, MODEL MINORITY, AND THE MYTH OF CASTE-LESSNESS

1. PTI, "Indian-Americans Make Up 1% of US Population but Pay 6% of Taxes: Congressman," January 13, 2023, *Business Insider India*, https://www.businessinsider.in/international/news/indian-americans-make-up-1-of-us-population-but-pay-6-of-taxes-congressman/articleshow/96954653.cms, accessed April 19, 2023.

2. Nikhil Inamdar and Aparna Alluri, "Parag Agrawal: Why Indian-Born CEOs Dominate Silicon Valley," December 4, 2021, BBC News, https://www.bbc.com/news/world-asia-india-59457015, accessed April 19, 2023.

3. AnnaLee Saxenian, *Silicon Valley's New Immigrant Entrepreneurs*, Public Policy Institute of California, 1999, https://www.ppic.org/wp-content/uploads/content/pubs/report/R_699ASR.pdf, accessed April 20, 2023.

4. Vivek Wadhwa, "How Indians Defied Gravity and Achieved Success in Silicon Valley," *Forbes*, October 15, 2012, https://www.forbes.com/sites/singularity/2012/10/15/how-indians-defied-gravity-and-achieved-success-in-silicon-valley/?sh=1cec462436d7, accessed April 19, 2023.

5. Economic Times HRWorld, "25% of Startups in US' Silicon Valley Managed by People of Indian Origin: Sitharaman," *Economic Times*, last updated September 12, 2022, https://hr.economictimes.indiatimes.com/news/industry/25-of-startups-in-us-silicon-valley-managed-by-people-of-indian-origin-sitharaman/94141044, accessed April 19, 2023.

6. Paresh Dave, "Indian Immigrants Are Tech's New Titans," *Los Angeles Times*, August 11, 2015, https://www.latimes.com/business/la-fi-indians-in-tech-20150812-story.html, accessed April 19, 2023.

7. Vivek Wadhwa, "Microsoft's Nadella, Google's Pichai, and Now Twitter's Agrawal: Why Indian-Born Leaders Dominate American Tech's Top Ranks," *Fortune*, December 3, 2021, https://fortune.com/2021/12/03/twitter-ceo-tech-industry-microsoft-google-silicon-valley-indian-born-leaders, accessed April 19, 2023.

8. Wadhwa, "Microsoft's Nadella, Google's Pichai, and Now Twitter's Agrawal."

9. Dileep Rao, "3 Skills That Have Helped the Growth of Indian-Origin CEOs," *Forbes*, December 14, 2022, https://www.forbes.com/sites/dileeprao/2022/12/14/the-3-skills-that-have-helped-the-growth-of-indian-origin-ceos/?sh=43630604823, accessed April 19, 2023.

10. Ajantha Subramanian, *The Caste of Merit* (Cambridge, MA: Harvard University Press, 2019), 281.

11. Subramanian, *The Caste of Merit*, 281.

12. Subramanian, *The Caste of Merit*, 283.

13. Subramanian, *The Caste of Merit*, 284.

14. Subramanian, *The Caste of Merit*, 284.

15. Abhinav Bhatt, "An IIT-Manipal 'Twitter War' over Satya Nadella," NDTV, February 10, 2014, https://www.ndtv.com/india-news/an-iit-manipal-twitter-war -over-satya-nadella-550344, accessed April 20, 2023.

16. Jyoti Thottam, "A Reunion at the 'MIT of India,'" *Time*, July 9, 2007, https://content.time.com/time/business/article/0,8599,1641232,00.html, accessed April 19, 2023.

17. Yashica Dutt, "Opinion: The Specter of Caste in Silicon Valley," *New York Times*, July 14, 2020, https://www.nytimes.com/2020d/07/14/opinion/caste-cisco -indian-americans-discrimination.html, accessed April 19, 2023.

18. Subramanian, *The Caste of Merit*, 296.

19. The Indus Entrepreneurs, "About," https://tie.org/about, accessed April 19, 2023.

20. Saxenian, *Silicon Valley's New Immigrant Entrepreneurs*; Inventus Capital Partners, "Kanwal Rekhi," https://www.inventuscap.com/kanwal-rekhi, accessed April 19, 2023.

21. Subramanian, *The Caste of Merit*, 295.

22. Times News Network, "The Indus Entrepreneurs Created $1 Trillion Value in 30 Years, Guns for 10m Startups," *Times of India*, December 13, 2022, https:// timesofindia.indiatimes.com/city/hyderabad/the-indus-entrepreneurs-created-1 -trillion-value-in-30-years-guns-for-10m-startups/articleshow/96184553.cms, ac- cessed May 29, 2022.

23. Vivek Wadhwa, AnnaLee Saxenian, Ben A. Rissing, and Gary Gereffi, "America's New Immigrant Entrepreneurs: Part I," *Duke Science, Technology & In- novation*, paper no. 23, Social Science Research Network, January 4, 2007, https:// doi.org/10.2139/ssrn.990152.

24. Saxenian, *Silicon Valley's New Immigrant Entrepreneurs*.

25. Saxenian, *Silicon Valley's New Immigrant Entrepreneurs*.

26. "Global Ties," *Forbes*, July 13, 2007, https://www.forbes.com/global/2007 /0723/068.html, accessed April 19, 2023.

27. Shahnawaz Islam, "Reservation Is Useless, Says IT Guru," *Times of India*, Mumbai edition, August 21, 2001, https://timesofindia.indiatimes.com/city /mumbai/reservation-is-useless-says-it-guru/articleshow/1793471367.cms, accessed April 20, 2023.

28. Subramanian, *The Caste of Merit*, 301.

29. Ambedkar King Study Circle (@akscsfba), "Open Casteist Call in a Tech Meet in Silicon Valley, USA—#BanCasteInUSA Raja Antony, Milpitas, CA," Twitter, February 4, 2023, 9:28 p.m., https://twitter.com/akscsfba/status/16220594 65582182400, accessed April 20, 2023.

30. Carla Power, "See How They Wander," *Newsweek*, July 7, 2000, https:// www.newsweek.com/see-how-they-wander-161717, accessed April 19, 2023.

31. Ullekh NP, "'Inside Big Tech, Privileged Caste Members Use Filters to Keep Others Out of Jobs, Promotions,'" August 20, 2022, *Open, The Magazine*, https:// openthemagazine.com/feature/marilyn-fernandez-professor-emerita-sociology -department-santa-clara-university-california, accessed April 19, 2023.

32. Ullekh NP, "'Inside Big Tech, Privileged Caste Members Use Filters to Keep Others out of Jobs, Promotions.'"

33. Vivek Wadhwa, "Indian Americans Will Rule Silicon Valley; They Help Each Other Regardless of Caste, Religion: Vivek Wadhwa," *Economic Times*, Feb-

ruary 3, 2014, https://economictimes.indiatimes.com/indian-americans-will-rule -silicon-valley-they-help-each-other-regardless-of-caste-religion-vivek-wadhwa /articleshow/29785052.cms, accessed April 19, 2023.

34. AnnaLee Saxenian, "Brain Circulation: How High-Skill Immigration Makes Everyone Better Off," *Brookings Review* 20, no. 1 (Winter 2002): 28–31, https://doi.org/10.2307/20081018, accessed April 19, 2023.

35. Subramanian, *The Caste of Merit*, 296.

36. Palashi Vaghela, Steven J. Jackson, and Phoebe Sengers, "Interrupting Merit, Subverting Legibility: Navigating Caste in 'Casteless' Worlds of Computing," *CHI '22: Proceedings of the 2022 CHI Conference on Human Factors in Computing Systems* (2022): 1–20, https://doi.org/10.1145/3491102.3502059.

37. Joseph Berger, "Family Ties and Entanglements of Caste," *New York Times*, October 25, 2004, https://www.nytimes.com/2004/10/25/nyregion/family -ties-and-entanglements-of-caste.html, accessed April 19, 2023.

38. Berger, "Family Ties and Entanglements of Caste."

39. Brahman Samaj of North America, *Brahma-Bharti* 1, no. 1 (January 1995), https://www.cs.umd.edu/~tripathi/bsna/bmbh5010.pdf, accessed April 19, 2023.

40. Neha Sahgal et al., *Religion in India: Tolerance and Segregation*, Pew Research Center, 2021, https://www.pewresearch.org/religion/2021/06/29/attitudes -about-caste/#fn-35266-12, accessed April 20, 2023.

41. Brahman Samaj of North America, "Mission," 2023, https://bsna.org /mission, accessed April 20, 2023.

42. B. R. Ambedkar, "Castes in India: Their Mechanism, Genesis, and Development," May 9, 1916, http://www.columbia.edu/itc/mealac/pritchett/00ambedkar/txt _ambedkar_castes.html, accessed April 19, 2023.

43. Brahman Samaj of North America, "Chapters," https://bsna.org/chapters, accessed April 19, 2023.

44. Agrawals of Washington, "Home page," updated January 28, 2023, https:// sites.google.com/site/agrawalsofwashington, accessed April 19, 2023.

45. Lavanga V. Wijekoon et al., "United States: Seattle Becomes the First U.S. Jurisdiction to Prohibit Caste Discrimination," *Mondaq*, March 7, 2023, https:// www.mondaq.com/unitedstates/discrimination-disability-sexual-harassment /1290114/seattle-becomes-the-first-us-jurisdiction-to-prohibit-caste-discrimination, accessed April 19, 2023.

46. Seattle Office of the City Clerk, Legislative Information Center, "An Ordinance Relating to Human Rights; Including Protections Against Discrimination Based on an Individual's Caste; [. . .]," Seattle City Council, record no. 120511, February 24, 2023, http://seattle.legistar.com/LegislationDetail.aspx?ID=6023482 &GUID=39536EA0-BE3C-4EA2-A619-EFDE7693B17C&FullText=1, accessed April 20, 2023.

47. Agrawal Samaj Dallas Forth Worth, "Home page," https://www.asdfw.org, accessed April 19, 2023.

48. Agrawal Samaj Dallas Forth Worth, "Home page."

49. Mary Hanna and Jeanne Batalova, "Indian Immigrants in the United States," Migration Policy Institute, October 16, 2020, https://www.migration policy.org/article/indian-immigrants-united-states-2019, accessed April 19, 2023.

50. Subramanian, *The Caste of Merit*, 267.

51. Dreambrew Technologies, "60 Minutes—IIT—World Imports Indian Engineers," June 24, 2016, video, 13:18, https://www.youtube.com/watch?v=O4Frq2SbvPY.

52. Julie Pitta, "The Venture Capitalist from Kanpur," *Forbes*, July 6, 1998, https://www.forbes.com/global/1998/0706/0107094a.html?sh=52e124e478c4, accessed April 19, 2023; Don Clark, "South Asian 'Angels' Reap Riches, Spread Wealth in Silicon Valley," *Wall Street Journal*, May 2, 2000, https://www.wsj.com /articles/SB957229182233249632, accessed April 19, 2023; Thottam, "A Reunion at the 'MIT of India'"; Subramanian, *The Caste of Merit* (*BusinessWeek* reference).

53. Melanie Warner, "The Indians of Silicon Valley: The Hidden Geniuses of the Tech Revolution Are Indian Engineers—Here's How One Bucked Stereotypes, Got Rich, and Has Become Godfather to a Generation of Immigrant Entrepreneurs," *CNN Money*, May 15, 2000, https://money.cnn.com/magazines/fortune /fortune_archive/2000/05/15/279748/index.htm, accessed April 19, 2023.

54. Hemali Chhapia, "Four Years On, 20% Women's Quota Fully Filled in Most IITs," *Times of India*, August 20, 2022, https://timesofindia.indiatimes. com/india/four-years-on-20-womens-quota-fully-filled-in-most-iits/article-show/93668336.cms, accessed April 19, 2023.

55. Vidya S., "India's IT Sector Has the Highest Women's Representation, Shows Study," *Business Today* (India), March 8, 2023, https://www.businesstoday .in/latest/corporate/story/indias-it-sector-has-the-highest-womens-representation -shows-study-372667-2023-03-08, accessed April 19, 2023.

56. "2022 Top Companies for Women Technologists," AnitaB.org, https://anitab .org/research-and-impact/top-companies/2022-results, accessed April 19, 2023.

57. Sarah K. White, "Women in Tech Statistics: The Hard Truths of an Uphill Battle," *CIO*, March 13, 2023, https://www.cio.com/article/201905/women-in-tech -statistics-the-hard-truths-of-an-uphill-battle.html, accessed April 20, 2023.

58. "America's Top 50 Women in Tech, 2018 Ranking," *Forbes*, https://www .forbes.com/top-tech-women-america/list/2/#tab:overall, accessed April 19, 2023.

59. Savita Patel, "'No Agency, Unpredictability': What Tech Layoffs Mean for Indian Women in US," March 8, 2023, *The Quint*, https://www.thequint.com /news/world/tech-layoffs-us-impact-on-indian-women-h1b-visas#read-more, accessed April 19, 2023.

60. Ari Hoffman and Jeanne Batalova, "Indian Immigrants in the United States," Migration Policy Institute, December 7, 2022, https://www.migration policy.org/article/indian-immigrants-united-states, accessed April 19, 2023.

61. Sanjoy Chakravorty, Devesh Kapur, and Nirvikar Singh, "America's 'Little Indias' Are High-Tech Hubs, Working-Class Neighborhoods, and Everything in Between," *Quartz*, January 20, 2017, https://qz.com/india/889483/from-25000 -to-250000-americas-little-indias-are-high-tech-hubs-working-class-neighborhoods -and-everything-in-between, accessed April 19, 2023.

62. Subramanian, *The Caste of Merit*, 269.

63. "United States v. Bhagat Singh Thind," Cornell Law School, Legal Information Institute, https://www.law.cornell.edu/supremecourt/text/261/204, accessed April 19, 2023.

64. Marian L. Smith, "Race, Nationality, and Reality: INS Administration of Racial Provisions in U.S. Immigration and Nationality Law Since 1898," *Prologue* 32,

no. 2 (2002), updated November 10, 2022, https://www.archives.gov/publications /prologue/2002/summer/immigration-law-1, accessed April 19, 2023.

65. Subramanian, *The Caste of Merit*, 280.

66. Arun Venugopal, "The Truth Behind Indian American Exceptionalism," *The Atlantic*, January/February 2021, published online December 19, 2020, https://www.theatlantic.com/magazine/archive/2021/01/the-making-of-a-model-minority /617258, accessed April 19, 2023.

67. Subramanian, *The Caste of Merit*, 293.

68. William Petersen, "Success Story, Japanese-American Style," *New York Times*, January 6, 1966, http://inside.sfuhs.org/dept/history/US_History_reader /Chapter14/modelminority.pdf, accessed April 20, 2023.

69. "Black Desi Secret History," https://blackdesisecrethistory.org, accessed April 19, 2023.

70. Jennifer Chowdhury, "A Conversation With: Author and Filmmaker Vivek Bald," *India Ink* (blog), *New York Times*, May 31, 2013, https://archive.nytimes.com /india.blogs.nytimes.com/2013/05/31/a-conversation-with-author-and-filmmaker -vivek-bald, accessed April 19, 2023.

CHAPTER 14: THE RECKONING OF CASTE IN TECH

1. Cisco, "Cisco Reports Fourth Quarter and Fiscal Year 2022 Earnings," news release, August 17, 2022, https://investor.cisco.com/news/news-details/2022/CISC O-REPORTS-FOURTH-QUARTER-AND-FISCAL-YEAR-2022-EARNINGS /default.aspx, accessed May 9, 2023.

2. Supriya Yelimeli, "Lakireddy Bali Reddy, Berkeley Landlord Convicted of Sex Trafficking, Dead at 84," *Berkeleyside*, November 13, 2021, https://www .berkeleyside.org/2021/11/12/lakireddy-bali-reddy-dead-berkeley, accessed May 9, 2023.

3. Viji Sundaram, "How an Infamous Berkeley Human Trafficking Case Fueled Reform," *San Francisco Public Press*, February 16, 2012, https://www.sfpublic press.org/how-an-infamous-berkeley-human-trafficking-case-fueled-reform, accessed May 9, 2023.

4. Swathi Moorthy, "After Cisco, HCL's US Unit Faces Lawsuit for Sacking Employee Based on Caste," *Moneycontrol*, August 5, 2020, https://www.money control.com/news/business/exclusive-after-cisco-hcls-us-unit-faces-lawsuit-for -sacking-employee-based-on-caste-5648071.html, accessed May 9, 2023.

5. "A Statement on Caste Bias in Silicon Valley from 30 Dalit Women Engineers," *Washington Post*, updated October 27, 2020, https://www.washington post.com/context/a-statement-on-caste-bias-in-silicon-valley-from-30-dalit -women-engineers/d692b4f8-2710-41c3-9d5f-ea55c13bcc50/?itid=lk_interstitial _manual_16, accessed May 9, 2023.

6. Maya Kamble, phone interview with author, July 2022.

7. Paresh Dave, "Caste in California: Tech Giants Confront Ancient Indian Hierarchy," *Reuters*, August 15, 2022, https://www.reuters.com/business /sustainable-business/caste-california-tech-giants-confront-ancient-indian -hierarchy-2022-08-15, accessed May 9, 2023.

8. "Amazon Supply Chain Standards," Amazon, https://sustainability.about amazon.com/amazon_supply_chain_standards_english.pdf, accessed May 9, 2023;

"Global Rights Principles," Amazon, https://sustainability.aboutamazon.com
/society/human-rights/principles, accessed May 9, 2023.

9. Pragyanshu Gautam, "Why Ambedkar Converted to Buddhism," *Outlook*,
updated April 15, 2022, https://www.outlookindia.com/national/why-ambedkar
-converted-to-buddhism-news-191616, accessed May 9, 2023.

10. Palashi Vaghela, Steven J. Jackson, and Phoebe Sengers, "Interrupting
Merit, Subverting Legibility: Navigating Caste in 'Casteless' Worlds of Computing," *CHI '22: Proceedings of the 2022 CHI Conference on Human Factors in Computing Systems* (2022): 1–20, https://doi.org/10.1145/3491102.3502059

11. Vinita Gopi, phone interview with author, July 2022.

12. Tanuja Gupta, "Tanuja Gupta's Goodbye Letter," DocumentCloud, contributed by Jai-Leen James (*Washington Post*), https://www.documentcloud.org
/documents/22050236-tanuja-gupta-goodbye-letter, accessed May 10, 2023.

13. Nitasha Tiku, "Google's Plan to Talk About Caste Bias Led to 'Division
and Rancor,'" *Washington Post*, June 2, 2022, https://www.washingtonpost.com
/technology/2022/06/02/google-caste-equality-labs-tanuja-gupta, accessed May 9,
2023.

14. "Twitter CEO Trolled for 'Smash Brahminical Patriarchy' Placard," *Al
Jazeera*, November 20, 2018, https://www.aljazeera.com/news/2018/11/20/twitter
-ceo-trolled-for-smash-brahminical-patriarchy-placard, accessed May 9, 2023.

15. K. Bhattacharjee, "Equality Labs and PJF: How a Nexus of
'Anti-Brahminism' Caste Activists, Khalistanis and Pakistan's ISI Is Working Together to Malign India Abroad," *OpIndia*, February 23, 2021, https://www.opindia
.com/2021/02/nexus-western-countries-usa-anti-brahminism-khalistanis-pakistan
-isi-caste-activists-equality-labs-suraj-yengde-pjf-ofmi, accessed May 9, 2023.

16. Shirin Ghaffary, "Google Is Cracking Down on Its Employees' Political
Speech at Work," *Vox*, August 23, 2019, https://www.vox.com/recode/2019/8/23
/20829430/google-new-community-guidelines-employees-political-speech
-internal-debate, accessed May 9, 2023; Gupta, "Tanuja Gupta's Goodbye Letter."

17. "Ending Forced Arbitration and Protecting Employees with Congress-
woman Cheri Bustos & Tanuja Gupta," Resilience, December 5, 2022, https://
www.ourresilience.org/ending-forced-arbitration-and-protecting-employees-with
-congresswoman-cheri-bustos-tanuja-gupta, accessed May 9, 2023; Tiku, "Google's
Plan to Talk About Caste Bias Led to 'Division and Rancor.'"

18. Press Trust of India, "Dalit Civil Rights Activist Accuse Google of a
Casteist and Hostile Workplace Practices," *Outlook India*, June 2, 2022, https://
www.outlookindia.com/business/dalit-civil-rights-activist-accuse-google-of-a
-casteist-and-hostile-workplace-practices-news-200026, accessed May 9, 2023.

19. Sakshi Venkatraman, "All Cal State Universities Add Caste to Anti-
Discrimination Policy," NBC News, January 19, 2022, https://www.nbcnews
.com/news/asian-america/cal-state-schools-add-caste-anti-discrimination-policy
-rcna12602#:~:text=California%20State%20University%20has%20become,they
%20regularly%20experience%20at%20school, accessed May 9, 2023.

20. Ryan General, "Professors Sue California State University System over
Caste Anti-Discrimination Policy," *Yahoo News*, October 20, 2022, https://news
.yahoo.com/professors-sue-california-state-university-221820540.html, accessed
May 9, 2023.

21. Harmeet Kaur, "Colleges and Universities Across the US Are Moving to Ban Caste Discrimination," CNN, January 30, 2022, https://www.cnn.com/2022/01/30/us/csu-caste-protections-universities-cec/index.html, accessed May 9, 2023.

22. Hannah Ellis-Petersen, "Death Threats Sent to Participants of US Conference on Hindu Nationalism," September 9, 2021, *The Guardian*, https://www.theguardian.com/world/2021/sep/09/death-threats-sent-to-participants-of-us-conference-on-hindu-nationalism, accessed May 9, 2023.

23. Niha Masih, "Under Fire from Hindu Nationalist Groups, U.S.-Based Scholars of South Asia Worry About Academic Freedom," *Washington Post*, October 3, 2021, https://www.washingtonpost.com/world/2021/10/03/india-us-universities-hindutva, accessed May 9, 2023.

24. Meghnad Bose and Sreya Sarkar, "'Family in Safe House Due to Threats': Dalit Scholar Fighting Google on Caste," *The Quint*, June 11, 2022, https://www.thequint.com/south-asians/dalit-scholar-thenmozhi-soundararajan-fighting-google-on-caste-interview, accessed May 9, 2023.

25. Isaac Chotiner, "Google's Caste-Bias Problem," August 11, 2022, *New Yorker*, https://www.newyorker.com/news/q-and-a/googles-caste-bias-problem, accessed May 9, 2023.

26. Shannon Newberry, email message to author, June 2022.

27. Tiku, "Google's Plan to Talk About Caste Bias Led to 'Division and Rancor.'"

28. "Google Has Just Shown Moral Courage on Caste We Hope Other Organizations Follow: HAF," Hindu American Foundation, June 3, 2022, https://www.hinduamerican.org/press/google-equality-labs, accessed May 9, 2023.

29. "A Conversation on Caste Equity in US Workplaces, BigTech and News Media," End Forced Arbitration, May 3, 2022, video, 55:50, https://www.youtube.com/watch?v=2xykx777qZM, accessed May 9, 2023.

30. Vaghela, Jackson, and Sengers, "Interrupting Merit, Subverting Legibility."

31. Rohit Chopra, "What Explains Indian-Americans Being Anti-Trump but Also Pro-Modi?" *Scroll.in*, March 2, 2021, https://scroll.in/global/988227/what-explains-indian-americans-being-anti-trump-but-also-pro-modi, accessed May 9, 2023.

32. Kamal, phone interview with author, September 2022.

33. *Guardian* Staff, "Seattle Becomes First US City to Ban Caste-Based Discrimination," *The Guardian*, February 21, 2023, https://www.theguardian.com/us-news/2023/feb/21/seattle-ban-caste-based-discrimination, accessed May 9, 2023.

34. Sakshi Venkatraman, "California Is One Step Closer to Banning Caste-Based Discrimination," April 26, 2023, NBC News, https://www.nbcnews.com/news/asian-america/california-one-step-closer-banning-caste-based-discrimination-rcna81555, accessed May 9, 2023.

EPILOGUE

1. Dhrubo Jyoti, "India's First Dalit Cricketer Palwankar Baloo Fought Against Caste Barriers on the Field and off It," *Hindustan Times*, September 16, 2018.

2. Jyoti, "India's First Dalit Cricketer Palwankar Baloo Fought Against Caste Barriers on the Field and off It."

3. Jyoti, "India's First Dalit Cricketer Palwankar Baloo Fought Against Caste Barriers on the Field and off It."

4. Rajesh Komath, "Castes of Cricket in India," *Round Table India*, September 23, 2017.

5. Kamalpreet Singh Gill, "India's First International Dalit Cricketer and the Breaching of the Caste Frontier," *Swarajya*, August 4, 2018. He has quoted "Cricket and Caste: The Heroic Struggle of the Palwankar Brothers" by Ramachandra Guha.

6. Jyoti, "India's First Dalit Cricketer Palwankar Baloo Fought Against Caste Barriers on the Field and off It."

7. Andrew Stevenson, "A Class Act? Opinions Differ," *Sydney Morning Herald*, January 5, 2008.

8. Amrit Dhillon, "Why No Dalit Cricketers in India?," *Sydney Morning Herald*, June 12, 2018.

9. Sanjjeev K. Samyal, "Vinod Kambli Embraces Christianity," *DNA*, September 9, 2010.

10. Stevenson, "A Class Act? Opinions Differ."

INDEX

ABOUT THE AUTHOR

Yashica Dutt, the award-winning author of *Coming Out as Dalit*, is an internationally acclaimed journalist and one of the world's leading feminist voices on caste. Dutt is a notable caste expert recognized for highlighting Dalit rights globally and her voice has been instrumental in understanding the realities of caste within the increasingly prominent Indian diaspora. Dutt's work has been published in the *New York Times*, *Foreign Policy*, and *The Atlantic*, and she has been featured on the BBC, *The Guardian*, and PBS *NewsHour*. Her writing has been part of PEN America's *India at 75 Anthology*, which featured prominent Indian writers looking back on India's history in its seventy-fifth year of independence, and a collection titled *Our Freedoms: Essays and Stories from India's Best Writers*. *Coming Out as Dalit*, Dutt's first book, is a best seller that is currently part of the curriculum in over fifty colleges and universities worldwide, including Harvard University, the University of California, Berkeley, and the University of California, Davis. Dutt was involved in the passage in February 2023 of the historic anti-caste bill in the city of Seattle, and her writing was instrumental in shaping the text of the first-in-nation law. She is working on a book on caste, to be published by Beacon Press in 2025. Dutt graduated from Columbia Journalism School and lives in Brooklyn, New York.